"I enjoy reading Phil Moore's books. He writes about Jesus and the Christian life with perception, wisdom and wit."
– Nicky Gumbel, Former vicar, HTB London

"In taking us straight to the heart of the text, Phil Moore has served us magnificently. We so need to get into the Scriptures and let the Scriptures get into us. The fact that Phil writes so relevantly and with such submission to biblical revelation means that we are genuinely helped to be shaped by the Bible's teaching."
– Terry Virgo, Founder of Newfrontiers

"Fresh. Solid. Simple. Really good stuff."
– R.T. Kendall, Author and speaker, former minister of Westminster Chapel, London

*"Most commentaries are dull. These are alive. Most commentaries are for scholars. These are for **you**!"*
– Canon Michael Green, Former evangelist, lecturer and apologist

"These notes are amazingly good. Phil's insights are striking, original, and fresh, going straight to the heart of the text and the reader! Substantial yet succinct, they bristle with amazing insights and life applications, compelling us to read more. Bible reading will become enriched and informed with such a scintillating guide. Teachers and preachers will find nuggets of pure gold here!"
– Greg Haslam, Former author and senior minister of Westminster Chapel, London

"A strong combination of faithful scholarship, clear explanation and deep insight make these an invaluable tool. I can't recommend them highly enough."
– Gavin Calver, Director of Mission, Evangelical Alliance

"The Bible is living and dangerous. The ones who teach it best are those who bear that in mind – and let the author do the talking. Phil has written these studies with a sharp mind and a combination of creative application and reverence."
– Joel Virgo, Leader of Newday Youth Festival

"Phil Moore's new commentaries are outstanding: biblical and passionate, clear and well-illustrated, simple and profound. God's Word comes to life as you read them, and the wonder of God shines through every page."

– **Andrew Wilson,** Author of *Incomparable* and *If God, Then What?*

"Want to understand the Bible better? Don't have the time or energy to read complicated commentaries? The book you have in your hand could be the answer. Allow Phil Moore to explain and then apply God's message to your life. Think of this book as the Bible's message distilled for everyone."

– **Adrian Warnock,** Christian blogger

"Phil Moore presents Scripture in a dynamic, accessible and relevant way. The bite-size chunks – set in context and grounded in contemporary life – really make the Word become flesh and dwell among us."

– **Dr David Landrum,** Director of advocacy and public affairs at Open Doors UK and Ireland

"Through a relevant, very readable, up-to-date storying approach, Phil Moore sets the big picture, relates God's Word to today and gives us fresh insights to increase our vision, deepen our worship, know our identity and fire our imagination. Highly recommended!"

– **Geoff Knott,** Former CEO of Wycliffe Bible Translators UK

"What an exciting project Phil has embarked upon! These accessible and insightful books will ignite the hearts of believers, inspire the minds of preachers and help shape a new generation of men and women who are seeking to learn from God's Word."

– **David Stroud,** Leader of Christ Church, London, and author of *Planting Churches, Changing Communities*

For more information about the Straight to the Heart series, please go to **www.philmoorebooks.com**.
You can also receive daily messages from Phil Moore on Twitter by following **@PhilMooreLondon**.

STRAIGHT TO
THE HEART OF

1 & 2
Chronicles

60 BITE-SIZED
INSIGHTS

Phil Moore

MONARCH
BOOKS

This book is dedicated to my wife, Ruth. Twenty-six out of twenty-six! You have been faithful in many small things, and faithfulness in a small thing is a big thing.

Published by **Monarch Books**

www.lionhudson.com

Part of the SPCK Group

SPCK, 36 Causton Street, London, SW1P 4ST

ISBN 978 0 85721 991 6

eISBN 978 0 85721 985 5

First edition 2022

Acknowledgments

Scripture quotations marked ESV from The ESV® Bible (The Holy Bible, English Standard Version®). ESV® Text Edition: 2016. Copyright © 2001 by Crossway, a publishing ministry of Good News Publishers. The ESV® text has been reproduced in cooperation with and by permission of Good News Publishers. Unauthorized reproduction of this publication is prohibited. All rights reserved.

Scripture quotation marked NET from the NET Bible® copyright ©1996-2017 All rights reserved. Build 30170414 by Biblical Studies Press, L.L.C.

Scripture quotations marked NIVUK from the Holy Bible, New International Version® Anglicized, NIV® Copyright © 1979, 1984, 2011 by Biblica, Inc.® Used by permission. All rights reserved worldwide.

A catalogue record for this book is available from the British Library

Printed and bound in the UK, September 2022, LH26

CONTENTS

PART THREE: SMALL THINGS ABOUT SOLOMON

PART FOUR: SMALL THINGS ABOUT JUDAH

About the
Straight to the Heart
Series

On his eightieth birthday, Sir Winston Churchill dismissed the compliment that he was the "lion" who had defeated Nazi Germany in World War Two. He told the Houses of Parliament that *"It was a nation and race dwelling all around the globe that had the lion's heart. I had the luck to be called upon to give the roar."*

I hope that God speaks to you very powerfully through the "roar" of the books in the *Straight to the Heart* series. I hope they help you to understand the books of the Bible and the message which the Holy Spirit inspired their authors to write. I hope that they help you to hear God's voice challenging you, and that they provide you with a springboard for further journeys into each book of Scripture for yourself.

But when you hear my "roar", I want you to know that it comes from the heart of a much bigger "lion" than me. I have been shaped by a whole host of great Christian thinkers and preachers from around the world, and I want to give due credit to at least some of them here: Terry Virgo, Dave Holden, Guy Miller, John Hosier, Adrian Holloway, Lex Loizides, Malcolm Kayes and all those who lead the Newfrontiers family of churches; friends and encouragers, such as Mike Betts, Simon Holley, Stef Liston, Joel Virgo, Stuart Gibbs, Scott Taylor, Nick Derbridge, Phil Whittall, and Kevin and Sarah Aires; Joshua Wells and all the team at SPCK, IVP and Monarch Books; my great friend Andrew Wilson – without all of your friendship, encouragement and example, this series would never have happened.

I would like to thank my parents, my brother Jonathan, and my in-laws, Clive and Sue Jackson. Dad – your example birthed in my heart the passion which brought this series into being. I didn't listen to all you said when I was a child, but I couldn't ignore the way you got up at five o'clock every morning to pray, read the Bible and worship, because of your radical love for God and for his Word. I'd like to thank my children – Isaac, Noah, Esther and Ethan – for keeping me sane when publishing deadlines were looming. But most of all, I'm grateful to my incredible wife, Ruth – my friend, encourager, corrector and helper.

You all have the lion's heart, and you have all developed the lion's heart in me. I count it an enormous privilege to be the one who was chosen to sound the lion's roar.

So welcome to the *Straight to the Heart* series. My prayer is that you will let this roar grip your own heart too – for the glory of the great Lion of the Tribe of Judah, the Lord Jesus Christ!

Introduction: The God of Small Things

"The events of King David's reign... together with the details of his reign and power."

(1 Chronicles 29:29–30)

It wasn't unusual for one of my father-in-law's friends to dig his own foundations for an extension to his home. As a close-knit community of North Dorset farmers, they resented paying professional builders to do work that they could do themselves. One month, my father-in-law's friends would dig with him in his garden. The next month, he would return the favour by driving his digger over to one of their homes.

What was unusual about this dig, however, was what John White found buried beneath the familiar turf of his backyard. The soil that he and his friends unearthed was peppered with so many brightly coloured little cubes that he eventually called a halt to his home extension and invited a team of archaeologists to come and dig over his garden instead. The BBC series *A History of the World in 100 Objects* would later place the Hinton St Mary Mosaic as number forty-four on its list of a hundred great historical finds. Underneath John White's unimpressive garden lay hidden the oldest and best-preserved mosaic of Jesus Christ in the entire Roman Empire. In the mosaic, Jesus stands in front of the Christian *chi-rho* symbol, as if waiting patiently for the diggers to locate him.[1]

---

[1] *A History of the World in 100 Objects* was broadcast on BBC Radio 4 in 2010. The Hinton St Mary Mosaic has now become one of the greatest treasures in the British Museum in London.

That's how we ought to regard 1 and 2 Chronicles. At first glance, these two books of the Bible appear as unimpressive as the grass in John White's backyard. Some readers complain that they begin with nine long chapters of genealogy. Others wonder why the books were written at all, given that their story has already been told in greater detail in Genesis, 1 and 2 Samuel, and 1 and 2 Kings. Originally a single book of the Hebrew Old Testament, it was split in two during the third century BC by the translators of the Greek Septuagint. They named it the *Paraleipomenon*, which means *Things Omitted Earlier*, or *Leftovers*, and which must surely qualify as the least inviting name of any of the books of the Bible![2] And yet, underneath the surface of these two unimpressive-looking books lies buried treasure. They are peppered with tiny details, each of which conveys big truth about God. They reveal him to be *the God of small things*.

Chronicles is the last book of the Hebrew Old Testament in many ancient manuscripts, reinforcing the idea that it was written as a supplementary appendix to the Old Testament as a whole. A long-held Jewish belief identifies Ezra as the author of 1 and 2 Chronicles and of Ezra and Nehemiah, and this is borne out by many striking similarities between those four books of the Bible.[3] At the very least, the Chronicler is a contemporary of Ezra who wishes to do more than merely write a history of Israel.[4] He is

---

[2] Ancient Hebrew omits vowels when written, so a lot of words could be fitted onto a single scroll. When the book of Chronicles was translated into Greek, it needed to be split in half and turned into two scrolls instead.

[3] Ezra and Nehemiah were also originally a single book of the Hebrew Old Testament. Manuscripts such as the Babylonian Talmud make Chronicles the final book of the Old Testament but, since the first verses of Ezra are almost identical to the final verses of 2 Chronicles, other manuscripts make Ezra–Nehemiah the final book, after Chronicles. Note the same peculiar name for the Holy Spirit – the "hand" of God/the Lord – in 1 Chronicles 28:19; Ezra 7:6, 9, 28; 8:18, 22 and 31 and Nehemiah 2:8 and 2:18. Note also the same peculiar way of describing his work – stirred/aroused/moved – in 1 Chronicles 5:26; 2 Chronicles 21:16; and Ezra 1:1 and 5.

[4] Ezra was the priest and scribe who led the second great return of the Jewish exiles back from Babylon in about 458 BC. Since the events of Nehemiah end in 432 BC, Ezra probably wrote all four books in about 430 BC.

like the Apostle John, who assumed his readers had already read Matthew, Mark and Luke, and therefore wrote a supplementary gospel which explored events and topics which had been omitted by the previous gospel-writers. The Chronicler goes back over the story of the Old Testament in order to highlight items in the ancient scrolls of Israel that were omitted earlier but which are of great significance to readers in his own day.[5]

The Chronicler wrote after the Jews had returned home to the Promised Land after decades of captivity in Babylon.[6] Many of the returning exiles wept with disappointment, for things were not as they expected.[7] Their new Temple and the new city walls of Jerusalem were much smaller than the ones destroyed by the Babylonians. Judea remained a subjugated province of the Persian Empire and the royal dynasty of David failed to produce a resurgent new king who could lead the Jewish nation to freedom. Many Jews became so disillusioned that they turned their backs on the Lord by marrying the foreign idolaters who had settled in the Promised Land during their long exile and by worshipping their idols. The Lord needed to warn them in Zechariah 4:10 that his plans for Israel were far from over. *"Who dares despise the day of small things...?"*

Into this context comes the Chronicler with a fresh retelling of the story of God's people. In **1 Chronicles 1–9**, he digs under the surface of Genesis and 1 Samuel to uncover **small things about Israel** which shed important light on what is happening in his own day. In **1 Chronicles 10–29**, he digs deeper into the events described in 2 Samuel, unearthing **small things about King David** that explain the disappointments of the present and unveil God's great promises for the future. In **2 Chronicles 1–9**, he digs deeper into the first chapters of 1 Kings to highlight

---

[5] The Chronicler names these old Jewish records as his primary sources in 1 Chronicles 9:1; 27:24 and 29:29, and 2 Chronicles 9:29; 12:15; 13:22; 16:11; 20:34; 24:27; 25:26; 26:22; 27:7; 28:26; 32:32; 33:18–19; 35:27 and 36:8.

[6] In 1 Chronicles 9:1–2, he describes the resettlement of the land by the returning Jewish exiles.

[7] See Ezra 3:12–13 and Haggai 2:1–3.

similar **small things about King Solomon**. In **2 Chronicles 10–36**, he unearths a host of buried treasures from the rest of 1 and 2 Kings, giving fresh hope to his readers through a myriad of omitted **small things about Judah**. In all of this, he echoes the words of Zechariah 4:10. He encourages the disappointed and disillusioned Jews after the exile that the Lord God of Israel is *the God of small things*.

The original Hebrew name for 1 and 2 Chronicles is *Dibrēy Hayyāmīm*, which means literally *The Things of the Days*. The Chronicler sweeps through many centuries of history, stopping frequently to focus the eyes of his readers on the little details of certain days in the past which shed great light on the problems of the present day. He uses each of these small details to convince his readers that they are still living at the heart of God's great story. The Lord is still fulfilling all his promises to his people.

The Chronicler uses events in the past to answer the big questions of the present. Who are we? Why are we here? What is God doing all around us? What should we do in response to him? These are all questions of worldview. The Chronicler uses the familiar stories of the past to bring clarity to the present and fresh energy for the future.

Like John White and his friends digging in their backyard, as we delve deeper into 1 and 2 Chronicles together, we will ultimately find revealed the face of Jesus Christ. As we reflect afresh on the stories of David, Solomon and the other kings of Judah, we will find that God has peppered their stories with tiny pieces of a great mosaic which points towards the life and ministry of his Messiah. Each of these tiny details matters greatly.

So let's get ready for some fruitful digging as we read 1 and 2 Chronicles together. Let's get ready to be inspired by each of the omitted details that the Chronicler adds back into the Jewish story. Let's get ready to enjoy the beautiful mosaic of God's plans for his people. Let's get ready to discover that the God of Israel is *the God of small things*.

Part One:

Small Things about Israel (1 Chronicles 1–9)

Un-tribal God
(1 Chronicles 1:1–54)

"Adam... Noah: Shem, Ham and Japheth...
Abraham: Isaac and Ishmael... Esau and Israel."

(1 Chronicles 1:1, 4, 28, 34)

There is a famous story about two friends who played a trick on their dim-witted neighbour. When the Amazon delivery man left a parcel for him at their home, they opened the package and switched the novel that he had ordered with an old telephone directory. A week later, they asked their neighbour how he was enjoying his new novel. "Well, I'll be honest with you," their dim-witted neighbour confessed to them. "I don't think much of the plot so far, but the opening cast list is incredible!"

16

The first nine chapters of 1 and 2 Chronicles are very similar. The story opens, not with action, but with a colossal list of names.[1] As a result, the eyes of many readers immediately glaze over, as they quickly flick forward to the start of the narrative in chapter 10. But to do so is to miss what the Chronicler is attempting to teach his readers. These opening chapters are more than just the cast list to his story. They are the story itself. The structure of these nine opening chapters reveals to us the God of small things.

| 1:1–54 | The un-tribal God |
| 2:1 – 4:23 | The royal tribe of Judah |

---

[1] Our English translations seek to soften this for us a little – for example, by adding an explanation to 1:4 that these are *"the sons of Noah"*. In the Hebrew text, the first four verses of 1 Chronicles are simply thirteen names.

Far from being dull and pointless, these nine opening chapters reveal a beautiful symmetry to God's purposes for his people. The Chronicler was probably Ezra the priest, so note the way in which the priestly tribe of Levi displaces the tribe of Dan to occupy the central place in this first section of the story.[2] The Chronicler wants to reassure his Jewish readers after the exile that it doesn't matter too much that no one from David's dynasty is ruling over an independent nation state of Israel. The centre of Jewish history was never a palace, but always the Temple. The fact that the Temple has been rebuilt after the exile means that the Lord now sits enthroned again in the midst of his people, even if Judea remains a minor province of the Persian Empire.

The priestly tribe of Levi is flanked on either side by the lesser tribes of Israel. These are flanked in turn by the two royal tribes of Israel – the families of King Saul and King David. These are flanked by people who enjoyed God's grace before and after the strict division of his people into twelve tribes. The returning exiles were known as the *Jews* and their province was known as *Judea* because they were largely the descendants of the tribe of Judah. Members of the tribe of Benjamin and of the other, lesser tribes of Israel lost much of their identity as they were absorbed

---

[2] Technically, Levi was not considered to be one of the twelve tribes, but Dan is also replaced by Levi in Revelation 7:4–8. Since Jacob prophesied in Genesis 49:16–17 that Dan would prove to be *"a snake by the roadside"*, it seems likely that the Danites never returned home from exile. Since the tribe of Zebulun is also missing, it may be that the Zebulunites failed to return too.

into this new Jewish nation.[3] The Chronicler therefore begins by reminding his readers that they have an un-tribal God.

In 1:1–3, we are reminded that the Lord walked with Adam, Enoch, Noah and their families long before he created the twelve tribes of Israel. In 1:4–27, we are reminded that the Lord was equally faithful to all three of Noah's sons. As many verses are devoted to describing the European descendants of Japheth and the African and Middle Eastern descendants of Ham as are devoted to describing the Israelite descendants of Shem.[4]

In 1:28–33, we are reminded that the Lord was faithful to all of Abraham's children. While it is true that Isaac was counted as Abraham's firstborn son when it came to inheriting his blessing (which is why he is listed before his older brother Ishmael), that doesn't mean the Lord despised the other sons of Abraham. The twelve sons of Ishmael are listed ahead of the twelve sons of Jacob. After all, the first person that the Lord ever named in the womb was Ishmael. The first appearance of one of his angels to anybody in the Bible was to Ishmael's mother Hagar.[5] In the same way, although Abraham should never have taken Keturah as his concubine and the Midianites she bore were bitter enemies to Israel, the Chronicler still lists her children ahead of Israel's tribes.[6]

This proclamation that the God of Israel is an un-tribal God becomes even clearer in 1:34–54. Isaac had twin sons. Esau was the eldest, so he is listed ahead of his brother Jacob, whom the Lord later renamed Israel. Esau sinned against the Lord by selling the blessing of the firstborn to his younger brother for

---

[3] We can tell from Luke 2:36; Romans 11:1 and Philippians 3:5 that the separate identities of the twelve tribes were not lost completely. But in the New Testament such tribal distinctions become few and far between.

[4] *Shem* is the root of our English word *Semitic*. Ham's descendants include the Egyptians who enslaved the Hebrews, the Philistines who repeatedly attacked them, and the nations which originally occupied the Promised Land. Ham's descendant Nimrod was also the founder of Assyria and Babylon. For more detail about the people in this list of names, see Genesis 5:1–32; 9:18 – 10:32 and 11:10–26.

[5] Genesis 16:1–16.

[6] The Chronicler lifts these two lists of names from Genesis 25:1–4 and 25:12–16.

a bowl of stew. Nevertheless, the Chronicler makes it clear that his unfaithfulness towards the Lord did not undo the Lord's faithfulness towards him.[7] The sons that Esau bore in his youth are listed in full in verses 35–37. The sons that he bore later, in the land that the Lord gave him in Seir, are listed in verses 38–42. The Chronicler even lists the kings of that land after it became the ancient kingdom of Edom, emphasising that *"These were the kings who reigned in Edom before any Israelite king reigned".*[8] By listing these non-Jews ahead of the twelve tribes of Israel, he helps his readers to grasp that the Lord is the God of all nations.[9]

So, if you find the opening chapter of 1 Chronicles a bit confusing, then you are in good company. So did its original Jewish readers after their return from exile in Babylon. As they stared with disappointment at their new Temple and lamented the fact that the twelve tribes of Israel were in disarray, the Chronicler surprised them with a careful retelling of the story of humanity. He pointed out that the God of small things has peppered the story of humanity with tiny details which together form a great mosaic of his purposes in history. He insisted that God's plan was never all about the twelve tribes of Israel. It was always about something far greater, for every nation.

It was the revelation of a God who does not play favourites, of a gloriously un-tribal God.

---

[7] See 2 Timothy 2:11–13.

[8] *Esau* means *Hairy* because his body was covered with thick red hair. Genesis 25:21–34 and 36:8 explain that he was also nicknamed *Seir* and *Edom*, which mean *Hairy* and *Red*, and these became the names of the land where he settled and of the kingdom that he founded there. For more detail on this list, see Genesis 36:1–43.

[9] God's grace is all the more remarkable in view of the fact that the Edomites helped the Babylonians to destroy Jerusalem and Judah in 586 BC. See Obadiah 1–21; Lamentations 4:21–22 and Malachi 1:2–5.

Revisionist History
(1 Chronicles 2:1 – 4:23)

*"These were the sons of David:… Solomon…
Rehoboam… Manasseh… Jehoiakim… Jehoiachin…
and Zedekiah."*

(1 Chronicles 3:1, 5, 10, 13, 16)

We live in an era of revisionist history. The heroes of the past are fast becoming the villains of today.

In 1895, a bronze statue of Edward Colston was erected in Bristol, England, to celebrate his philanthropy towards the city's poor. In 2020, his statue was toppled, defaced and thrown into Bristol Harbour by an angry crowd because the money which he used to help the poor of Bristol had been earned through his involvement in the transatlantic slave trade. In 1973, a similar statue of Sir Winston Churchill was erected outside the British Houses of Parliament to commemorate the role he played in winning World War Two. In 2020, it was graffitied with the words "Churchill was a racist" because of his harsh response to Mahatma Gandhi's call for Indian independence after the war.

In the second, third and fourth chapters of 1 Chronicles, the Lord performs some revisionist history of his own. He warns the returning Jewish exiles that their memory of their nation's past is wrong. When the Chronicler lists the twelve tribes of Israel in 2:1–2, the Lord inspires him to name them, not by the order of their birth, but by their mothers.[1] First come Jacob's six

---

[1] Paul insists in 2 Timothy 3:16–17 that the Lord inspired the Chronicler as he wrote. This is therefore not just the Chronicler's revisionist take on history. The Lord is revealing to us what truly happened.

sons by Leah. Then come his two sons by Rachel, sandwiched between his two sons by her maidservant Bilhah. Then come his two sons by Leah's maidservant Zilpah.[2] This is meant to signify to the readers of 1 Chronicles that the history of Israel is the story of God's grace towards all twelve sons of Jacob.

After the exile, the Jews believed that the hope of the world lay in the resurgence of the tribe of Judah. On one level, they were right. The southern kingdom of Judah had indeed followed the Lord after the northern kingdom of Israel turned to idols. Furthermore, the Messiah would indeed come into the world as the heir to David's royal dynasty of Judah. Yet the Chronicler needs to point out that they are wrong if they imagine that this has anything to do with Judah's own inherent goodness.

In 2:1–4, the Chronicler reminds his readers that Judah broke the Lord's command from the very outset by marrying a Canaanite idolater. When two out of three of their sons died as a result of sin, Judah out-sinned them both by having sex with his widowed daughter-in-law, then attempted to excuse his sin by claiming that he mistook her for one of the prostitutes who sold their bodies at the shrines of pagan idols.[3] In 2:5–9, the Chronicler reminds his readers that it was Achan of the tribe of Judah who brought trouble on the twelve tribes of Israel in the days of Joshua by stealing plunder from the ruins of Jericho.[4] Nothing but God's mercy could ever bring a Saviour out of such a wicked tribe, conceived in sin and still giving birth to sin.

In 2:10–17, the Chronicler focuses on the family of David. If any family might be found in Judah that was devoted to the Lord,

---

[2] See Genesis 29:31 – 30:24 and 35:16–26. Note that the Chronicler refers to Jacob in 1:34 and 2:1 by the other name God gave him: *Israel*. This is not just the history of a man, but the history of an entire nation.

[3] That's really not an acceptable excuse! You can read about the deaths of Er and Onan in Genesis 38:1–30.

[4] *Achar* in 2:7 instead of *Achan* in Joshua 7 reflects the way in which the Chronicler uses lots of variant Hebrew names. English Bible translators normally ignore those variants and render each name as it appears throughout the rest of the Bible – for example, *Jeconiah* in 3:16–17 becomes the *Jehoiachin* of 2 Kings.

then the Jews believed it would be this one, yet the revisionist history continues. David's older brothers were rejected by the Lord. Eliab even tried to talk him out of tackling Goliath.[5] Furthermore, the sons of David's sisters, Zeruiah and Abigail, often proved to be thorns in his side throughout his reign.

In 2:18–55, the Chronicler turns to the family of Caleb, a descendant of Judah through his son Perez.[6] The purpose of these verses is not to tell us about the younger and more famous Caleb, who fought alongside Joshua and who appears in chapter 4 with his nephew Othniel, whom he raised up as the first Judge of Israel by promising him his daughter Aksah in marriage if he conquered a difficult section of the Promised Land. The purpose of these verses is to tell us that this older Caleb was the ancestor of Bezalel, who oversaw the building of the Tabernacle at Mount Sinai.[7] Other than that, Caleb is a bit of an Ordinary Joe. He has no inherent goodness in him either.[8]

In 3:1–24, the Chronicler turns to the family of King David, the greatest hero of the tribe of Judah. After the exile, the Jews were convinced that salvation would only come to Israel through the revival of David's royal dynasty, so note the way in which the Chronicler also revises David's history. He was guilty of taking many wives and concubines. Some of these were pagan women, one of the most serious sins that Ezra and Nehemiah

---

[5] 1 Samuel 17:28. David has seven older brothers in 1 Samuel 16. The Chronicler ignores one of them to make David the seventh son of Jesse, the Hebrew number of perfection, as a tiny prophetic picture of Jesus as the true and perfect Son of David. This is picked up by New Testament verses such as Matthew 1:1; 12:23 and 21:9.

[6] This Caleb cannot be the friend of Joshua, since 2:18–20 says he was the great-grandfather of Bezalel, a contemporary of Moses. For more on Bezalel, Caleb and Othniel, see Exodus 31:1–11 and 35:30–35; Numbers 13:1 – 14:38 and 34:16–19; Joshua 14:5–15 and 15:13–19, and Judges 1:12–15 and 3:7–11.

[7] The Kenites and Rekabites who are mentioned in 2:55 are not descendants of Caleb, but descendants of Jethro, the Midianite father-in-law of Moses, who lived among Caleb's descendants. See Numbers 10:29; Judges 1:16; 2 Kings 10:15–17 and Jeremiah 35:1–19.

[8] Caleb's family tree gives us an interesting insight into the life of Abraham, since 2:34–35 shows us how important it was for a Hebrew man to have a male heir – even if it meant having sex with a female slave.

confronted amidst the returning Jewish exiles.[9] The Chronicler mentions Bathsheba, the wife of one of David's close friends, as a reminder that David had his friend killed to cover up the fact that he had made Bathsheba pregnant.[10] If salvation were to come from David's dynasty, then it could only be as an act of utter mercy from the Lord.

As for the royal descendants of David, these include kings such as Solomon and Rehoboam, whose folly divided the twelve tribes of Israel into two kingdoms, and Manasseh, who sacrificed his babies to the idol Molek and filled Jerusalem with the blood of his political purges. They also include Jehoiakim, Jehoiachin and Zedekiah, the last three kings of Judah, whose sins provoked the final destruction of Jerusalem. Based on the names on this list, the restoration of David's dynasty would do more harm than good to Israel. Their hope was not in David, but in the God who had such mercy on him.

In 3:17–24, the Chronicler lists the leaders of David's dynasty after the return from exile. His mention of Zerubbabel, who rebuilt the Temple, reminds us that he failed to become anything more than a Temple-Builder.[11] Although he served a term as governor, he was unable to make his children the hereditary rulers of an independent Judah. Instead, they became like the rest of the tribe in 4:1–23 – a bunch of very ordinary Jews.[12] Other than Caleb, the friend of Joshua, and Othniel, the

---

[9] Ezra 9:1–10:44 and Nehemiah 10:30 and 13:23–29. Might the sins of Absalom be attributed to the influences of his pagan mother? The names of David's nineteen sons in 3:1–9 are largely lifted from 2 Samuel 3:2–5 and 5:13–16.

[10] The Chronicler also mentions Tamar, who was raped by David's eldest son in 2 Samuel 13, marking another low point in his fumbling reign and fallen dynasty.

[11] Zerubbabel was the heir of Jehoiachin's eldest son Shealtiel (Ezra 3:2, 8 and 5:2; Nehemiah 12:1; Haggai 1:1, 12–14; 2:2 and 23, and Matthew 1:12). The Chronicler adds in 3:19, however, that Zerubbabel was the biological son of Jehoiachin's third son Pedaiah and was adopted by the heirless Shealtiel. This little extra detail offers us another prophetic picture of Jesus, who was not the biological son of Joseph the carpenter.

[12] In the same way that the tribe of Levi occupies the central place in the wider account of Israel in 1 Chronicles 1–9, the family of David occupies the central place in the account of Judah in 1 Chronicles 2–4.

first Judge of Israel, we know nothing about any of the people who are listed here.

So let's not rush over these three chapters of ancient Jewish genealogy. The Chronicler is setting the scene for a fresh retelling of the story of Israel. When salvation comes into the world through the tribe of Judah and its royal dynasty of David, then his readers must be under no illusions. The tribe of Judah has no inherent goodness of its own to offer. The salvation that it brings will be a mark of God's amazing grace and mercy.

Let's Get Personal
(1 Chronicles 4:9–10)

"Jabez cried out to the God of Israel, 'Oh, that you would bless me and enlarge my territory!'"

(1 Chronicles 4:10)

It's ironic when modern readers complain that the message of 1 and 2 Chronicles isn't relevant to them because they feel a million miles away from the world of David, Solomon and the other kings of Judah. Such a comment merely proves how much they need these two books of the Bible, because that's precisely how the world of David, Solomon and the other kings of Judah felt to the original readers of 1 and 2 Chronicles.

The Jews had returned home from their exile in Babylon, but they remained subjects of the Persian Empire. They felt a million miles away from a world in which the twelve tribes of Israel were ruled by godly kings in pursuit of God's glory. The Chronicler therefore retells the story of a distant past in order to teach his readers how to live their lives effectively in a very different present. That's why we need to pay close attention, especially when he halts his genealogies to invite us to make a personal response to God. These two verses about Jabez may seem throwaway and inconsequential, but the Chronicler remains insistent that the Lord Almighty is the God of small things.

Jabez has the briefest of Bible biographies. He is mentioned nowhere else in Scripture outside these two verses. He represents the many ordinary believers within the tribe of Judah before the exile who made active personal responses to God. The Chronicler uses his example to encourage us to make an active personal response of our own.

Jabez illustrates for us that *our little actions matter deeply to God*. Nowhere in the grand sweep of world history in his opening four chapters does the Chronicler pause to describe the cataclysmic Flood which destroyed the earth in the days of Noah – and yet he takes a time-out here to record the simple faith-filled actions of Jabez![1] If there is one thing that we are meant to learn from these two books of the Bible, then it is this: the little actions of our lives matter deeply to God because he is the God of small things.

Jabez also illustrates for us that *the history of the world pivots on people's prayers*. Nowhere in these first four chapters does the Chronicler mention wars or earthquakes or big business decisions or any of the other things that fill up our daily newsfeeds. Yet he stops here to turn the spotlight onto prayer, because that is how the Lord invites people to shape the events of world history with him. We know very little about Jabez except that he *"cried out to the God of Israel... and God granted his request."* Perhaps that's all that we need to know. If we cry out to God like Jabez, then God can grant our requests too.

Jabez illustrates for us that *the Lord loves to turn our pain around for good*. His name comes from a Hebrew word that can be translated *Pain* or *Grief* or *Misery*, and his mother evidently gave it to him after many hours of painful labour.[2] Imagine what a moniker it must have been for her son to bear. *Meet my baby – his name is Misery. We're allocating new learning partners today at school – great news: yours is Misery. Hi, I'd like permission to marry your daughter – my name is Misery, and you can trust me to make her happy.* The life of Jabez must have been the ancient equivalent of the Johnny Cash song about "A Boy Named Sue".

---

[1] Some readers see a reference to the start of different language groups at the Tower of Babel after the Flood, since we are told in 1:19 that in the days of Peleg *"the earth was divided"*.

[2] The curse reversed by his prayer is therefore not just that of his mother, but also that of Genesis 3:16.

And yet, the Lord evidently met with Jabez in his trauma. The God of small things always seems to seek out those whom this world disregards as worthless. He explains in Isaiah 57:15 that *"I live in a high and holy place, but also with the one who is contrite and lowly in spirit."* Jesus proves it in the gospels by gravitating towards the leprous, the lame, the lost, the least and the lonely. When Jesus does so, he is not revealing something new about God. He is simply proving what Jabez discovered in these verses.

The Lord found Jabez to be *"more honourable than his brothers"*. He became like the beggar in Jesus' famous parable in Luke 16:19–31, who lifted up his eyes to heaven because he lacked the luxuries that kept the eyes of his rich neighbour looking down at his table. He became like the tax collector in another parable of Jesus in Luke 18:9–14. While his brothers might pray prayers puffed up with pride, Jabez knew his place and pleaded for mercy. *"Oh, that you would bless me and enlarge my territory!"* he begs the Lord. *"Let your hand be with me and keep me from harm so that I will be free from pain."*[3] The Jews who returned from exile placed their hope in the fact that they were part of the tribe of Judah, but not Jabez. His painful life humbled him and, as he confesses his state of weakness, he finds to his surprise that he is honoured by the Lord.[4]

Jabez therefore illustrates that *the Lord longs to bless us, if only we will let him.* The Israelites believed that a name shaped a person's life and destiny, but Jabez refuses to buy that idea. He believes that the name of the Lord trumps every human name.[5] He cries out *"to the God of Israel"* – that is, to the one who changed the name of Jacob (which means *Deceiver*) to Israel

---

[3] Based on Ezra's other writings, this mention of the "hand" of the Lord may be a reference to the Holy Spirit. See 1 Chronicles 28:19; Ezra 7:6, 9, 28; 8:18, 22 and 31, and Nehemiah 2:8 and 2:18.

[4] Jesus makes this the conclusion to his Parable of the Pharisee and the Tax Collector, in Luke 18:14 – *"All those who exalt themselves will be humbled, and those who humble themselves will be exalted."*

[5] This principle is fleshed out in Psalm 9:10; 20:7; 54:1 and 124:8; Proverbs 18:10 and John 17:11–12.

(which means *One Who Rules as a Prince with God*). He prays literally in Hebrew, *"Oh, that you would bless me with blessing... that I would be free from pain"* – in other words, that God would replace his cursed name with a double blessing. He makes three specific requests as part of this. First, a larger share of the Promised Land. Second, a deeper experience of God's presence. Third, a practical enjoyment of God's protection. We are told that *"God granted his request"* (singular) because these are not three separate things. A bestselling Christian book teaches people how to use the prayer of Jabez to get more out of God, but what the Chronicler teaches here is far more radical.[6] He insists that the greatest thing that we can get from God is God himself. God uses our requests about our little earthly lives to catch us up into his great plans for eternity.

The Lord granted Jabez the additional territory that he asked for. You may have noticed in 2:55 that one of the towns of Judah was named Jabez, presumably in honour of its founder. But the greatest thing that Jabez achieved through his troubled life and anguished prayer was a deep relationship with the Lord. Think about it: God enjoyed his friendship with Jabez so much that he decided to make mention of it in the Bible!

We are about to carry on our journey through the genealogies which form the first nine chapters of 1 Chronicles. Before we do so, take a moment to respond to the Chronicler's call for you to make its message personal. Cry out to God with Jabez. Tell the Lord that you trust in his name and that you want to enjoy a similar deep friendship with him too.

---

[6] See Bruce Wilkinson's *The Prayer of Jabez: Breaking Through to the Blessed Life* (Colorado: Multnomah Publishers, 2000).

The Missing
(1 Chronicles 4:24 – 5:26)

"The descendants of Simeon… the Reubenites, the Gadites and the half-tribe of Manasseh."

(1 Chronicles 4:24, 5:18)

Not all of the tribes that went into exile in Assyria and Babylon made it back home to the Promised Land with Zerubbabel, Ezra and Nehemiah. One of the things that made the Jewish survivors weep the loudest was the fact that many of the tribes of Israel were missing. The Chronicler reflects on those missing tribes in this section of his genealogy.[1]

In 4:24–43, he focuses on the tribe of Simeon, which had been the southernmost tribe in the days before the exile. Simeon had lied to his Canaanite neighbours in order to slaughter them in his anger. He pretended that he did so out of holy passion for the Lord, but this pretence was soon exposed when he made a Canaanite idolater the mother of his son Shaul.[2] His father Jacob had cursed him for his sin, and that curse caused the scattering of the Simeonites throughout Judah in the days before the exile. The curse reached its fullness when no known Simeonites returned home from Babylon. The Chronicler underscores the horror of this by quoting from the annals of King Hezekiah that the Simeonites expanded their territory to the south and

---

[1] It is likely that a few survivors from these missing tribes did return from exile, but if they did so then they had lost their distinct identity and had become swallowed up into the other tribes of Israel.

[2] See Genesis 24:1–8; 28:1–2; 34:1–31; 46:10 and 49:5–7. The tribe of Simeon continued to take a lead in this same sin in Numbers 25:14. The Chronicler copies these genealogies from Genesis 46:10; Exodus 6:15 and Numbers 26:12–13, adding in a lot of extra detail along the way.

that *"they have lived there to this day"*.[3] The original readers of 1 Chronicles knew full well that this was no longer the case. The Simeonites had not returned to reclaim their territory after the exile. Their lands in Israel were now inhabited by pagan Idumeans.[4]

In 4:27, the Chronicler offers us one of the reasons for this. Simeon had a prolific descendant named Shimei, who fathered sixteen sons and six daughters, but none of his other descendants multiplied as quickly as the other tribes of Israel. This is a helpful reminder for our own day that a handful of super-evangelists can never take and hold new territory on their own. The Great Commission is an every-member ministry. If the bulk of Christians ignore God's plan for their lives, then our churches will end up like the tribe of Simeon. The Chronicler grieves over the fact that it is among the missing.

In 5:1–10, he moves on to the tribe of Reuben, the eldest son of Jacob, who was also cursed for having sex with one of his father's concubines.[5] For this reason, Reuben forfeited the double-blessing of the firstborn son, and his descendants forfeited something even greater when they refused to cross the River Jordan to make their homes in the Promised Land, settling in lands east of the river instead.[6] Although they scored some early victories over the Amorites and the descendants of Hagar, they were unprotected by the River Jordan and were among the first tribes to go into exile.[7] The Reubenites are never mentioned again in the Bible. They, too, are among the missing.

---

[3] He does this again in 2 Chronicles 5:9. His original readers knew full well when he was talking about their day and when he was quoting verbatim from ancient royal records as a lament for the old days.

[4] This is borne out by the list of resettled towns in Ezra 2:21–35 and Nehemiah 7:26–38. None of the towns listed are south of Hebron, in the former territory of the tribe of Simeon.

[5] Genesis 35:22–23.

[6] Genesis 48:1–22 and 49:3–4; Numbers 32:1–42 and Deuteronomy 21:17.

[7] The descendants of Hagar are mentioned in Psalm 83:6 as enemies of God's people. The Chronicler explains in 5:18–22 that the Reubenites defeated them by crying out to the Lord in battle. However, he also records in 5:6 that they were defeated in turn by Tiglath-Pileser III of Assyria, who reigned from 745 to 727 BC. Protected by the River Jordan, the western tribes of Israel were able to hold out longer, until 722 BC.

In 5:11–22, the Chronicler moves his focus onto the tribe of Gad, which also settled on the east side of the River Jordan, to the north of Reuben. The Gadites enjoyed some early military victories and expanded their territory by crying out to the God of Israel in battle and by trusting him to help them defeat their enemies *"because the battle was God's"*. Sadly, this is all that the Chronicler can say positively about them. He can tell us that the Gadites *"occupied the land until the exile"*, but he isn't able to record their triumphant return. The tribe of Gad was also counted among the missing.[8]

In 5:23–26, the Chronicler records the fate of the half-tribe of Manasseh, which chose to settle in lands east of the River Jordan and to the north of the Gadites and Reubenites. At first, this appeared to be a wise move, since they quickly multiplied in number and were able to expand their territory to the slopes of Mount Hermon, on the modern-day border between Lebanon and Syria. However, unlike the half-tribe of Manasseh which went west, they were unprotected from the pagans by the River Jordan. First, the Eastern Manassites fell spiritually by worshipping the pagan idols of their neighbours. Next, they fell militarily, when King Tiglath-Pileser III of Assyria carried them off into exile along with the Gadites and Reubenites. They were never to return. We can sense the tears in the Chronicler's eyes when he solemnly informs us that the Assyrians *"took them to Halah, Habor, Hara and the river of Gozan, where they are to this day."*

The saddest statement of all is when the Chronicler informs us that their descendants are missing from the ranks of Israel because *"the God of Israel stirred up the spirit"* of King Tiglath-Pileser against them. Tragic though their fate is, he insists that they got what was coming to them as a result of their sin and compromise and rank idolatry. This is a sobering reflection, not

---

[8] Instead of copying the genealogy of Gad from Genesis 46:16 and Numbers 26:15–18, the Chronicler lists its chieftains under King Jeroboam II of Israel (793–753 BC), Gad's final heyday before it went into exile.

just for the twelve tribes of Israel many centuries ago, but also for the struggling churches of our own day.

For Simeon, lying to his neighbours and lusting after pagan women was a small thing. For Reuben, a little dalliance with his father's concubine was a small thing too. For the Reubenites, the Gadites and the eastern half-tribe of Manasseh, the decision not to settle in the Promised Land west of the River Jordan was also a small thing. But that's the Chronicler's point. The Lord Almighty is the God of small things. Each of our little acts of disobedience therefore assumes an untold enormity before him.

As you read these verses about the missing tribes of Israel, take a moment to consider whether there is any little sin or compromise in your own life. Jesus warns us in Matthew 7:21–23 that the Lord Almighty is still the God of such small things:

> *Not everyone who says to me, "Lord, Lord," will enter the kingdom of heaven, but only the one who does the will of my Father who is in heaven. Many will say to me on that day, "Lord, Lord, did we not prophesy in your name and in your name drive out demons and in your name perform many miracles?" Then I will tell them plainly, "I never knew you. Away from me, you evildoers!"*

Centre Story
(1 Chronicles 6:1–81)

"The sons of Levi…"

(1 Chronicles 6:1)

The sixth chapter of 1 Chronicles is the longest. Unless we understand the context which inspired the Chronicler to retell the Jewish story, then we may also think it the most tedious. When we realise, however, that he placed these eighty-one verses at the heart of the symmetrical structure of the first section of his story, we begin to grasp why he gave his readers such a detailed family tree of the tribe of Levi. It is a physical statement of one of the Chronicler's biggest themes – that in the history of Israel it has always been the priesthood, and not just the monarchy, which has held the central place in the story.

33

1:1–54	**The un-tribal God**
2:1 – 4:23	**The royal tribe of Judah**
4:24 – 5:26	**The lesser tribes of Israel**
	(Simeon, Reuben, Gad and Eastern Manasseh)
6:1–81	**The priestly tribe of Levi**
7:1–40	**The lesser tribes of Israel**
	(Issachar, Benjamin, Naphtali, Western Manasseh, Ephraim and Asher)
8:1–40	**The royal tribe of Benjamin**
9:1–34	**The un-tribal God once more**

In his first five chapters of genealogy, the Chronicler pointed out that the Lord has always loved and blessed people who are not part of the twelve tribes of Israel, that he hasn't always found the royal tribe of Judah to be faithful, and that he may not be planning to bring some of the disobedient tribes of Israel back home. In chapters 7–9, he does the same thing in reverse – focusing on the other tribes of Israel, including the fallen royal tribe of Benjamin, before concluding that the Lord again wants to reveal himself to the world as the un-tribal God. The Chronicler places the priestly family of Levi at the centre of this symmetrical retelling of the history of Israel to point out that the Temple, not just the palace, lies at the centre of God's great purposes for humanity.

This was important for the Jews after the exile because many of them were bitterly disappointed with what life was like for them back in the Promised Land. Their reading of the Old Testament prophets had led them to believe that a new king of Judah from David's royal dynasty ought to be ruling over an independent land of Israel. Instead, Judea remained a minor province of the Persian Empire and included only a fraction of the historic territory of the tribes of Israel. With no new king and no new kingdom, many of the Jews had concluded that the Lord's plans for his people must have failed.

That's why, in 6:1–15, the Chronicler uses the family tree of Levi to prove to his readers that the priesthood, not the monarchy, always lay at the centre of the Jewish story. Centuries before the tribes of Israel sinned against the Lord by demanding that he give them a king, the Lord had chosen the tribe of Levi to serve as his priests and worship leaders. The family tree in these verses takes us from Aaron (the elder brother of Moses and the first high priest at his Tabernacle) to Eleazar (who helped Joshua to conquer and divide the Promised Land between the twelve tribes) to Phinehas (who served as high priest in the days of the Judges) to Zadok (who served as high priest for King David and King Solomon) to Azariah (who served as the first high priest at Solomon's new Temple) all the way down to Seraiah (the last high priest before the exile, who was executed by the Babylonians).[1]

This long list of names reaches a grand finale in verse 15, where the Chronicler informs us that *"Jozadak was deported when the Lord sent Judah and Jerusalem into exile by the hand of Nebuchadnezzar."* First, this is a statement that the Lord himself sent the tribes of Israel into exile. The strong arm of the king of Babylon was just a tool wielded by the far stronger arm of the Lord.[2] Second, it is an affirmation of the Lord's continued faithfulness towards the Jewish nation, since everybody knew that Joshua son of Jozadak was the high priest who led the first wave of exiles back from Babylon and built the Second Temple with Zerubbabel. The emergence of a Second Temple was as much a sovereign work of the Lord as the destruction of the First Temple. It didn't matter, then, that there wasn't a king from David's dynasty on the throne of an independent Jewish nation. The Temple, and not just the palace, always lay at the centre of the Jewish story.[3]

In 6:16–30, the Chronicler points out to his readers that the Lord has been equally faithful in bringing home the other Levites to assist the descendants of Aaron at the Temple.[4] This list of names includes Korah (who led a rebellion against Moses in the desert) and Samuel (the last of the Judges of Israel) and his two sons (whose lack of devotion to the Lord provoked the Israelites to demand that God grant them a king). The list breaks off at this point as another poignant

---

[1] 2 Kings 25:18–21. This list of high priests may seem long, but the Chronicler has actually abridged it for us. For example, he misses out the high priests Jehoiada and Uriah, who appear in 2 Kings 12:2 and 16:10–16.

[2] The Chronicler can say this on the basis of Jeremiah 25:9; 27:6; 43:10; 51:7 and 20–23.

[3] Ezra 3:2. The descendants of Jozadak remained high priests until the destruction of the Temple in 70 AD.

[4] The Chronicler builds this list from Exodus 6:16–19; Numbers 3:17–20; 16:1–2 and 26:57–58, and 1 Samuel 8:1–22. As usual, he makes a few slight alterations to the names as he does so.

reminder that the monarchy of Israel had a chequered history. The Temple was God's throne room and it lay at the true centre of the story.[5]

In 6:31–48, the Chronicler reminds his readers that King David and King Solomon both affirmed the central place that the Temple played in the Jewish story. They appointed Levites to lead worship at their new Tabernacle and Temple in Jerusalem.[6] David rejoiced in the Law which declared that the Lord's purpose in saving Israel was *"that I might dwell among them"*. Solomon affirmed the response of Moses to this declaration:

> *"If your Presence does not go with us, do not send us up from here. How will anyone know that you are pleased with me and with your people unless you go with us? What else will distinguish me and your people from all the other people on the face of the earth?"*[7]

In 6:49–53, the Chronicler rejoices in the continuity between the actions of the priests and Levites at Solomon's First Temple and at Zerubbabel's Second Temple. Everything was done there *"in accordance with all that Moses the servant of God had commanded"*. In 6:54–81, he lifts from Joshua 21 the list of Levite settlements throughout the land of Israel, so that the Jewish survivors can rejoice at how faithful God has been in bringing the Levites back to those same towns – even to towns that lie within the territory of the missing tribes which are yet to return home from the exile.

There is a lot of detail in this chapter, but it all boils down to something very simple: the Lord's promises to his people have not failed because there is no king on the throne of an

---

[5] Ancient thrones often had a footstool as well as a seat (2 Chronicles 9:18). God's Temple in Jerusalem was therefore considered to be the earthly footstool of his heavenly throne (1 Chronicles 28:2; Psalms 99:5 and 132:7, and Lamentations 2:1).

[6] Some of the men listed here were big names in Israel's history, writing Psalms 42–50, 73–85 and 87–89. The Chronicler will make David's Tabernacle and Solomon's Temple the central focus of parts 2 and 3 his story.

[7] Exodus 29:46 and 33:15–16.

independent nation state of Israel. The priesthood of Aaron lies as much at the centre of the Jewish story as the dynasty of David. Israel's salvation lies in the fulfilment of both strands of its history. Far greater than the presence of an earthly king within a palace is the Presence of Almighty God within the throne room of his Temple.

Seven-and-a-Half
(1 Chronicles 7:1 – 9:44)

"The first to resettle on their own property in their own towns were some Israelites… from Benjamin, and from Ephraim and Manasseh."

(1 Chronicles 9:2–3)

Each of the twelve tribes of Israel had a distinct history before they went into exile. We have already seen that the tribe of Judah settled in the south, near the city of Jerusalem. We have also seen that the tribe of Simeon settled further south and was found missing after the return from exile. Also missing were the tribes of Reuben and Gad, along with the half-tribe of Manasseh, since they settled in lands east of the River Jordan and soon fell victim to foreign idols and to foreign armies.

This leaves the seven-and-a-half tribes which formed the northern kingdom of Israel on the west side of the River Jordan before the exile. It is to these tribes that the Chronicler now turns in chapter 7. Having dedicated a hundred verses to Judah and eighty-one verses to Levi, he deals with each of these remaining tribes rather rapidly. Issachar receives five verses. Benjamin receives seven. Naphtali gets only one, which is more than Dan or Zebulun, who receive no mention at all. Those two tribes settled in the extreme north of Israel so, like Simeon in the extreme south, they fell foul of foreign idols, foreign women and foreign conquest. They too are counted among the missing.[1]

---

[1] Joshua 19:10–16; Judges 18:1–31 and 2 Kings 15:29. Naphtali lay north of Zebulun and south of Dan. It appears that Naphtali survived, but barely, since it receives only a single verse in chapter 7.

The western half of the tribe of Manasseh receives six verses, in which the Chronicler points out that women played a vital role in its history. Ephraim receives ten verses, in which the Chronicler remembers that this was the tribe of the hero Joshua. Asher receives eleven verses, which ends with the number of its fighting men and rounds off an important theme throughout this chapter.[2] It doesn't matter if you are regarded as mighty (like Joshua) or disregarded by everyone (like the women of Manasseh). The Lord knows every ordinary foot soldier in his Kingdom and has a plan for their life.[3] Whenever you feel small and insignificant, remember that he is the God of small things.

In chapter 8, the Chronicler backtracks to focus again on the tribe of Benjamin. He lists the family tree of King Saul as a symmetrical counterpart to the family tree of King David in chapter 3.[4] Together with its repeat in 9:35–44, this forms a bridge between the first and second sections of 1 Chronicles, transitioning the story from genealogy to a narrative that begins with the downfall of King Saul. The royal family of Benjamin is also a reminder that the monarchy was never quite as rosy as the Jews who returned from exile imagined. King Saul had led their nation away from the Lord. He had even murdered the Lord's priests at his Tabernacle. The restoration of God's presence within his Temple was every bit as important to Israel as a restoration of its monarchy.

In 9:1, the family tree of King Saul culminates with a statement that these seven-and-a-half tribes *"were taken captive*

---

[2] The source for the numbers of fighting men in chapter 7 is probably David's census. 1 Chronicles 21:6 does not say that Joab failed to number the men of Benjamin, but simply that he failed to pass it on to David.

[3] Whatever else we grasp from these first nine chapters of 1 Chronicles, we mustn't miss the obvious – that the Lord keeps an eternal record of the individual actions of everybody who forms part of his people.

[4] Benjamin's genealogy is the hardest of all the tribes to understand, since Genesis 46:21 lists his ten sons, 1 Chronicles 7:6–12 lists only three of those sons, and Numbers 26:38–39 and 1 Chronicles 8:1–2 list only five sons. Some of their names change here too, as do the names of King Saul's sons when compared to 1 Samuel.

to Babylon because of their unfaithfulness".[5] The exile had not been proof that the gods of Babylon were stronger than the God of Israel, but proof that God meant what he said when he called the tribes of Israel to be holy because his presence dwelt among them.

In 9:2–34, the Chronicler rejoices that the Lord has been faithful to these seven-and-a-half tribes despite their unfaithfulness towards him. This is more than just a random list of families who resettled in the towns of Judah and in the ruins of Jerusalem during the first great return of the exiles from Babylon under the leadership of Zerubbabel.[6] Among the names of those from the royal tribe of Judah and the priestly tribe of Levi, we are told that some were "Israelites... from Benjamin, and from Ephraim and Manasseh". Since Luke 2:36 adds that some were also from the tribe of Asher, we should take this to mean that all of these seven-and-a-half tribes returned to the Promised Land under Zerubbabel, Ezra and Nehemiah.[7] One of the great themes of 1 and 2 Chronicles is that God will always judge people who are unfaithful to his Word, but another great theme is that God will never stop being faithful towards them.[8]

The Apostle Paul puts it this way in 2 Timothy 2:11–13:

> "Here is a trustworthy saying: If we died with him, we will also live with him; if we endure, we will also reign with him. If we disown him, he will also disown us; if we are faithless, he remains faithful, for he cannot disown himself."

---

[5] The northern kingdom of Israel was actually exiled to Assyria in 722 BC, but the Chronicler is arguing that this was part and parcel of the exile of the southern kingdom of Judah to Babylon in 586 BC.

[6] A similar list appears in Nehemiah 11:3–19. The names there are different because it lists the names of those who settled in Jerusalem almost a century later under Nehemiah.

[7] We can also tell this from Esther 2:5; Romans 11:1 and Philippians 3:5.

[8] We can see this especially in 9:19, where the descendants of Korah, who rebelled against the Lord by demanding equal access to the Tabernacle in Numbers 16, are restored as the gatekeepers of God's Temple!

The Chronicler seeks to prove this through the restoration of the Temple gatekeepers after the exile. He points out that these were first appointed for the Tabernacle by the third high priest Phinehas.[9] They continued their work during the days of the Judges, when Samuel reaffirmed the importance of their role. King David followed this up by reaffirming them again. Although he built a new Tabernacle on Mount Zion, he reassigned gatekeepers to the Tabernacle of Moses and gave directions for the gatekeepers of the future, after the two Tabernacles had been combined into one new Temple. The Chronicler's point here is that the descendants of those gatekeepers returned from the exile and were reappointed to those same posts in Zerubbabel's Temple. It didn't matter that there was no new king as yet on the throne of Israel. It was always the Temple, and never just the palace, which was central to the Jewish story.

The stage has now therefore been set for the narrative of 1 Chronicles to begin – a fresh retelling of the history of Israel for the Jews after the exile. Well done for wading through the detail of these first nine chapters. I hope that you have found the effort rewarding, because these chapters are far more than a dry telephone directory of ancient Israel. They are an affirmation that the continuity between God's people before and after the exile, is not so much found in the royal palace as it is in the Lord's Temple.

The Lord is the true King of Israel and his Presence returned with the exiles to the Promised Land. Jewish history restarted when he made his Temple in Jerusalem once more the earthly footstool to his heavenly throne.

---

[9] This happened as a result of the Lord's blessing on him in Numbers 25:1–13. Phinehas had assumed the role of spiritual gatekeeper for the twelve tribes of Israel by the time of Joshua 22:9–33.

Part Two:

Small Things about David (1 Chronicles 10–29)

The Messiah
(1 Chronicles 10:1–14)

"Saul died because he was unfaithful to the Lord…
So the Lord put him to death and turned the kingdom
over to David."

(1 Chronicles 10:13–14)

There was a special Hebrew word that the Israelites used to describe Saul as the first king of Israel. They called him the *messiah* – a word that is used to describe him eight times in 1 Samuel and which means *The Chosen One* or *The Anointed One* of the Lord.[1]

Sadly, Saul did not live up to the name he had been given. The Chronicler emphasises this by beginning the narrative of the second section of his story with the downfall of King Saul at the Battle of Mount Gilboa. He makes no mention of the good old days, when the Holy Spirit anointed Saul to prophesy words from the Lord, or when the Holy Spirit empowered him to deliver Israel from the hand of the Ammonites in fierce battle. Instead, the Chronicler fast-forwards to the very last day of Saul's reign. His narrative begins where 1 Samuel ends, with King Saul's final downfall.

The Lord's *messiah* was meant to deliver the tribes of Israel from their bitterest enemies, the Philistines.[2] Instead, we find Saul on the run from the Philistines. They massacre

---

[1] In the Hebrew text of 1 Samuel, Saul is described as the Lord's *messiah* in 12:3, 5; 24:6, 10; 26:9, 11, 16 and 23. David is described as the Lord's *messiah* in 16:6 and throughout 2 Samuel.

[2] The Lord says in 1 Samuel 9:16 that Saul's calling as *messiah* is to rescue Israel from the Philistines.

his army, slaughter his three sons and bring his kingdom to a shameful end.[3] They then move in on Saul for the kill. The tribe of Benjamin was famous for the accuracy of its archers and its slingers, so it is deeply ironic when Saul is driven back and wounded by the Philistine bowmen and forced to make his final stand amid their arrows.[4]

The Lord's *messiah* was meant to be a man of prayer, who ruled the tribes of Israel for God. He is described in the Hebrew text of 1 and 2 Samuel, not just as a *melek*, which means *king*, but as a *nāgīd*, which means *viceroy* or *deputy*.[5] Saul refused to rule this way, so he was told in 1 Samuel 13:14 that *"Your kingdom will not endure; the Lord has sought out a man after his own heart and appointed him ruler [nāgīd] of his people, because you have not kept the Lord's command."* The Chronicler demonstrates how unwilling Saul was to submit to the Lord's authority by telling us that, even on the brink of death, he refused to repent of his sins and to plead with the Lord to rescue him.[6] He would literally rather die than hand his life over to the Lord, so in the end that's precisely what he did.

The *messiah* was meant to partner with the Lord to conquer the remaining pockets of the Promised Land which had held out stubbornly against Joshua and the Judges. Instead of inspiring the twelve tribes of Israel to do so, we meet Saul's army in full flight. In a tragic reversal of God's plan for Israel, it is the Philistines who expand their borders to possess a greater share of the Promised Land.

---

[3] Saul's dynasty was not quite wiped out, since 9:39 says he also had a fourth son. 2 Samuel 1–4 explains that Esh-Baal (also known as Ish-Bosheth) ruled over the northern tribes of Israel for the next seven years.

[4] Their skill with the bow and sling is celebrated in 12:2. It is equally ironic when Saul commits suicide, since he has been self-harming the royal dynasty of Benjamin throughout his sinful reign.

[5] The word *nāgīd* is used in 1 Samuel to describe both Saul (9:16 and 10:1) and David (25:30). It is used in 1 Chronicles to describe both Solomon (29:22) and the many deputies who helped David govern Israel (13:1).

[6] Even the sinful Reubenites, Gadites and Manassites were helped by the Lord, in 5:18–22, *"because they cried out to him during the battle"* as a sign that *"they trusted in him"*. Saul stubbornly refuses to do so here.

The *messiah* was meant to demonstrate to the world that the God of Israel was far stronger than any pagan idol. Instead, the Philistines return to the battlefield to mutilate Saul's corpse, and to put his severed head and armour on display as victory trophies in the temples of their false gods.[7] We are meant to be horrified that they *"sent messengers throughout the land of the Philistines to proclaim the news among their idols and their people"*. In all of this, the Chronicler is seeking to remind his readers that Israel's salvation never lay in a merely human king sitting on its throne, but in the Presence of the Lord turning its Temple into the footstool of his far greater throne.

In case we miss this lesson, the Chronicler states it very plainly in verses 13–14. If the Jews are harking back to the days of the monarchy, then they need to remember what those days were truly like. *"Saul died because he was unfaithful to the Lord; he did not keep the word of the Lord and even consulted a medium for guidance, and did not enquire of the Lord. So the Lord put him to death and turned the kingdom over to David son of Jesse."*

We can almost hear his readers rushing to respond that they did not wish for a return to the monarchy of Saul, but to the monarchy of David. After all, the word *messiah* is also used throughout the Hebrew text of 1 and 2 Samuel to describe David. He was a man of prayer, who consciously ruled as God's deputy.[8] He defeated not just the Philistines, but all the other enemies of God's people too. He extended the territory of Israel to its greatest ever boundaries, and as he did so he brought back the pagan idols of his foes along with treasure plundered from their temples as victory trophies for the Lord.[9]

But such a response ignores the strange verb that the Chronicler uses in verse 2 to describe the Philistines in hot

---

[7] The Lord had caused a statue of the Philistine idol Dagon to bow down before him in 1 Samuel 5. Now, because of Saul's unfaithfulness, the world is falsely led to assume that Dagon is stronger than Yahweh, until the men of Jabesh Gilead, who were rescued by Saul in 1 Samuel 11, put an end to this shame.

[8] Psalms 5:2 and 145:1.

[9] 2 Samuel 5:21 and 8:11, and 1 Chronicles 14:12.

pursuit of the *messiah*. The Hebrew word *dābaq* states literally that they *clung* or *stuck like glue* to King Saul and his sons. Whenever we set up someone as an earthly saviour, the Lord allows the Devil to pursue that person closely until everybody grasps that the best of men are never more than men at best. This happens to King David in 1 Chronicles 21:1, because he is not the true *Messiah* who will save God's people. Nor are any of the other kings of Judah, which is why the Lord did not restore their dynasty to the throne when the Jews returned from exile in Babylon.

The downfall of King Saul paves the way for the Chronicler to retell the story of King David, so let's not make the same mistakes as the Jews after the exile by imagining that he is the *messiah* we are looking for. The Chronicler omits to mention his many years as a fugitive, his seven years of rejection by the northern tribes of Israel, his shocking sin with Bathsheba or the repeated rebellions of his sons because he wants to use King David, not just as a historical figure, but as a prophetic picture of the true *Messiah* who is to come.

Matthew picks up on this at the start of his gospel by beginning with seventeen verses of genealogy which echo 1 Chronicles 1–9. This leads into narrative in which Matthew tells his readers that Jesus is the true *Messiah* of 1 Chronicles 10–29. Matthew is looking back to the retelling of the story of King David in 1 Chronicles when he starts his gospel with a cry of triumph: *"This is the genealogy of Jesus the Messiah"*!

Choose Your King
(1 Chronicles 11:1 – 12:40)

"These are the numbers of the men armed for battle who came to David at Hebron to turn Saul's kingdom over to him."

(1 Chronicles 12:23)

There is an important spiritual principle for anyone who seeks to follow the Lord. We should expect a lengthy gap between the promise and the payoff. David discovered this after Samuel anointed him as *messiah*. He was forced to spend many years as a fugitive on the run from a jealous King Saul. When Saul died, David was rejected by the northern tribes of Israel. Only the tribe of Judah chose to receive him as their king; the northern tribes preferred a son of Saul.

The Chronicler says very little about this period. Having started this second section of his story with a narrative that echoes 1 Samuel 31, he now fast-forwards to events that echo 2 Samuel 5. He acknowledges that David recruited a rabble army at his hideout in the cave of Adullam, and that David ruled over the tribe of Judah from the southern city of Hebron until the northern tribes were willing to receive him as their king. But his focus in these two chapters is less on the gap between the promise and the payoff than it is on the fact that this gap gives us an opportunity to choose our king.[1] He tells the Jews after the exile, who are lamenting the demise of David's dynasty,

---

[1] Our best Christian discipleship takes place at times when God doesn't give us what we want – at least, not straightaway. It is in those moments that he purifies our hearts, as we surrender everything to him.

that their disappointment is an invitation from God to set their eyes towards a better King.

In 11:1–3, the northern tribes finally decide to make David the new king of Israel. Saul's last surviving son has been assassinated, so they have little choice about it, yet they still try to play hardball with King David. They tell him that they are choosing him because he is an Israelite with a great track record of leadership and a prophetic calling from the Lord – yet those three things have been true of David for the past seven years![2] They are only willing to anoint him king after they have negotiated a covenant with him.[3] What follows in the next two chapters is meant to be a counter to this. The Chronicler lists those who willingly chose David as their king, long before the reluctant leaders of Israel.

In 11:4–9, he retells the story of how David conquered Jerusalem from the Jebusites.[4] It is lifted from 2 Samuel 5:6–10, but with one obvious difference. In 2 Samuel, it is David who captures Jerusalem, but in 1 Chronicles it is David's nephew Joab, who chose to side with David when he was on the run from Saul and who is now rewarded by being made commander-in-chief of the army. Similarly, in 2 Samuel it is David alone who fortifies Jerusalem as his capital, whereas Joab gladly does it with him in 1 Chronicles.[5]

---

[2] The Hebrew phrase which describes David's leadership in 11:2 means literally that he *"brought out and brought in Israel"*. This is what Christian leaders do. They lead people *out* of Satan's schemes and strongholds and *into* all the blessings that God has for them in Jesus.

[3] They know full well that he is the Lord's *messiah* because they use the Hebrew word *nāgīd* in 11:2, meaning *viceroy* or *deputy*, when recalling what God prophesied over him through Samuel.

[4] The city's ancient name was *Salem*, which means *Peace*, in the days when it was ruled by a God-fearing king named Melchizedek (Genesis 14:18–20). David seems to have sensed that he needed to deliver the city from the pagans who renamed it Jebus, in order to make himself a prophetic picture of the *Messiah* to come (Psalm 110 and Hebrews 6:20). Having done so, he renamed it *Jerusalem*, which means *Foundation of Peace*.

[5] A less obvious difference is that the Chronicler changes *"the king and his men"* in 2 Samuel 5:6 to *"David and all the Israelites"*. These chapters rejoice over those who gladly chose King David from the eleven northern tribes.

In 11:10–47, the Chronicler lists the mighty warriors who chose to receive David as their king while he was still a fugitive from King Saul. We don't need to understand how Jashobeam and Abishai were each able to skewer 300 foes with their spears in a single battle or how Eleazar could help David to hold off the entire Philistine army on his own.[6] Nor do we need to understand which of these fifty-three men were counted among the Three and the Thirty.[7] We are simply meant to view this list as an invitation to fix our eyes on the true *Messiah*, instead of looking to earthly saviours like King Saul.[8] Many of these warriors came from the northern tribes of Israel, yet they gladly chose to receive David as their true king. They lavished their love upon him (11:15–19) and they laughed off good excuses not to follow him (11:22).[9] *"They, together with all Israel, gave his kingship strong support to extend it over the whole land".*[10]

In 12:1–22, the Chronicler lists other rank-and-file soldiers who also chose to receive David as their true king while he was on the run from Saul. These included men from Saul's own tribe of Benjamin (12:1–7, 16–18) and from the

---

[6] The Chronicler says literally in Hebrew that Jashobeam and Abishai *"woke up"* their spears. Sleepy Christians need to wake up to the fact that God has fully armed them to push back the Devil (Ephesians 6:10–18). He will even enable them to turn Satan's own weapons back on him (11:23 and Habakkuk 3:13–14).

[7] We find out more about the exploits of Sibbekai, who is listed in 11:29, when he reappears in 20:4.

[8] The mention of Uriah the Hittite in 11:41, who was murdered on David's instructions in 2 Samuel 11, reminds us that the real King David was a sinner like King Saul. These chapters give us a prophetic picture of the true *Messiah*, who does not need our help (11:9), but who grants us the privilege of siding with him.

[9] We would have excused Benaiah for waiting for the snow to thaw before confronting a lion. But Benaiah grasped that the only day on which we have power to serve the Messiah is today.

[10] To serve the *Messiah*, our focus needs to be on extending his Kingdom, and not on extending our own profile. David is not just served by men from the tribes of Reuben and Benjamin (11:31 and 42), but also by out-and-out foreigners, such as *Ammonites*, *Hittites* and *Moabites* (11:39, 41 and 46).

tribe of Gad (12:8–15).[11] Although their tribe had settled on the wrong side of the River Jordan, the Gadites were so quick and courageous that they crossed the river while it was in full flood to stand shoulder-to-shoulder with David as their true king. Others came from the tribe of Manasseh and even from among the Canaanites of Gibeon (12:4, 19–21). This chapter isn't really about King David, who was as much a sinner as King Saul.[12] The Chronicler explains to us that these soldiers are a prophetic picture of *"the army of God"*. They are meant to stir our hearts to turn our backs on the world and to make the *Messiah* our king.

In 12:23–40, the Chronicler moves on to list those warriors who chose to side with David during the seven years that he reigned over Judah from the city of Hebron. He tells us that 337,000 men came to join him from all twelve tribes of Israel, as well as from the tribe of Levi, because they were *"fully determined to make David king over all Israel"* and *"to turn Saul's kingdom over to him.*[13] After using the army at the cave of Adullam as a picture of the true *Messiah*'s army in chapter 11, the Chronicler ends chapter 12 by making the joyful feasting of this army at Hebron a prophetic picture of the banquet to which the *Messiah* invites all those who gladly choose him as their King.[14]

When the Chronicler tells us in verse 31 that these thousands of soldiers were *"designated by name"*, he seems to

---

[11] The Hebrew word *bādal* in 12:8 tells us that these Gadites *separated* or *divided* themselves from their brothers to receive David as their king. The Lord had parted the River Jordan in flood in Joshua 3:15–16, but these Gadites didn't wait for a miracle – they acted in faith. With such courage, determination and sense of urgency, it is no wonder that each of the Gadites was a match for 100 or 1,000 normal soldiers.

[12] The Chronicler alludes to this by reminding us that David foolishly ended up fighting for the Philistines against the tribes of Israel. The Lord needed to save David from himself in 2 Samuel 27–29.

[13] By the time the leaders of the northern tribes finally anointed David as king, *"all the rest of the Israelites were also of one mind to make David king"* (12:38). Even those who could not fight for David supplied his army with food.

[14] Note in 12:38 that each of these soldiers *volunteered*. We can read more about this joyful messianic banquet in Isaiah 25:6–8; Matthew 8:11–12 and 22:1–14; Luke 14:15–24 and Revelation 19:7–9.

be encouraging us that the true *Messiah* is calling us to add our own name to this list too. He is inviting us to ask the Holy Spirit to stir in us the song he stirred in the heart of Amasai in verse 18: *"We are yours!... We are with you!... Success, success to you, and success to those who help you, for your God will help you."*[15]

[15] The Hebrew text of 12:18 says literally that the Holy Spirit *"clothed"* Amasai – the same vivid metaphor which is used in Judges 6:34; 2 Chronicles 24:20 and Luke 24:49. Saul could only muster an army of 600 men in his own strength (1 Samuel 13:15), but God's Spirit stirs people to devote themselves gladly to his *Messiah*.

Three Histories
(1 Chronicles 12:32–33)

"From Issachar, men who understood the times and knew what Israel should do."

(1 Chronicles 12:32)

The Bible has three different ways of looking back on Israel's history. None of the basic facts are altered with each retelling, but the Bible writers emphasise different aspects of what happened, depending on which of three distinct goals they have in view.

A lot of the time, the Bible seeks to give us a *doxological history*. It tells the story of Israel in a way that celebrates the glory of God viewed through his faithful rule over the world. Deuteronomy 32, Psalm 105 and Daniel 2 are all great examples of this, since those three chapters seek to convince us that all history is "his story". They call us to cry out with them: *"Ascribe greatness to our God!... His work is perfect."*[1]

At other times, the Bible seeks to give us a *prophetic history*. It tells the same story of Israel, but in a way that garners lessons for the present from what happened in the past. By recording positive outcomes from other people's faith and obedience, the Bible writers encourage us to walk in similar faith and obedience ourselves. By recording negative outcomes from other people's disobedience, they warn us not to copy those

---

[1] Deuteronomy 32:3–4 in the English Standard Version (ESV).

same sins ourselves. A clear example of this is Psalm 106.[2] So is much of Joshua, Judges, 1 and 2 Samuel, and 1 and 2 Kings – all books which are categorised among the "Former Prophets" in the Hebrew Old Testament. The New Testament writers often quote from such books in order to warn their readers that *"these things occurred as examples to keep us from setting our hearts on evil things as they did."*[3]

At still other times, the Bible seeks to give us a *genealogical history*. It tells the story of how God's people came to be where they are today. Often it begins with the moment when the Lord called Abraham to leave Ur of the Chaldees to become a wandering nomad. Then it recalls what happened to the patriarchs in Canaan, to the Hebrews during the Exodus and to the twelve tribes of Israel after they entered the Promised Land. Great examples of this type of history telling are found in Nehemiah 9 and Acts 7.

You might be tempted to assume that 1 and 2 Chronicles is an example of *prophetic history*, since it frequently uses what happened to God's people before the exile as a warning for those who live after it. *"They were unfaithful to the God of their ancestors and prostituted themselves to the gods of the peoples of the land… so the God of Israel… took the Reubenites, the Gadites and the half-tribe of Manasseh into exile." "Saul died because he was unfaithful to the Lord; he did not keep the word of the Lord… so the Lord put him to death."*[4] But although the Chronicler does this, the Hebrew Old Testament categorises his books, not with the "Former Prophets", but with the "Other Writings". It should be fairly obvious from its first nine chapters that 1 and 2 Chronicles is *genealogical history*. It seeks to use the past to teach us God's eternal purposes for his people. It calls us to

---

[2] Psalms 105 and 106 are intentionally placed next to one another in order to show that these three ways of telling history are complementary, not contradictory. With just doxological history, we become happy-clappy. With just genealogical history, we become tribalistic. With just prophetic history, we become shrill.

[3] 1 Corinthians 10:6; Romans 15:4; 1 Corinthians 10:11; Hebrews 4:8–11 and 6:12.

[4] 1 Chronicles 5:25–26 and 10:13–14.

live all out for those priorities during our own moment in the history of God's people.

That's why we need to sit up and take notice, in the Chronicler's list of warriors who chose David to be their king, when he mentions a group of 200 chiefs *"from Issachar, men who understood the times and knew what Israel should do"*. This might appear at first to be a throwaway comment, but the Chronicler insists that the God of Israel is the God of such small things. He is writing for a group of confused Jews after the exile, so he makes this comment an invitation for his readers to consider their response to what the Lord is doing in their own present day.

The men of Issachar *understood the times*. That is, they grasped the route that the twelve tribes of Israel had taken to end up where they were. They recognised that the Lord had always been the true King of Israel and that their ancestors sinned against him when they asked for a king like the other nations.[5] It was an idolatrous attempt to succeed in the world by pursuing the same form of leadership as the pagans, rather like a church which pursues the appointment of a CEO, rather than a pastor, as its leader today. To most of their contemporaries, King Saul seemed head-and-shoulders better than his peers.[6] But to the men of Issachar, he embodied the self-reliance that had been the bane of the tribes of Israel. In David, however, they saw something of the Lord's true *Messiah*.

The men of Issachar also *knew what Israel should do*. They were more than just researchers of the past and commentators on the present. They were men who knew how to make plans for the future based on what they saw. When King Saul died, they knew what needed to be done. The northern tribes needed to repent of having crowned his son as king. They ought to rush south to Hebron to crown David instead. The men of Issachar also knew the five priorities which the new King David needed

---

[5] Numbers 23:21; Deuteronomy 33:1–5; 1 Samuel 8:4–7 and 12:17–19, and Psalms 5:2, 47:1–9 and 145:1.

[6] This is implied by 1 Samuel 9:2 and 10:23.

to pursue once he had reunified the twelve tribes of Israel under his rule. Those five priorities form the basis of the next few chapters of 1 Chronicles. He was to pursue:

The Presence of God (13:1 – 14:17)
The House of God (15:1 – 16:43)
The Heart of God (16:8–36)
The Son of God (17:1–27)
The Plan of God (18:1 – 20:8)

Following hot on the heels of these men of Issachar come the men of Zebulun, in 12:33. If the men of Issachar know how to apply the lessons of genealogical history, then the men of Zebulun demonstrate the attitude with which we need to do so. We are told that they are *experienced*. They are not idealists when it comes to accomplishing the plans of God. They know how things work in the real world. We are told that they are *prepared for battle*.[7] They know that accomplishing the plans of God is unlikely to be an easy ride. We are told that they can fight *with every kind of weapon*. They are versatile enough to serve the Lord however he may lead. We are told that they offer themselves to David *with undivided loyalty*.[8] They are determined that nothing should distract them from their goal.

So as we step forward into the main narrative of 1 Chronicles, about the reign of the great King David, let's ask the Lord to make us like the men of Issachar and the men of Zebulun. Let's ask him to help us to fight well for our own *Messiah* in our present hour.

---

[7] The Hebrew phrase for this means literally that they were able to *"keep rank"* under pressure.

[8] The Hebrew phrase for this means literally that they helped David *"without a double heart"*. They were so focused on the prize which lay before David that they would rather die than think of running away.

The Presence of God (1 Chronicles 13:1 – 14:17)

"Bring up from there the ark of God the Lord, who is enthroned between the cherubim – the ark that is called by the Name."

(1 Chronicles 13:6)

If you have ever watched the Indiana Jones movie *The Raiders of the Lost Ark*, then you can guess the biggest disappointment that faced the Jews who made it home from the exile. It wasn't simply that Zerubbabel's Temple was smaller and less splendid than Solomon's. Nor was it that some of the tribes of Israel seemed to be missing from their worship services. It was the fact that the Ark of the Covenant had gone missing. The Presence of God had been said to dwell above the lid of that great golden box within the inner sanctuary of the Temple, but it had disappeared in the destruction of Jerusalem.[1]

The Chronicler addresses this disappointment by recalling that King David was a man who held the Ark of the Covenant in great esteem. Although Saul ignored the Ark throughout his reign, content for it to remain in the house of a man named Abinadab in the hilltop town of Kiriath Jearim, David dreamed about it constantly.[2] Psalm 132 tells us that he made a vow after Samuel singled him out as the Lord's new *messiah*. He looked

---

[1] Exodus 25:16–22 and Numbers 7:89. The last mention of the Ark is in 2 Chronicles 35:3. It is likely that it was hidden to avoid its capture by the Babylonians, then lost when those who hid it died in the slaughter.

[2] 1 Chronicles 13:3 is ambiguous. It could either mean that people failed to enquire of *"it"* (of the Ark) or to enquire of *"him"* (of the Lord in general). Either way, it is a terrible verdict on Saul's forty-year reign.

up at the lights of Kiriath Jearim, 8 miles away from the fields where he tended his father's sheep near Bethlehem, and swore that when he became king: *"I will not enter my house or go to my bed, I will allow no sleep to my eyes or slumber to my eyelids, till I find a place for the Lord, a dwelling for the Mighty One of Jacob."* David never forgot that the Presence of God lay right at the heart of Israel's story, so he vowed that he would bring the Ark of the Covenant back to the centre of Israel's life as one of his first actions as king.[3]

That's why 1 Chronicles 13 begins with great celebration. David cries, *"Let us bring the ark of our God back to us"*, and the twelve tribes of Israel respond by gathering in great number to bring back *"the ark of God the Lord, who is enthroned between the cherubim – the ark that is called by the Name"*.[4] Since the Presence of God dwelt between two ornately crafted cherubim angels on the lid of the Ark, the Israelites are rejoicing that the Lord is coming to Jerusalem to make their capital city his new home.

What happens next is therefore hugely surprising. King David and the Israelites place the Ark on a cart and worship their way from Kiriath Jearim to Jerusalem. Suddenly the oxen pulling the cart stumble. Uzzah instinctively stretches out his hand to stop the Ark from falling – and is immediately struck down dead by the Lord![5] David is so confused by what has happened and so furious with God that he calls off his plan to bring the Ark back to Jerusalem altogether. Instead, he stows

---

[3] Exodus 29:46 and 33:15–16. David's main complaint in 1 Samuel 26:20 about his life as a fugitive from Saul was that it meant he had to live *"far from the presence of the Lord"*.

[4] The normal stock phrase for the whole of Israel gathering together is that people came *"from Dan to Beersheba"* – the northernmost and southernmost cities of Israel. The Chronicler refers to places that are even further north and south than this, because King David extended Israel's borders beyond their historic limits.

[5] The Ark came to Abinadab's house in about 1080 BC, after it was returned by the Philistines in 1 Samuel 6–7. It is now about 1000 BC, so his sons or grandsons Uzzah and Ahio have become its new guardians (2 Samuel 6:3).

it safely at the nearby house of Obed-Edom and returns to Jerusalem without this symbol of the Presence of God.

Or so he thinks. The Chronicler applauds David's good intentions, but we can tell that he wants to correct him from the fact that, while 2 Samuel devotes one chapter to the return of the Ark to Jerusalem, the Chronicler gives it four. David made two mistakes here. First, he *forgot how holy God's Presence is.* He consulted with his army officers but failed to consult with the Lord. He put the Ark on a cart pulled by oxen *"because it seemed right to all the people"* and because the Philistines did so in 1 Samuel 6. He forgot that the Lord commanded in the Law of Moses that the Ark must be wrapped up in the Tabernacle curtains and carried on poles by the Levites whenever it needed to be moved. It was too holy to travel on public transport – much less behind the buttocks of a team of oxen! David and Uzzah were sincere in their actions, but they trifled with God's Presence. His Ark needed to be transported in *"the prescribed way."*[6]

The second mistake that David made was to *assume that the Presence of God was confined* to such a golden box at all. To help us see this, the Chronicler rearranges the order of events as they appear in 2 Samuel. The family of Obed-Edom is blessed during the three months that he guards the Ark for David, which is ironic, since he is a Gittite – he comes from the Philistine city of Gath, where the Ark caused misery in 1 Samuel 5.[7] Meanwhile, we discover that David's family is equally blessed too. His brand new palace and his many sons bear witness to the fact that *"the Lord had established him as king over Israel"* and that *"his kingdom had been highly exalted for the sake of his people Israel."* David finds that he is able to live in the good of God's Presence, even without the Ark.

---

[6] Exodus 25:10–15; Numbers 4:5–15 and 1 Chronicles 15:13–15. David learned this lesson before he tried a second time to bring the Ark of the Covenant to Jerusalem.

[7] Obed-Edom was a foreigner whose name means *Servant of Edom*, yet he was rewarded for guarding the Ark by being made an honorary Levite at David's Tabernacle (15:18–24; 16:4–8 and 37–38).

When the Philistines invade his territory, David does not make the mistake that the Israelites made in 1 Samuel 4. Although the Philistines bring their idols onto the battlefield to help them, David does not send for the Ark as if it were a talisman guaranteeing victory. Instead, he prays for God's Presence to help him without it. Note the deliberate contrast in literal meaning between *Perez Uzzah* in 13:11, where the Lord *Breaks Out Against Uzzah* for touching the Ark, and *Baal Perazim* in 14:11, where *The Lord Breaks Out* for Israel, without it.[8]

David remembers this lesson when the Philistines invade his territory a second time. He prays again and quickly hears God's Presence rushing through the tops of the trees to help him.[9] The Chronicler rejoices that *"David's fame spread throughout every land, and the Lord made all the nations fear him"*, without a golden box in sight. He wants his readers to grasp that their missing Ark of the Covenant is, in fact, a great blessing. It is a sign to them from God that his Presence isn't confined to the sanctuary of his Temple.

In other words, the day about which the Lord prophesied in Jeremiah 3:16–17 was on its way: *"People will no longer say, 'The ark of the covenant of the Lord.' It will never enter their minds or be remembered; it will not be missed, nor will another one be made. At that time they will call [the whole of] Jerusalem The Throne of the Lord."*

That day came at Pentecost, in 30 AD. We are to live in the good of this by making the holy Presence of God our top priority – not by confining it to Sundays and special meetings, but by being filled with his Holy Spirit each day. This lies at the heart of what God taught the returning Jewish exiles. It is how we carry on their story today.

---

[8] The Hebrew word *ba'al* means *lord*, and we can tell from the names of Saul and Jonathan's sons in 8:33–34 that it was only later that the name was hijacked to become exclusively the name of a false god.

[9] King Saul enquired very little of the Lord (10:14 and 13:3), but King David enquired constantly. Even when the Philistines camped in the same place with the same intent, David sought fresh guidance from the Lord.

The House of God
(1 Chronicles 15:1 – 16:43)

"After David had constructed buildings for himself in the City of David, he prepared a place for the ark of God and pitched a tent for it."

(1 Chronicles 15:1)

David had done more than dream about the Presence of God while tending his father's sheep in the fields outside Bethlehem. Psalm 132 tells us that he swore an oath about his first actions as king. *"I will not enter my house or go to my bed, I will allow no sleep to my eyes or slumber to my eyelids, till I find a place for the Lord, a dwelling for the Mighty One of Jacob."* The Chronicler therefore tells us about David's Tabernacle, the new dwelling-place that he built for the Lord in Jerusalem, where everybody could come to worship him.

The Philistines had destroyed the Tabernacle of Moses at Shiloh, but the Israelites restored it, first at Nob and then at Gibeon.[1] We are told in 1 Samuel 22:15 that David was a regular worshipper at this Tabernacle, so we should not regard his new tent as a replacement for the one built by Moses. He wished his new tent to be used alongside it as a vivid proclamation that a better day was coming, when the Presence of God would be a gift for everyone. Unless we grasp this, we will make no sense of 1 Chronicles 15–16.

We will not understand why David is so excited about his second attempt to bring the Ark of the Covenant to Jerusalem. We have just seen that he learned to enjoy the Presence of the Lord

---

[1] 1 Samuel 1:24; 4:3–4 and 22:11; 1 Chronicles 16:37–42 and 21:29, and 2 Chronicles 1:3–7.

without it, so why does he dance with such joyful abandon that his wife despises him for behaving in an undignified manner?[2] We need to grasp that David knew his reign was a prophetic picture of a greater *Messiah*.[3] That's why, this time around, he does everything *"in accordance with the word of the Lord"*.[4] The Ark is carried on the shoulders of the Levites, who are accompanied by hundreds more Levites as worship leaders.[5] They blow trumpets made of ram's horns – an instrument taken from the corpse of a dead sheep, which is used throughout the Old Testament as a prophetic proclamation that the *Messiah* is coming to be the atoning Lamb of God.[6] In case we miss this, the priests also offer blood-sacrifices by the side of the road.

Unless we grasp that David's Tabernacle was a proclamation that a great day of salvation was coming, we will fail to understand why he wears an *ephod* (the clothing of a high priest) and why he personally offers the blood-sacrifices at his new Tabernacle and personally speaks the priestly blessing over the worshippers there. We are told in 15:11 that the high priest Zadok is present, so this is deliberate. We find out why in Psalm 110. Evidently, David was inspired by the days when a man named Melchizedek was both king and high priest in Jerusalem. Melchizedek served bread and wine to Abraham in Genesis 14:18–20 as a sign that God's *Messiah* would offer his body and

[2] Michal was the first of David's wives and a daughter of Saul – both by birth and by character. We are given more detail about this incident in 2 Samuel 6:16–23. Michal hated to see David acting as a *nāgīd* – as God's *deputy*. The world praises Christians for their charity work but hates to see them worshipping Christ as Lord.

[3] The Apostle Peter insists in Acts 2:25–35 that David grasped this far more clearly than most of us realise.

[4] The Chronicler is firm with his readers that sincerity does not equal truth. If we want to seek God and find him, then we need to study the Gospel and come to him in his prescribed way – only through his *Messiah*.

[5] Heman, Asaph and Ethan were all mentioned as worship leaders in 1 Chronicles 6. Together, they wrote fourteen of the Psalms. Kenaiah was *"in charge of the singing… because he was skilful at it"* (15:22). One of the ways we tell how God has called us to serve him is to have a go and find out what we are and aren't gifted at doing!

[6] John 1:29 and 36. The Hebrew word for this ram's horn trumpet is *shōphār*, and examples of it being used to proclaim the *Messiah*'s victory over his enemies can be found in Leviticus 25:9; Joshua 6:20 and Judges 6:34.

blood as a sacrifice for sin outside the walls of his city. David was a prophet, so in Psalm 110 he reveals that Melchizedek is still a picture of the *Messiah* who is to come. The New Testament picks up on this, declaring that Jesus is the fulfilment of David's Tabernacle: *"Jesus... has become a high priest for ever, in the order of Melchizedek".*[7]

The Law of Moses strictly forbade any king of Israel from offering blood-sacrifices at his Tabernacle on Mount Gibeon, yet David offers the one-off blood-sacrifices that inaugurate his new Tabernacle on Mount Zion.[8] In doing so, he prophesies that the *Messiah* is going to offer a once-for-all blood-sacrifice for sin to inaugurate a New Covenant with God's people. The only sacrifices that are offered after this at David's Tabernacle are sacrifices of grateful thanks and praise, which looks ahead to the day when the *Messiah* will shout from the cross that *"It is finished"* – a triumphant declaration that a new era of God's salvation has begun.[9]

Unless we grasp this, we will not understand how David is able to invite ordinary Israelites to step into his tent and to stand before the Ark of the Covenant. In the Tabernacle of Moses, the Ark had been hidden away in an inner sanctuary, far away from the ordinary worshippers of Israel. Only the high priest was permitted to enter that inner sanctuary, and even he could only enter on one day of the year. What a contrast, then, at David's Tabernacle, where there is no inner sanctuary and where everyone can dance the night away in worship before the Ark![10] David's Tabernacle points to a day when the dividing

---

[7] Hebrews 4:14 – 5:10 and 6:13 – 7:28. Acts 15:16 also says that Jesus rebuilt *"David's fallen tent"*.

[8] Numbers 3:10 and 18:7, and 1 Chronicles 16:39–42. Solomon would repeat what his father did in 1 Kings 3:15, offering sacrifices at the start of his reign and never again. Moses' Tabernacle remained Israel's *sacrifice centre* whilst David's Tabernacle became its *worship centre*. Solomon's Temple would combine both.

[9] Psalm 27:6; 40:6–8; 51:17 and 141:2; John 19:30; Hebrews 7:27; 10:1–10 and 13:15, and Revelation 5:8.

[10] The Hebrew word *tāmîd* in 16:6 does not so much mean *regularly* as *continually*. David called for a 24/7 worship celebration to begin at his new Tabernacle on Mount Zion.

curtain which Moses hung between God and his people will finally be torn away.[11]

We know that the Chronicler loves to give his readers lengthy lists of drawn-out detail. We will be reminded of this later by his long description of Solomon's Temple. It is remarkable, therefore, that he gives no detail here at all about the dimensions and design of David's Tabernacle. It is as if he wants to keep our focus, not on how this tent was constructed, but on how to imitate the type of worship which took place inside it.

For this is how the Lord wishes our churches to be today. Places from which the Good News constantly rings out about the *Messiah*'s once-for-all blood-sacrifice for sin. Places where everyone is invited to come and enjoy the Presence of God. Communities where each believer serves as a priest before the Lord by bringing him the sacrifices of their grateful praise. Places that are filled with joyful worship that glorifies Jesus as the long-awaited Son of David, and as the eternal High Priest in the order of Melchizedek.[12]

---

[11] Matthew 27:51, and Hebrews 9:1–12 and 10:19–22.

[12] Israel's worship is described in 15:16, 25 and 28–29 as *joyful* and *loud*, and full of *dancing*, *rejoicing* and *celebration*. Christian worship can be quiet and reflective, but this is the exception rather than the norm.

The Heart of God
(1 Chronicles 16:7–36)

"All you families of nations, ascribe to the Lord glory and strength... bring an offering and come before him."

(1 Chronicles 16:28–29)

When Hernán Cortes and the other Spanish conquistadors landed in Mexico, its native people were so surprised to see a man on horseback that they could not fathom what they saw. Bernal Díaz del Castillo wrote in his record of the expedition that *"The natives had not seen horses up to this time and thought that the horse and rider were all one animal."*[1]

David's Tabernacle on Mount Zion represented a far greater revolution for Israel's thinking than mounted conquistadors did for the people of Mexico. For 650 years they had been told that God's Presence needed to be shut away inside the inner sanctuary of the Tabernacle of Moses, accessed only by the high priest on a single day of the year. The idea that every commoner from each of their twelve tribes had now been granted an "Access All Areas" pass to enjoy God's Presence was mind-blowing. But that wasn't even the half of the revolution which David's Tabernacle was to bring about in their thinking. The Chronicler says that David gave them a song to sing at his new Tabernacle to help them fathom the scale of change that the *Messiah* would bring.[2]

---

[1] The conquistador records this in his *True History of the Conquest of New Spain* (1568).

[2] By giving this psalm to the worship leader Asaph, King David is declaring that it is for congregational singing. Asaph and his associates would later split it into three expanded Psalms. Verses 8–22 became Psalm 105:1–15, verses 23–33 became Psalm 96, and verses 34–36 became Psalm 106:1 and 47–48.

In 16:8–11, the first stanza of the song comes straight out with the essence of the revolution. It reveals that God's heart is to save people, not just from the twelve tribes of Israel, but from every pagan people group of the world. If you have any doubt about how revolutionary it was for the Israelites to sing, *"Make known among the nations what he has done"*, then just read 1 Chronicles 18–20. They expected the God of Israel to help them slaughter pagans, not invite them to become part of his family!

While the Israelites are still reeling from this revelation of the heart of God, David gives them a list of ten things in 16:8–11 that God wants his Israelite and Gentile worshippers to do as they gather together. First, they are to *give him thanks and praise*. The Hebrew word *yādāh* means literally *to fire an arrow*, so the idea here is that those who love the Lord will want to fill the skies with a volley of grateful praise. Second, they are to *proclaim his name*. The Hebrew word *qārā'* means *to call* or *to cry out*, so it could either refer to laying hold of God's Name in fervent prayer or shouting loudly to the pagans that God's Name is far more beautiful than any of the names of their idols. Third comes an explicit command to *make known among the nations* what the Lord has done. The news about God's goodness to Israel and about what David's Tabernacle signifies is too world-changing for the Israelites to keep it to themselves.

Fourth and fifth, they are to *sing* and to *sing praise* to the Lord. Two different words are used for this in Hebrew, although the distinction between them isn't very clear.[3] Sixth, they are to *meditate* on his amazing deeds. The Hebrew word *sīah* means literally *to ponder* or *to discuss*, because our worship becomes shallow when we merely repeat the same old songs without thought. Sharing our testimonies and reflections keeps it alive.[4]

---

[3] The same thing is true of the musical terms used in 15:20–21. What matters is that God wants us to sing!

[4] This list of ten things warns us not to divide worship, prayer, Bible study and evangelism into separate distinct things. All of them are the overflow of God's heart towards us and our heart towards God.

Seventh, they are to *boast* in the Lord's name. They are to find their identity in God and to resist the false humility that makes believers keep their changed lives to themselves.[5] Eighth, they must *rejoice* in him. Ninth and tenth, they must *look to the Lord's strength* and *seek his face always* in a desire to know him more.[6] This is a rich recipe for our worship!

In 16:12–22, the next three stanzas of the song come as a bit of relief to the Israelites at David's Tabernacle. Those stanzas reassure them that they are God's chosen people, heirs to the *"everlasting covenant"* that he made with Abraham, Isaac and Jacob.[7] Verse 22 describes their ancestors as *messiahs* living under the protection of the Lord.[8] They can rest assured, as the offspring of the patriarchs, that the Saviour towards whom David's Tabernacle points is the Jewish *Messiah*.

In 16:23–36, however, in the last five stanzas, the heart of God towards the nations comes back centre stage. The song calls *"all the earth"* to sing to the Lord and to *"declare his glory among the nations"* to *"all peoples"*, because *"all the gods of the nations are idols"*.[9] The song calls *"all you families of nations"* to ascribe to the Lord the glory that he is due from all humanity.[10] David's Tabernacle is for *"all the earth"* and for anybody who

---

[5] It is in this sense that the Bible writers encourage us to *"boast in the Lord"*. See Psalm 34:2 and 44:8; Isaiah 45:25; Jeremiah 9:23–24 and 1 Corinthians 1:27–31.

[6] In 16:6, the Chronicler used the Hebrew word *tāmīd*, which means *continually*, to describe the 24/7 worship at David's Tabernacle. Now he uses the same word again, in 16:11, to instruct people to urge one another to become part of it. This is what we are also told to do in Hebrews 10:24–25.

[7] The Hebrew text of 16:15 does not actually say that God remembers his covenant, but that he calls *his people* to remember it. Forgetfulness is never a danger with God; only with those who claim to worship him.

[8] The Greek word for *Messiah* is *Christ*, so when we call ourselves Christians we are claiming to be God's little anointed ones too. See John 20:21–22.

[9] We see in 16:23–24 a great summary of what evangelism means: we proclaim God's salvation by telling people about his glorious character and his marvellous actions on behalf of humanity. The song's stark denunciation of pagan idols warns us not to mistake mere interfaith dialogue for evangelism.

[10] The Hebrew word *mishpāhāh* in 16:28 means *family*, *clan* or *class*. In other words, God wants to do more than save people from every nation. He wants to save people from every tribe and class within those nations.

is willing to *"say among the nations, 'The Lord reigns!'"* In case we are in any doubt that the Lord wants to gather a company of worshippers from every nation, the song even calls the sea creatures, the plants of the field and the trees of the forest to join in this worship song. It invites every pagan to cry out to the God of Israel to *"Save us, God our Saviour; gather us and deliver us from the nations, that we may give thanks to your holy name".*[11]

Can you see now why the Apostle James, quoting from Amos 9 in Acts 15:16–18, describes the start of Church history as the rebuilding of *"David's fallen tent"* because *"the rest of mankind"* are finally coming to know God – *"even all the Gentiles who bear my name"*? Can you see that it comes right from the heart of God when Jesus gives his followers the Great Commission, in Matthew 28:18–20, to take his Gospel to every nation?

When a twenty-five-year-old shoemaker named William Carey stood up at a meeting of English church leaders in 1786 and asked them to take seriously the fact that three quarters of the world had not yet heard the Good News about Jesus, one of them responded angrily: *"Young man, sit down, sit down! You're an enthusiast. When God pleases to convert the heathen, He'll do it without consulting you or me."*[12] So whose side are you on? That of the man who told William Carey that the Great Commission was an inconvenient suggestion, or that of the shoemaker who refused to take no for an answer and who went on to become known as "the father of modern missions"?

Make no mistake about it: this is our song. The Israelites sang it at a Tabernacle which merely pointed to a glorious Gospel that is ours today. So come on, let's go out and sing!

---

[11] Tragically, when David went home to bless his family in 16:43, we are told in 2 Samuel 6:16–23 that his own wife Michal rejected this Gospel invitation.

[12] Quoted by S. Pearce Carey in his biography simply entitled *William Carey* (1923).

The Son of God
(1 Chronicles 17:1–27)

"He said to Nathan the prophet, 'Here I am, living in a house of cedar, while the ark of the covenant of the Lord is under a tent.'"

(1 Chronicles 17:1)

I don't know how you like to spend your summer holidays, but my family and I love to build sandcastles on the beach together. When we work well as a team, it takes us just a few hours to construct an impressive fortress, but then we always hit the same big problem. Sooner or later, the tide comes in and washes away whatever we have built together, removing every trace of our busy craftsmanship on the smooth sand.

This became David's concern after he had finished building his new Tabernacle on Mount Zion and calling everyone to come and worship the Lord with him there. He suddenly started worrying that his prophetic picture of the *Messiah* would be swept away without a trace when he died. He needed to build something longer-lasting in Jerusalem. He couldn't live in a palace built of cedarwood while the Ark of the Covenant stood in a flimsy tent nearby. David therefore decided that he would build a mighty Temple, better than those of the pagan idols, in order to combine the Tabernacle of Moses on Mount Gibeon and his own Tabernacle on Mount Zion into one single, solid spiritual legacy for the people of God after he died.[1]

---

[1] Since the Psalms refer forty times to Mount Zion and never to Mount Gibeon, it is easy to assume that David lost interest in the Tabernacle of Moses. However, this isn't true. He asked the high priest Zadok to continue offering sacrifices there and he installed worship leaders for the first time on Mount Gibeon (16:39–42).

When David shared his plan with the prophet Nathan, he received a positive reply: *"Whatever you have in mind, do it, for God is with you."*[2] While this might be a helpful general maxim for Christian ministry, Nathan actually spoke too hastily and he is forced to backtrack the following morning after hearing God speak in the night.[3] He reminds David that the Lord is unlike the pagan idols, which demand fancy houses of their worshippers. The true God moves about freely among his people, upping his tent pegs at will. He has never asked any of Israel's rulers to upgrade his Tabernacle into a Temple. David's Tabernacle is a one-generation foretaste of the day when he will come and dwell within the heart of everyone who worships him. There will come a moment for the two Tabernacles to be combined into a single Temple, but it isn't today.[4] David will not build a house for God; God will build a house for David!

The Lord reminds David that he promoted him from lowly shepherd boy to mighty ruler because he wanted a *deputy* who was willing to serve his purposes, not because he needed a *king* to lend him a helping hand. David is a man of action who is accustomed to asserting his will violently on the battlefield, but now he needs to surrender his plans to the far greater plan of the Lord.[5] God intends for David's Tabernacle to be swept away like a sandcastle. It will barely outlive him, because it is a prophetic picture of a day far in the future when the true *Messiah* will finally come. Until then, the Ark of the Covenant must go

---

[2] Nathan and Gad were the two main prophets of David's reign (1 Chronicles 29:29). Nathan was not afraid to challenge David when he forgot that he ruled as the Lord's deputy. See 2 Samuel 12:1–14.

[3] What God puts in a Spirit-filled heart is normally a good gauge of his guidance (Psalm 16:7). He tends to guide us as we put our desires into action, but beware the double warning in Proverbs 14:12 and 16:25.

[4] Solomon's Temple would be structurally like the Tabernacle of Moses, but it would be marked by the same vibrant worship as David's Tabernacle (1 Chronicles 23:3–5 and 25:1–31, and 2 Chronicles 29:25–26). Once completed, Solomon would move the Ark into it and dismantle both Tabernacles (2 Chronicles 5:5).

[5] We are told in 22:6–10 and 28:2–7 that one of the main reasons why David needed to leave the Temple-building to his son Solomon (whose name means *Peaceful*) was that David was a self-assertive man of war.

back behind the curtain in the inner sanctuary as a reminder to the tribes of Israel that the covenant he made with them at Mount Sinai needs to be upgraded into something better. As if to prove it, the Lord suddenly announces that he is making a better covenant with the dynasty of David, right here and right now.

"I declare to you that the Lord will build a house for you", Nathan prophesies, as a deliberate rejoinder to David's idea that he will build a house for the Lord. *"I will make your name like the names of the greatest men on earth"* – not as a Temple-Builder, but as a prophetic picture of the far greater Temple-Builder who is to come.[6] In the short-term, this will be David's son Solomon, the builder of the First Temple. In the longer-term, however, it will be a far greater Son of David, one about whom the Lord can say without any caveats or qualifiers in verses 13–14: *"I will be his father, and he will be my son... I will set him over my house and my kingdom for ever; his throne will be established for ever."*

Far from being disappointed that the Lord has just forbidden him from upgrading his Tabernacle into a Temple, David is overwhelmed with joy over God's grace towards him. He stumbles from his palace to the Tabernacle so that he can sit in awestruck wonder in the Presence of the Lord. *"Who am I, Lord God, and what is my family, that you have brought me this far?"* he marvels, before revealing that he understands full well why his Tabernacle needs to be swept away like a brief sandcastle. In a literal translation of the Hebrew text of 17:17, he prays, *"You, Lord God, have regarded me as a picture of the Man who is on high."* David does not simply praise God here for treating him better than he does most other people. As a prophet, he praises

---

[6] The New Testament quotes from 17:13 and applies it to Jesus in Luke 1:32–33 and Hebrews 1:5. The Chronicler also gives us further clues by omitting the reference in 2 Samuel 7:14 to the Son of David sinning, and by changing *"your house and your kingdom"* in 2 Samuel 7:16 to *"my house and my kingdom"* here.

God because he grasps that the Son he has been promised is not merely Solomon, but the true and long-awaited *Messiah*.[7]

David sits, but he is not passive. He is happy for his Tabernacle to be swept away like a sandcastle, but he is determined that nothing shall ever sweep away the Lord's plans for his coming *Messiah*. He therefore prays fervently that God will do all that he has promised.[8] He prays with abject humility, referring to himself ten times in these few verses as the Lord's *"servant"*, and reminding God that his deepest desire is that *"your name will be great forever. Then people will say, 'The Lord Almighty, the God over Israel, is Israel's God!'"* Then, after pleading strongly, David ends his prayer by resting in faith that whatever the Lord has covenanted with him is guaranteed to be fulfilled: *"Now you have been pleased to bless the house of your servant... and it will be blessed forever."*

Are you sitting comfortably? Then you are like David at the end of this chapter – in the perfect position to pray similar prayers of your own. The Chronicler wrote these verses to encourage the Jews after the exile that the *Messiah* was coming, but he is able to say something far greater to you and to me: The *Messiah* has now come! So give yourself no rest till you have pleaded with the Lord, just like King David, to do all that he has promised. Pray that he will establish the throne of Jesus in your own generation.

---

[7] The Hebrew word for *offspring* in 17:11 is *zera'*, which literally means *seed* and is the same word that God uses throughout Genesis to describe both Isaac and Jesus at the same time. See Galatians 3:16, 19 and 29.

[8] David teaches us in 17:25 that God makes promises to his people, not so that they can become passive, but in order to stir them with greater courage to pray!

The Plan of God
(1 Chronicles 18:1 – 20:8)

"King David dedicated these articles to the Lord, as he had done with the silver and gold he had taken from all these nations."

(1 Chronicles 18:11)

A friend of mine told me recently that he could not accept the Christian message because God appears too judgmental. Why is he so concerned with what people do, and how could a good God ever send people who don't believe in him to hell? I tried to explain to my friend that God opens his arms to receive everyone, but that he forces himself upon no one. If a person decides that they want to live without God, in spite of his pleadings, then a day will finally come when God gives that person what they have desired.

This has never been a very popular aspect of the Bible's teaching, which is why the Chronicler gives us three whole chapters that describe the military conquests of King David. He uses this *messiah* to give his readers a full picture of God's plan for his *Messiah*.

First, we need to recognise that none of the foreigners who die in these chapters needed to do so. We have already seen that David welcomed Moabites, Canaanites, Hittites, Philistines and Ammonites to become important members of his team.[1] We have also seen that he instructed the Israelite worshippers at his new Tabernacle to go out and proclaim the Good News among the nations so that many pagans could be saved. The fact

---

[1] 1 Chronicles 11:39, 41, 46; 12:4 and 13:13.

that so many of them are slaughtered in this chapter is meant to signify that the *Messiah* who comes to save the world will also come a second time to judge it.[2]

These verses make uncomfortable reading for our twenty-first-century eyes because we have forgotten what these nations did to Israel. The Philistines had repeatedly attacked them, the Moabites had tried to curse them and to seduce them into sexual sin, and the shameful way in which the Ammonites treat the Israelites in chapter 19 is indicative of how the other pagan nations acted towards them.[3]

Second, we need to recognise that the battles which take place in these chapters are spiritual as well as physical. In the same way that the Philistines brought back Saul's plunder to the temple of their false god Dagon in 10:9–10, in order to proclaim to the world that their idols had proved more powerful than the God of Israel, the Chronicler is quick to emphasise that each of David's victories was a chance to prove that the opposite was true. After he plunders the defeated armies of Philistia, Moab, Aram, Edom, Ammon and Amalek, we are told in 18:8 and 11 that *"King David dedicated these articles to the Lord"* and that the plunder was used to build King Solomon's Temple.[4] We might say that David is evangelising the pagan nations for the God of Israel. They have rejected his soft invitation to throw away their idols and to serve the Lord, so he follows it up with a second, firmer invitation. He topples their idols by force so that

---

[2] The *Moabites* and *Ammonites* were the descendants of Lot to the east. The Aramean cities of *Zobah*, *Damascus* and *Hamath* were in the north. The *Amalekites* and *Edomites* were descendants of Abraham in the south, and the *Philistines* were in the west. The *Messiah*'s judgment will therefore reach in all directions.

[3] Numbers 22–25. Before you dismiss David as heartless and persuade yourself that you live in a more compassionate age, remember that David was one-eighth Moabite through his great-grandmother Ruth.

[4] 1 Chronicles 18:12 is a great example of a supposed Bible contradiction which is not a contradiction at all. It says that Abishai killed 18,000 Edomites in the battle, whereas 2 Samuel 8:13 says that David killed them and the title of Psalm 60 says that Joab killed 12,000. What must have happened was that David's general Joab killed 12,000 Edomites in battle and his lieutenant Abishai killed 6,000 more in the rout which followed.

they will see those false gods for what they truly are.[5] Isn't this how the Lord often appeals to us too?

Whether or not they are willing to respond to his second, firmer invitation, David remains passionate to prove that the Lord is the true God of gods.[6] Our disgust at these chapters may simply signify that we are less eager than David to see the whole earth filled with the knowledge of the glory of God.[7] The single, overriding aim of his foreign policy is to prove what he declares at the start of Psalm 24: *"The earth is the Lord's, and everything in it."* He can no more accept that parts of the world belong to Baal and Dagon than we should accept terms such as "the Muslim world" or "post-Christian Europe".[8] The Devil is just as active in the world today as he was through the demon-gods of old. Are we as ready to engage him in spiritual warfare as is Joab in 19:13? *"Be strong, and let us fight bravely for our people and the cities of our God."*

Third, the Chronicler is clearly idealising the *messiah* David as a prophetic picture of the ultimate *Messiah*.[9] For a start, he sanitises his retelling of the story by refraining from mentioning any of David's sin with Bathsheba, which comes at this point in the story in 2 Samuel.[10] If you have ever sung the hymn "Crown Him with Many Crowns", then you should rejoice to see your prayers answered prophetically on the battlefield in 20:2. If you

---

[5] Hadadezer means *Hadad Is My Helper*, and Hadad was another name for *Baal*.

[6] Israel's battles with the nations are presented throughout Scripture primarily as battles between the true God and false idols. See Exodus 12:12 and 18:11; Numbers 33:4; 1 Samuel 5:7 and 6:5, and 1 Chronicles 14:12.

[7] We can tell how much David cared for God's glory from the way that he disables most of the horses he captures in 18:4, in obedience to Deuteronomy 17:16, so that he trusts in the Lord alone (Psalm 20:7).

[8] For an insight into David's motivation, read Psalm 60, which he wrote during these military campaigns.

[9] We see this in 18:14, which highlights that David the *messiah* did *"what was just and right for all his people"*. The *messiah* is tasked with defeating the Philistines in 1 Samuel 9:16 and 2 Samuel 3:18. The *Messiah* succeeds in defeating the Devil and his demons (Colossians 2:15).

[10] In 20:4–8, the Chronicler also chooses not to copy from 2 Samuel 21:15–22 an example of David's weakness in old age. He prefers to use David in his own account as a prophetic picture of the *Messiah*.

have ever prayed for Satan's strongholds to be defeated, then you should thank God when he promises to answer your prayers by empowering David's soldiers to dispatch several giant-sized problems in 20:4–8.[11] If you have ever prayed for God's Kingdom to come on the earth as it is in heaven, then be encouraged by his repeated answer in 18:6 and 18:13: *"The Lord gave David victory wherever he went."* These chapters promise you that, through Jesus, the Lord will grant you the same victory too.[12]

We began reading 1 Chronicles 13–20 by praying that the Lord would make us like the men of Issachar, who understood the times that they were living in and knew what God's people should do. I hope that your prayers have been answered and that you now have a greater grasp of God's priorities for his people in your generation. If we pursue the Presence of God and devote ourselves to building the House of God, then we will see the heart of God fulfilled among the nations, as they embrace the plan of God to save them through the Son of God,.

Jesus commissions us to join his world-conquering Gospel army in Matthew 28:18–20:

All authority in heaven and on earth has been given to me. Therefore go and make disciples of all nations, baptising them in the name of the Father and of the Son and of the Holy Spirit, and teaching them to obey everything I have commanded you. And surely I am with you always, to the very end of the age.

[11] These include the giant-sized brother of Goliath. If you are in any doubt that these chapters represent our own spiritual warfare, then remember that Goliath *"cursed David by his gods"* and that David retorted that he would kill him so that *"the whole world will know that there is a God in Israel"* (1 Samuel 17:26, 36, 43–47).

[12] A literal translation of the Hebrew verb in 18:6 and 13 is that *"the Lord saved David wherever he went"*. These chapters are less about slaughter than about God's promise to save people if we fight hard for their souls.

The Enemy of God
(1 Chronicles 21:1 – 22:1)

"Satan rose up against Israel and incited David to take a census of Israel."

(1 Chronicles 21:1)

In the mid-1990s, a shadowy terrorist cell began to set off bombs across London. The police knew that the cell was part of the Provisional IRA, but they knew nothing more than that. They could only wait and hope that the attacks would somehow end.

I was living overseas at the time, but I was praying with a friend when the news came through that another bomb had devastated the Canary Wharf area. Suddenly, I felt the Spirit of God stir the anger of God within me. I prayed for the bombings to end, quoting the words of Jesus back to him from Matthew 26:52, that *"All who draw the sword will die by the sword."* Eventually, my friend and I sensed that God had heard our fervent prayers. A few days later, the news came through that, whilst attempting to plant a bomb on the number 171 bus, the leader of the terrorist cell had blown himself up instead. With his death, the attacks came to an immediate end.

Whatever you make of a story like that, you can't deny that the Devil's plans backfire on him spectacularly in 1 Chronicles 21. For many readers, this is one of the most problematic passages in the book, since it seems to contradict the parallel passage in 2 Samuel 24. But if we understand it properly, then it reveals a glorious truth to us.

The final chapter of 2 Samuel begins by telling us that *"The anger of the Lord burned against Israel, and he incited David*

against them, saying, 'Go and take a census of Israel and Judah.'"
At a superficial glance, the Chronicler appears to contradict this
by telling us that *"Satan rose up against Israel and incited David
to take a census of Israel."* So which one is it? Was it God who
incited David, or Satan who incited David? The answer is: *both.*

The Chronicler is extraordinarily generous towards King
David in his retelling of Israel's history. He skirts over his years
as an outlaw on the run from Saul. He says very little about his
adultery with Bathsheba and the subsequent murder of one
his close friends. He glosses over the fact that several of his sons
rebelled against him in the latter years of his reign, hoping to
supplant Solomon as his successor, even while David was still
alive.[1] But the Chronicler makes full mention of David's proud
self-reliance because it provoked the enemy of God to overplay
his hand very foolishly against him. It was through David's sinful
pride that the Lord finally laid the groundwork for his Temple.

The Devil longs to hurt those who are close to God. Knowing
that he cannot touch the Lord himself, he causes him pain by
waging war on his people. He does this by deceiving them and
tempting them so that he can parade their guilt before God,
which is why he is knowns as *Satan* and *the Devil* – both of which
come from Hebrew and Greek words for *the Accuser.*[2] Martin
Luther referred to the Devil as *"God's Satan"* because the book of
Job reveals that he can only act on the Lord's say-so. He is Christ's
defeated foe, who can only work within the strict parameters
that he is given, like a fierce dog on a tight leash.[3] The writer
of 2 Samuel records that the Lord decided that it was time to

---

[1] He also glosses over the unruliness of Joab towards David, although we catch a hint of it in 21:6. The numbers here are the real numbers, while the numbers in 2 Samuel are Joab's adjusted numbers. We are told in 2 Samuel 24:8 that it took Joab nine months and twenty days to complete the census – a massive undertaking.

[2] In Job 1–2 and Zechariah 3:1–2, he is called *"the satan"* – that is, *the Accuser* or *the Fault Finder*. By the time that 1 Chronicles 21:1 and the New Testament were written, *Satan* had morphed into a proper name.

[3] We see those parameters clearly in 1 Samuel 16:14; Judges 9:23; 1 Kings 22:19–22; 2 Chronicles 18:19–22; Job 1:12 and 2:6; Matthew 8:29–32; Luke 8:28–33 and 22:31; 2 Thessalonians 2:11 and Revelation 12:12.

expose King David's pride, but he doesn't fully tell us why. As the Chronicler copies down those verses from 2 Samuel, he makes some changes to the text that explain what happened. Through the Tempter would come the impetus for building the Temple.

In 21:1–7, the Devil strikes. There was nothing sinful about conducting a national census, in and of itself (the Lord commands Moses to conduct censuses in Numbers 1 and 26), but as commander-in-chief of David's army, Joab can tell immediately that the king has allowed Absalom's rebellion to rob him of his confidence in the Lord.[4] The Chronicler explains in 27:23 that *"the Lord had promised to make Israel as numerous as the stars in the sky"*, but David feels the need to check up on that promise. He wants to rest easy in his palace by relying on the size of his army, not on the greatness of his God.[5]

In 21:8–15, David confesses his sin and asks for forgiveness. The Lord responds with immediate mercy but explains through the prophet Gad that, for David to be forgiven, a blood-sacrifice must be made to atone for his sin.[6] He offers David a choice between three years of death through famine, three months of death through civil war or three days of death through plague. David's response is brilliant – he will accept any judgment, just so long as it comes from the just, measured hand of the Lord.

In 21:16–30, the Lord forgives David and stops the plague while it is still in mid flow.[7] David is too afraid of the Lord's judgment to leave Jerusalem to offer blood-sacrifices at the Tabernacle of Moses on Mount Gibeon. Instead, he pleads with the Lord, *"Let your hand fall on me and my family"*. The Lord accepts this intercession by directing him to sacrifice at the

---

[4] The normal Hebrew word for *counting* in a census is *pāqad*, which carries the sense of *to care for*. Here and in 2 Samuel 24:10, however, *sāphar* is used instead, a word normally used for counting property and cattle.

[5] For us, the equivalent would be to rely on our bank balances. See 1 Timothy 6:10 and Hebrews 13:5–6.

[6] Gad was the second prophet of David's reign, mentioned alongside Nathan in 29:29.

[7] Since *seven* was the number of perfection in Hebrew thinking, *70,000* deaths was a large number but not an arbitrary number. God's judgment would have been much worse but for his mercy.

threshing-floor of Araunah, one of the Jebusites who survived the capture of the city by King David. As soon as David offers blood-sacrifices as instructed, the Lord commands his angel to sheath his sword and the plague is over.

In 22:1, we are told how. This verse forms the grand finale to the story and the eight chapters which follow unpack it in more detail. The Chronicler rejoices that *"David said, 'The house of the Lord God is to be here, and also the altar of burnt offering for Israel.'"* In case we miss the significance of this, he repeats in 2 Chronicles 3:1 that King Solomon built *"the temple of the Lord in Jerusalem on Mount Moriah, where the Lord had appeared to his father David. It was on the threshing-floor of Araunah the Jebusite, the place provided by David."*

The threshing-floor of Araunah was on Mount Moriah, the mountain in Genesis 22 where the Lord provided an innocent sheep for Abraham to sacrifice instead of Isaac. One of the outcrops of Mount Moriah was called *Calvary*, where Jesus would one day die for the sins of the world. When David cried out, *"Let your hand fall on me and my family"*, he spoke more truly than he knew. God used this incident to ensure that the Temple was built on the mountain where Jesus would one day die as the Lamb of God.

To the Jews after the exile, confused that they remained part of the Persian Empire, this offered a revolutionary conclusion. The enemy of God is "God's Satan", who can do nothing without his say-so, and who only ever looks like he is succeeding when the Lord knows how to turn Satan's worst around for his own best for his people. Like the mighty warrior Benaiah in 11:23, the Lord loves to snatch the Devil's weapon from his hands and to turn it back against him. He loves to make the Devil's tactics backfire on him.

It still is a revolutionary conclusion for us today. No matter how confusing we may find our own circumstances, it means that the Lord is in control. If the enemy of God seems to be winning, then it can only be because the Lord has found a way to turn the Devil's worst around for our good. Trust in the Lord, even when you are attacked by his enemy.

Costly Worship
(1 Chronicles 21:15–30)

"King David replied to Araunah, 'No, I insist on paying the full price. I will not... sacrifice a burnt offering that costs me nothing.'"

(1 Chronicles 21:24)

Do you ever have moments when you don't feel like worshipping God at all? Perhaps it is on a cold winter's morning when you wake up and feel that you would rather do just about anything else other than pray. Perhaps it is at a church service at the end of a difficult week, when you feel more like shouting at God than singing to him.

Whatever the detail, if – like me – you ever feel sluggish and reluctant in your worship, then you will love what the Chronicler teaches us about true worship here. These are the verses which inspired C.S. Lewis to argue that *"Prayers offered in a state of dryness are those which please him best."*[1] He unpacks what he means:

> *What seem our worst prayers may really be, in God's eyes, our best. Those, I mean, which are least supported by devotional feeling and contend with the greatest disinclination. For these, perhaps, being nearly all will, come from a deeper level than feeling. In feeling there is so much that is really not ours – so much that comes from weather and health or from the last book read... God*

---

[1] Lewis says this in *The Screwtape Letters* (London, Geoffrey Bles, 1942).

sometimes seems to speak to us most intimately when He catches us, as it were, off our guard.[2]

King David is having a very bad day. He can't have felt like worshipping at all. Although he grasps in verse 13 that God's mercy is very great towards us when we sin, he is still grief-stricken at the thought that 70,000 Israelites have died in three days of plague directly caused by his sin.[3] That's why he and the elders of Israel have clothed themselves in sackcloth as an expression of their repentance. It is also why David is following the angel of the Lord as he sweeps his way across Jerusalem destroying people with the plague.[4] Suddenly, David sees a glimmer of hope. It looks as though the Lord may be relenting. David and his elders quickly bow down on their faces and begin to express their willingness to offer a costly sacrifice to God.[5]

David is a prophet who received a promise from the Lord in chapter 17 about his Son being the true *Messiah* and Saviour of the world. Does he have this promise in mind as he pleads with the Lord: *"I, the shepherd, have sinned and done wrong. These are but sheep. What have they done? Lord, my God, let your hand fall on me and my family, but do not let this plague remain on your people"*? We cannot know for certain, but what we do know is that this act of intercession paves the way for

---

[2] Lewis adds this explanation in his *Letters to Malcolm: Chiefly on Prayer* (London, Geoffrey Bles, 1964).

[3] Since the Lord listed all three of the options that he gives David in 21:11–12 in his curse upon sin in Deuteronomy 28:15–25, there can have been no doubt in David's mind that their deaths were his fault.

[4] The Israelites were not innocent of sin themselves. 2 Samuel 24:1 seems to suggest that the Lord was angry with them for neglecting his Tabernacle and returning to the ways of Saul. The mention of the destroying angel also reminds us of Exodus 12:13 and 12:23 – in other words, sinful Israel has become like Egypt! Some readers also think the Israelites sinned by taking a census without collecting the redemption money which pointed to the death of the *Messiah* (Exodus 30:12), although the Chronicler does not name that as a sin here.

[5] The Hebrew verb *nāham* in 21:15 means *to change one's mind* or *to regret* or *to repent* or *to be checked by compassion*. The Lord is slow to anger and quick to forgive, so he helps David to find mercy (Exodus 34:6–7).

the forgiveness which follows, because someone from David's family would indeed soak up God's judgment on a sinful world.

The Lord tells his angel, who tells Gad, who tells David to build an altar of blood-sacrifice on the threshing-floor of Araunah the Jebusite.[6] If this feels like an overly elaborate chain of communication, then bear in mind that this is one of the holiest moments in Israel's history. The Lord had guided Abraham to sacrifice his son Isaac on a specific mountain in Genesis 22. After the Lord provided him with an innocent ram to sacrifice instead of Isaac, Abraham named that mountain *Moriah* – which means *The Lord Will Provide*. Perhaps his son tried to correct his tenses on their way back down the mountain, since Genesis 22:14 clarifies that his future tense was deliberate: *"On the mountain of the Lord it **will be** provided."*[7]

The pagan Jebusites had threshed their wheat and barley on Mount Moriah before David captured Jerusalem, since it was one of the highest and breeziest points of the city. Araunah is still using the site for that purpose when the Lord declares that it will now become the place where he threshes the sin out of his people. Malachi 4:1 recalls this when it prophesies that the *Messiah* will come to divide the wheat from the chaff among God's people. John the Baptist recalls it too when he prophesies about the *Messiah* in Matthew 3:12 that *"His winnowing fork is in his hand, and he will clear his threshing floor, gathering his wheat into the barn and burning up the chaff with unquenchable fire."* When Araunah sees the angel, he gladly accepts this mandatory change-of-use for his property. He offers David the site for free, as well as oxen and wheat and wood for the offering.

But King David will have none of it. He tells Araunah that *"I insist on paying the full price. I will not take for the Lord what is yours, or sacrifice a burnt offering that costs me nothing."* This is

---

[6] The Chronicler often uses variant names when copying passages from other parts of the Old Testament. Here he refers to Araunah as *Ornan*, but most English translators stick to the name as it appears in 2 Samuel.

[7] Jesus explains in John 8:56 that *"Abraham rejoiced at the thought of seeing my day; he saw it and was glad."*

the verse which made C.S. Lewis conclude that the Lord is most pleased with our prayer and worship when we least feel like praying and worshipping. The Lord cannot be duped. A sacrifice is not a sacrifice if it comes cheaply to the worshipper. David pays 7 kilograms of gold to Araunah for the site of the future Temple.[8] After sacrificing the oxen and arranging the wood for the burnt offering as a high priest in the order of Melchizedek, he calls for fire to fall from heaven as a sign of things to come. This is what had happened on the bronze altar at the Tabernacle of Moses in Leviticus 9:24, and it is what will happen on the bronze altar at Solomon's Temple in 2 Chronicles 7:1. All three of these occasions are prophetic pictures of the true Lamb of God dying at Calvary, an outcrop of Mount Moriah, as the Son of God who has come down from heaven.

In that sense, the Lord leads the way for us in our worship. He doesn't merely ask us to bring him our costly worship. He paid the greatest price himself when he sent his beloved Son to die at Araunah's threshing-floor to atone for the sins of the world.

So be encouraged. The times when you struggle the most to pray and worship are not times best forgotten, which you should rush through until you feel in a better state to pray and worship on another day. They are the times when your prayer and worship delight the Lord the most!

For the Jews after the exile, worshipping God through their disappointment, this mattered hugely. It matters just as much for you and me today. It means that, no matter what our circumstances and no matter how little we feel like worshipping, God delights in what we bring.

So put down this book and take some time to bring your costly worship to the Lord.

---

[8] The Chronicler deliberately changes the price from the 575 grams of silver mentioned in 2 Samuel 24:24. That was just the price of the threshing floor; this is the price paid to Araunah for the Temple site as a whole.

How's Your Zeal?
(1 Chronicles 22:1 – 29:30)

*"Then David said, 'The house of the Lord God is to be
here, and also the altar of burnt offering for Israel.'"*

(1 Chronicles 22:1)

I'll be honest with you. I'm not always as eager to help people
as I appear. If I offer to lend you money and you decline politely,
then I probably won't offer a second time. If I begin to put
out the rubbish and one of my children offers to do it for me,
then the job is theirs as quick as you can say, "You're not like
King David, are you?" You see, David didn't just offer to build a
Temple for the Lord. He was consumed with an insatiable zeal
to build it.

The first verse of chapter 22 forms the grand finale to
chapter 21. It also forms a springboard into the eight chapters
which follow. David submits to the Lord's decree that his
son Solomon must build the Temple instead of him, but he is
determined to do everything the Lord permits, short of actually
laying the Temple's foundation stone. He freely confesses
to the Lord in Psalm 69:9 that *"Zeal for your house consumes
me"*.[1] Buying the Temple site from Araunah the Jebusite for 7
kilograms of gold (about £250,000 in today's money) is only the
beginning of his busy activity.

In 22:2–19, David gathers together a team of builders and
many of the raw materials that Solomon will require to build
the Temple. He demonstrates his zeal by contributing very
generously to this new stockpile: over 3,000 tons of gold, almost

---

[1] Yes, this verse is applied to Jesus in John 2:17, but it is part of a psalm of David and
originally about him.

35,000 tons of silver, and so much bronze, iron, wood and stone that even the Chronicler (who likes his lists!) cannot count them for us. David accepts that *"This word of the Lord came to me: 'You have shed too much blood and have fought too many wars... Solomon... is the one who will build a house for my Name...'"* – but he does not allow it to dampen his zeal as a Temple-Builder. He commands Israel's leaders to help his son Solomon to build the Temple just as eagerly as they would have helped him.

In 23:1 – 26:32, David draws together rosters for the Levites who will serve in the Temple. It doesn't matter that he will never live to see it. David is so zealous for the house of the Lord that nothing can hold him back from doing all he can. In chapter 23, he divides the various Temple tasks between the three clans of Levites who were counted in his recent census. In chapter 24, he divides the tasks which only priests can perform between the twenty-four surviving clans of Aaron's family. In chapter 25, he appoints many of the Levites to serve as worship leaders and musicians. In chapter 26, he sets the remaining Levites to work as gatekeepers, treasurers and teachers of the twelve tribes of Israel. If you find these chapters a bit long-winded, then rest assured that they are the last long lists in 1 and 2 Chronicles. But don't skim-read them. Allow David's zeal to inspire you.

In 27:1–34, David continues to compile rosters for the other tribes of Israel. He decides who will lead the different divisions of his militia army, who will lead each of the twelve tribes of Israel, and who will oversee the royal palace and its royal property. For the original readers of 1 Chronicles, these chapters were a vital link back to their past. There may not be a king from David's dynasty on the throne, but everything which takes place at Zerubbabel's new Temple is done as King David stipulated in great detail. For us, these detailed chapters can feel harder going, but don't miss the big picture of what the Chronicler is saying to you. If King David was this zealous for a Temple that was made of stone and would stand for less than 400 years before it was destroyed by Babylon, then how much more should we be zealous for the true and better Temple that Jesus is building right now across the world!

At the start of Jesus' ministry, he entered the Temple courtyards and began to demonstrate that he was every bit as zealous for God's house as had been his famous ancestor. We are told in John 2:17 that, after watching him drive out the merchants and overturn the tables of the moneychangers, *"His disciples remembered that it is written: 'Zeal for your house will consume me.'"* They saw in Jesus the fulfilment of Psalm 69:9, as well as Isaiah 56:7 and 59:17. He had *"wrapped himself in zeal as in a cloak"* in order to accomplish his Father's longing that *"My house will be called a house of prayer for all nations."*

It is true that the final eight chapters of 1 Chronicles are hard going. There are a lot of lists of names in the rosters that David zealously prepares for the Temple of the Lord. But all of this detail aims to stir up the same zeal that was stirred in David. It seeks to make us like the Sons of Korah, who wrote in wonder in Psalm 84:

> *How lovely is your dwelling-place, Lord Almighty! My soul yearns, even faints, for the courts of the Lord... Blessed are those who dwell in your house... I would rather be a gatekeeper in the house of my God than dwell in the tents of the wicked... Better is one day in your courts than a thousand elsewhere!*

In 28:1 – 29:30, when David hands over his throne to Solomon, it is remarkable how focused he is on the building of God's Temple. Solomon will have royal palaces to live in, royal properties to manage, and a mighty army to lead, yet they barely get a look-in here. David is totally focused on his son's role as God's chosen Temple-Builder. As he gives Solomon a blueprint for the construction of the Temple which is as detailed as the one that the Lord gave to Moses for the Tabernacle, David explains to him in 28:19 that *"All this... I have in writing as a result of the Lord's hand on me, and he enabled me to understand all the details of the plan."*[2] With his dying breaths, David empties his personal treasury to add it to the many tons of gold and silver that are ready for his Temple-building son once he is gone. Zeal for God's house consumes King David to the very end.

The Chronicler uses this to encourage his original readers. They mustn't despair that there is no king from David's dynasty reigning over Judah, because they have the Temple which consumed the thoughts of King David, both day and night, until he died.

What he writes in these chapters also serves to encourage us, the followers of the true Son of David, the *Messiah* who told his followers in Matthew 16:18 that *"I will build my church and the gates of Hades will not overcome it."* It stirs our hearts to be as eager to build this new and living Temple as David was to build a lesser Temple out of lifeless stone.[3]

The Apostle Paul adds his own encouragement in Romans 12:11 for us to do this: *"Never be lacking in zeal, but keep your spiritual fervour, serving the Lord."*

---

[2] *"The Lord's hand"* is a description of the Holy Spirit, who gave David crystal-clear detailed guidance for the Temple. See Ezra 7:6, 9, 28; 8:18, 22 and 31; Nehemiah 2:8 and 2:18; Luke 1:66 and Acts 11:21.

[3] 1 Corinthians 3:16–17; 2 Corinthians 6:16; Ephesians 2:19–22 and 1 Peter 2:4–6.

Succession
(1 Chronicles 22:1–19)

"Now, my son, the Lord be with you, and may you have success and build the house of the Lord your God, as he said you would."

(1 Chronicles 22:11)

Success without a successor spells failure. If David didn't know that from the very start, then he certainly knew it after the Lord revealed that his Temple would be built by David's son. That's why it's helpful for us to remember that 1 and 2 Chronicles were originally a single book. The final eight chapters of 1 Chronicles begin with a verse which fires the starting gun on the building of the Lord's Temple in Jerusalem. They celebrate the way that David handed over his kingdom to the successor to his throne, before we read about Solomon's reign in the first nine chapters of 2 Chronicles.

The Chronicler has a very different take on this handover from the writers of 2 Samuel and 1 Kings. While they tell us that David had Solomon crowned king in a hurry to stave off a rebellion by his eldest surviving son, Adonijah, the Chronicler focuses instead on the fact that David began his handover many years before Adonijah forced his hand.[1] Although the final coronation of Solomon was rushed, the Chronicler describes the way in which David painstakingly prepared and commissioned Solomon to reign as king.

---

[1] The Chronicler knows that his readers have access to 2 Samuel and 1 Kings, so he retells the story in a way that points more clearly to the coming of the *Messiah* and his Temple.

Throughout chapter 22, there are deliberate echoes of the famous handover from Moses to Joshua in Deuteronomy 31 and Joshua 1. For a start, David uses the same Hebrew words when he charges the young Solomon in verse 13 to *"Be strong and courageous"* in leading Israel forward into God's purposes. He also echoes Moses when he tells Solomon not to be afraid or discouraged because the Lord will be with him constantly to help him, just so long as he remains true to the Law. David even reminds Solomon that the Lord has given the whole of the Promised Land into the hands of his people. In all of this, by imitating the example of Moses and Joshua, David seeks to convince the next generation of Israelites that the Lord has sovereignly chosen Solomon to be his *messiah*.

To emphasise this further, David discloses new information which consolidates Solomon's claim to the throne. In chapter 17, the Lord tells David that he is not destined to be the Temple-Builder, without explaining to us why. Now David discloses, in verse 8, that the Lord explained that *"You have shed much blood and have fought many wars. You are not to build a house for my Name, because you have shed much blood on the earth in my sight."*[2] In chapter 17, the Lord tells David that one of his sons will be the Temple-Builder, but he does not reveal which one. Now David discloses to us that – like Ishmael, Isaac, John the Baptist and Jesus – the Lord named Solomon before his birth.[3] He decreed that he should have a name which means *Peaceful*, so that his life and reign could serve as a prophetic picture of Jesus, the Prince of Peace who was to come.[4]

David is aware that his son is young and inexperienced, so he pressgangs the Canaanite survivors into serving Solomon

---

[2] David repeats this again in 28:3–7. The wars described in 1 Chronicles 18–20 were not sinful, but David's violence made him a flawed reflection of the Prince of Peace who was to come.

[3] Genesis 16:11 and 17:19; Matthew 1:21 and Luke 1:13.

[4] Isaiah 9:6–7. Don't miss the future tenses in 22:9 and 2 Samuel 7:12. Solomon was only aged around eighteen when he became the new king of Israel in 970 BC.

as heavy lifters and stonecutters.[5] This is also why he stores up vast quantities of gold, silver, bronze, iron, masonry and cedarwood, so that nothing will hinder his son from building the Temple right from the very start of his reign. It is also why David assembles all the leaders of Israel in order to assure them that the Lord will be with them as they build with King Solomon:

> *Now devote your heart and soul to seeking the Lord your God. Begin to build the sanctuary of the Lord God, so that you may bring the ark of the covenant of the Lord and the sacred articles belonging to God into the temple that will be built for the Name of the Lord.*

Under Solomon, the Israelites would complete what they had started through the construction of David's Tabernacle.

Having done all that he can personally do to hand over well to Solomon, David prays that the Lord will do the rest by making his son a successful Temple-Builder. He asks the Lord to grant Solomon *"discretion and understanding"* – a prayer that will be answered beyond David's wildest dreams when the Lord blesses Solomon with such wisdom at the start of his reign that he becomes *"wiser than anyone else"* who has ever lived before him.[6] David also prays – poignantly – that this wisdom will enable his son to follow the Law of Moses all his days. This is something that Solomon will fail to do.

Don't miss this, because it forms a vital aspect of a subplot which runs through this handover chapter. In verse 14, David declares that he has stored up expensive raw materials for the building of the Temple during his *'onī* – that is, during his final years of reigning over Israel in the midst of *trouble* and

---

[5] This had begun already in Deuteronomy 29:11 and Joshua 9:21, but Solomon would take it to a new level in 2 Chronicles 8:7–10.

[6] 22:12; 1 Kings 3:12; 4:29–34 and 5:12, and 2 Chronicles 2:12; 9:1–8, and 22–23. David also uses the Hebrew adjective *hākām*, meaning *wise*, here in 22:15 to describe the *skilfulness* of the Temple craftsmen.

misery and *pain*. This is the closest that the Chronicler gets to recording the rebellions of David's sons against him, each of them hoping to overturn the Lord's decree that their little brother should inherit the throne.[7] It goes alongside the none-too-subtle premonition in verses 12–13 that Solomon will drift from the Law of Moses and begin to worship the foreign idols of his pagan wives. Together, these verses are here to remind us that, whilst King Solomon was the *son of David*, he was not the true *Son of David*. He was the *messiah*, but not the true *Messiah*.[8]

The true Temple-Builder would only be born in a stable in Bethlehem a thousand years after David's handover to Solomon. Also named by God before his birth, he would distinguish himself from Solomon as the true Prince of Peace by never once straying from the Law of Moses. Instead of pressganging the nations to build his New Covenant Temple with him, Jesus would draw the willing worship of the nations through the beauty of his character. He would declare himself to be the true Son of David and the Successor about whom this handover chapter prophesies, when he called the crowd to look to him as their Saviour in faith, because *"something greater than Solomon is here"*![9]

---

[7] Adonijah confesses that he knows the Lord's decree in 1 Kings 2:13–15.

[8] We can also see this in 22:10, since Solomon's sons would not rule *"over Israel for ever"*, other than through Jesus. Upon Solomon's death, Israel and Judah would be divided into two rival and opposing kingdoms.

[9] Matthew 12:42 and Luke 11:31. Isaiah 60:9–16 picks up on 1 Chronicles 22 by prophesying that the nations will not need to be pressganged into building with the true *Messiah*. They will gladly volunteer.

What Priests Do
(1 Chronicles 23:13)

*"Aaron was set apart… to consecrate the most holy
things, to offer sacrifices before the Lord, to minister
before him and to pronounce blessings in his name."*
(1 Chronicles 23:13)

Have you noticed how some of the little words in the Bible
require a lot of unpacking? We can read the word *grace* over
a hundred times in the Bible, without ever truly grasping what
the grace of God means for us. In the same way, we can read the
word *priest* several hundred times without understanding what
those priests were actually called to do. That's why I love the
explanation that the Chronicler gives us midway through his
long roster of priests in chapters 23–24. It's so brief that you
might miss it, but I'm sure that you have learned by now that the
Lord is the God of such small things.

Many readers speed through these two chapters because
they imagine that what the priests did at the Temple is irrelevant
to their own lives. That's tragic, because right from the start of
Israel's history the Lord made it clear that what those priests
did was a picture of his purposes for us all. He promised the
Israelites at Mount Sinai that *"You will be for me a kingdom of
priests and a holy nation."* In case we see this as a promise just
for ancient Israel, the New Testament repeats that it remains
God's plan to make his people *"a royal priesthood"* – that is,
"kings and priests to serve our God".[1] When we look at the priests

---

[1] Exodus 19:6; 1 Peter 2:9 and Revelation 1:6 and 5:10. Some Greek manuscripts of
Revelation read *"a kingdom and priests"*, but other manuscripts read far more simply:
basileis kai hiereis – "kings and priests".

of ancient Israel, we are meant to see a picture of what the Lord has now commissioned every single follower of Jesus to do.[2]

First, the Chronicler tells us in 23:13 that priests were set apart *"to consecrate the most holy things"* to God. Since the Hebrew phrase that is used here is *qodesh qādāshīm* and is the normal phrase used to describe the *Holy of Holies* (the inner sanctuary of the Tabernacle of Moses and the Temple of Solomon), we might equally read this to mean that they were *"to consecrate the Most Holy Place"*. As followers of Jesus, we are called to honour heavenly things as holy, and we are called to become the new Holy of Holies on the earth today. *"Don't you know that you yourselves are God's temple and that God's Spirit lives among you?"* the Apostle Paul asks in one of his letters. *"For God's temple is sacred and you together are that temple."*[3] Don't speed-read through these chapters so quickly that you forget your calling to be a carrier of the Presence of the Lord wherever you go.

Second, the Chronicler tells us in 23:13 that priests were set apart *"to offer sacrifices before the Lord"*. We can tell from what David did in dedicating his Tabernacle that Jesus has changed this for us today. There is no longer any need for his followers to offer sacrifices for their sins, because Jesus *"sacrificed for their sins once for all when he offered himself."*[4] Instead, we are cleansed freely from our sins and empowered by God's Spirit to offer him the same sacrifices that were offered in David's Tabernacle – sacrifices of shouts of joy, of an obedient spirit, of hands lifted up in thankful praise and of fervent prayer.[5]

Third, the Chronicler tells us in 23:13 that the priests of God were set apart *"to minister before him"*. The Hebrew word

[2] The "priesthood of all believers" was one of the cardinal doctrines of the Protestant Reformation in the sixteenth century. Martin Luther argued, in his pamphlet *On the Babylonian Captivity of the Church* (1520), that *"We are all equally priests, as many of us as are baptised... We are all priests, as many of us as are Christians."*

[3] 1 Corinthians 3:16–17; 2 Corinthians 6:16; Ephesians 2:19–22 and 1 Peter 2:4–6.

[4] Hebrews 7:27; 9:11–15, 24–28 and 10:1–12.

[5] Psalm 27:6; 40:6–8; 51:17 and 141:2; Hebrews 13:15; 1 Peter 2:9 and Revelation 5:8–9.

shārat, means *to serve*, and it is far less a piece of religious jargon than the English word "minister". It is the word used elsewhere to describe Joseph attending to the mundane needs of his slave master Potiphar and to the humdrum needs of his fellow prisoners in a dungeon.[6] This helps us understand the very practical ways in which the New Testament says we can minister to the Lord – by caring for his people, by proclaiming his Word to nonbelievers, by fervently praying and fasting for his Great Commission to be completed in the world, and by serving him diligently in our workplaces.[7] The Lord is so mighty that he needs nothing from his people, yet he grants us the privilege of pleasing him by making his deepest concerns our own.

Fourth, the Chronicler tells us in 23:13 that the priests of God were set apart *"to pronounce blessings in his name"*.[8] We are not just to enjoy him for what his Presence means to us. We are to emerge from his Presence to do what David did when he emerged from his Tabernacle in 16:2. We are to proclaim the goodness of God to those who are on the outside, reassuring them that God's Name is powerful enough to meet their every need.[9] As followers of Jesus, this means more than proclaiming the Gospel and praying for people. It means demonstrating the Gospel through such miracles as healing and deliverance from demons. We can tell from the psalm in chapter 16 that the message of David's Tabernacle was *Come And See*. At the end of Matthew and Mark's gospels, we find that the message of Jesus to his followers has now become *Go And Tell*.

---

[6] Genesis 39:4 and 40:4.

[7] In Romans 15:16, Paul uses the Greek word *hierourgeō*, which means *to serve as a priest*, to describe the sacrifices which Christians make for the sake of serving the Lord today. Their prayer and fasting is likened to priestly offerings in Acts 13:2, and in Revelation 5:8 and 8:3.

[8] The roster in 24:6–18 for which priests offered incense on which weeks of the year proves important in Luke 1:5–9. John the Baptist's father belonged to the family of Abijah, so he entered the Temple at the just right time to meet the angel Gabriel and to begin the chain of events which led to the birth of the *Messiah*.

[9] We can also see this in Leviticus 10:8–11; Numbers 6:22–27 and Deuteronomy 31:9–13.

Fifth, the Chronicler tells us in 23:13 that the priests were to do these things *"forever"*. We find a clue in 23:25, which treats the Temple of King Solomon as a *"forever"* building, that the priests of ancient Israel were a temporary picture of something which continues in another form through Jesus Christ.[10] This is underlined for us again in Malachi 2:5–9, which lists these four priestly roles a second time at the end of the Old Testament to clear the stage for the arrival of the true *Messiah*. Malachi says that the priests of Israel were called to display God's holiness, to rejoice in God's presence, to partner with God in his purposes and to proclaim God's Word. This remains our own calling today.

So praise God for these long chapters which record the names of the many individuals who served as priests in the time of King David and King Solomon. Don't complain about how long they are; rejoice in the fact that each name on the list proclaims that the Lord has called you to serve as a valued member of his massive priestly team.[11]

Priest. It's such a little word, but the Lord is the God of small things. Through chapters such as these, he is calling you to display his holiness, to rejoice in his presence, to partner with him in his purposes and proclaim his Word to everyone around you today.

---

[10] Forever does not mean unchanging. The mobile Tabernacle of Moses (described as *"the tent of meeting"* in 23:32) was becoming a static Temple, so David adjusts the tasks of the 38,000 adult Levites in 23:3–5.

[11] Having counted 38,000 male Levites aged over thirty in 23:3, David discovers that he needs more than this, so he lowers the age limit to twenty in 23:24. He also establishes an important principle for God's team of priests in 24:31 – that the old and the young are of equal value in their service to him. See also 25:8 and 26:13.

Worship God Wants (1 Chronicles 25:1–31)

*"David… set apart some of the sons of Asaph,
Heman and Jeduthun for the ministry of prophesying,
accompanied by harps, lyres and cymbals."*

(1 Chronicles 25:1)

Worship leader and author Jeremy Riddle observes:

*Mankind has been worshipping since the beginning of
time, busily crafting all manner of gods and an endless
variety of accompanying religious rituals and practices
for the sake of appeasing, connecting with, and
entreating those same gods. The important thing to note
is, whatever the worship practice may be, it's consistently
subject to the gods themselves. Even pagan worship has
understood that the only one who can determine whether
an act of worship is actually "worshipful" is the one being
worshipped… Though the worship of our God – the One,
True, Living God – is distinct in almost every way, in this,
it is the same… If God doesn't like it… it's not worship.*[1]

That's why it is so helpful to us that the Chronicler records in
quite some detail what the sung worship was like at David's
Tabernacle. Although the long list of names in chapter 25 can
appear tedious in places, it contains several little clues about
the type of worship that the Lord enjoys, and we have learned
that he is the God of small things. This chapter may not be as

---

[1] Jeremy Riddle says this in his book *The Reset,* Anaheim, Wholehearted Publishing
(2020). If you don't believe him, take a look at Amos 5:21–24.

exciting as the one in John's gospel where Jesus declares that *"God is spirit, and his worshippers must worship in the Spirit and in truth"*, but it is nonetheless full of important insight into Israel's worship, if we pay attention to detail.[2]

First, this chapter shows us that *the Lord loves variety* in our worship. None of the worship leaders at David's Tabernacle led on their own. They led as part of three families of worship leaders: Asaph and his sons, Jeduthun and his sons, and Heman and his sons.[3] (In case our modern ears are offended by the male leadership structures of ancient Israel, note that the daughters of Heman are given special mention in verse 5.[4]) Nor do these diverse worship leaders all use the same instruments. We are told in this chapter that they led bands of skilled musicians who played harps, lyres and cymbals.[5]

Second, this chapter shows us that *the Lord loves to hear the unique voice of each worshipper*. Heman means *Faithful* and he wrote Psalm 88, so he had a claim to be the greatest worship leader. Jeduthun means *Praise Man* and was a nickname given to Ethan, the writer of Psalm 89. Since other worship leaders dedicated Psalms 39, 62 and 77 to him, he might have argued that his leadership gift warranted even greater room than that of Heman. Asaph means *Gatherer* and he wrote not just one psalm, but twelve – Psalms 50 and 73–83. It is therefore a mark of the immense humility on the part of these three gifted men that one of their twenty-four sons was equally likely to lead the crowds in worship at David's Tabernacle. The Chronicler is revealing the type of worship that the Lord desires when he records in

---

[2] John 4:19–26. Jesus tells the Samaritan woman that he is the true *Messiah* and is building a better Tabernacle.

[3] Aaron had three sons and each of these three families came from a different clan descended from those three sons. These three chief worship leaders are also mentioned in 6:31–47; 15:17–22; 16:4–7 and 37–42.

[4] It was the male Levites who served at the Tabernacle and Temple, but we have great examples of female worship leaders elsewhere in ancient Israel. See Exodus 15:20–21 and Judges 5:1–31.

[5] The Chronicler emphasises their gifting as musicians in 25:7. The Lord loves the sound of our worship, regardless of our skill, but greater gifting is needed on the part of those he calls to lead others. See 15:22.

verse 8 that *"Young and old alike, teacher as well as student, cast lots for their duties."* The Lord loves to hear the unique voice of every worshipper.

Third, this chapter shows us that *the Lord loves to break into our worship with gifts of the Holy Spirit*. David doesn't just set apart Heman, Jeduthun, Asaph and their sons to lead the people in singing worship songs. He sets them apart *"for the ministry of prophesying"*. Throughout the Old Testament, there is a strong link between singing worship songs to the Lord and his responding to those songs through the gift of prophecy. In 1 Samuel 10:5, a team of prophets bring God's word to people to the sound of *"lyres, tambourines, pipes and harps"*. In 2 Kings 3:15, the prophet Elisha asks a harpist to play for him to help him hear the voice of God. It shouldn't surprise us that God's Presence is felt most keenly in our worship, because it is a theme which runs throughout the Psalms.[6] Asaph even breaks off midway through one of them to explain that *"I heard an unknown voice say"* a word of prophecy by which the Lord responded to his singing (Psalm 81:5–16).

If the worshippers at David's Tabernacle expected God's Spirit to inspire them to prophesy words of encouragement to one another as they sang together, then how much more should we who live on the other side of the Day of Pentecost. The Apostle Peter encourages us to believe that *"Your sons and daughters will prophesy, your young men will see visions, your old men will dream dreams."* The Apostle Paul agrees: *"When you come together, each of you has a hymn, or a word of instruction, a revelation, a tongue or an interpretation. Everything must be done so that the church may be built up."*[7] Who knows how much blessing we forfeit by making too little room for each spiritual gift to be exercised?

Fourth, this chapter shows us that *the Lord loves us to worship him in an orderly way*. Having told the Corinthian church

---

[6] For example, in Psalm 14:5 and 22:3. This is one of the reasons why we always worship better when we gather to sing together, rather than simply worshipping on our own.

[7] Acts 2:17 and 1 Corinthians 14:26. Peter adds in Acts 2:39 that this is a promise for every generation of Christians.

to make room for every gift of the Holy Spirit to be exercised, Paul ends the chapter by reminding them that *"Everything should be done in a fitting and orderly way."*[8] We see the same principle at work here at David's Tabernacle, where everything is done *"under the supervision of Asaph"* or Heman or Jeduthun – men who themselves are *"under the supervision of the king"*. Freedom in worship should never mean a free-for-all. Prophecies need to be weighed. Worshippers need to be led in response to God. It isn't easy to get the balance right between freedom and supervision, but this chapter encourages us that it is possible.

Fifth, this chapter shows us that *the Lord loves worship which forms a conversation between him and his people.* Scripture reading tends to be one-way, as the Lord speaks timeless words to a group of worshippers. Singing tends to be one-way in reverse, as those worshippers respond to what God's Word says. It is easy for us to think that prophesying is one-way traffic too – the Lord responding to his people as they respond to his timeless Word. However, verse 3 seems to suggest that Jeduthun was also given prophetic words from the Holy Spirit that formed "new songs" for the people to sing back to God in thanks and praise. What we see here is worship as a fluid conversation.[9]

So don't speed-read through the list of names in chapter 25. Put down your book and let this list of names inspire you to spend time worshipping the Lord today. These verses teach us five of the things that the Lord loves to hear in our worship. So let's allow ourselves to be led by Asaph, Heman and Jeduthun. Let's truly worship the Lord.

---

[8] 1 Corinthians 14:32–33 and 40.

[9] Asaph is referred to as a *"seer"* or *"prophet"* in 2 Chronicles 29:30. We are also told in Matthew 13:35 that one of Asaph's worship songs foretold the future ministry of the *Messiah* (Psalm 78:2). For examples of their emphasis on "new songs" of worship, see Psalms 33:3; 40:3; 96:1; 98:1; 144:9 and 149:1.

Multiply
(1 Chronicles 25:5)

"All these were sons of Heman the king's seer. They were given to him through the promises of God to exalt him. God gave Heman fourteen sons and three daughters."

(1 Chronicles 25:5)

Every single second, your body produces 25 million new cells. Let me say that again: every single second. So cut yourself a little slack the next time your body feels tired!

The way in which our bodies multiply new cells is both mind-boggling and utterly commonplace. All of us do it. We each began life as a single cell in our mother's womb. That cell quickly multiplied into two, then those two cells multiplied into four, and so on. Before we knew it, nine months later, we had two trillion cells and were ready to be born.

The hard work didn't stop there. By the time a person reaches adulthood, those 2 trillion cells have multiplied to become 37 trillion cells or more. We produce 25 million new cells every second to replace old cells that die. In order to grow, the bodies of children and teenagers work much harder. It's as if the Lord designed our bodies to be a proclamation that God created us to go forth, increase and multiply.[1]

This much becomes obvious in the lists of names in the final chapters of 1 Chronicles. Many readers miss the little throwaway comments along the way, but we know by now

---

[1] For more on this, see Bill Bryson's excellent book *The Body* (New York, Doubleday, 2019).

that such little details matter. The Lord is the God of such small things.

In 23:10, the Chronicler informs us that a man named Shimei had four sons – enough to make him a mighty clan leader amongst the Levites who ministered at the Temple. However, because *"Jeush and Beriah did not have many sons... they were counted as one family with one assignment."* Everybody needs to multiply if they want their clan to grow. This verse reminds us of an earlier throwaway comment, in 4:27, where the Chronicler recorded the offspring of another man named Shimei, this time a member of the tribe of Levi. *"Shimei had sixteen sons and six daughters, but his brothers did not have many children; so their entire clan did not become as numerous as the people of Judah."*

In 23:17, the Chronicler highlights the flip side to this principle. Moses had a son named Eliezer, who only gave him one grandson. Nevertheless, he became a mighty clan leader among the Levites because *"Eliezer had no other sons, but the sons of Rehabiah were very numerous."* Eliezer reminds me of the famous story about Albert McMakin, a farmer from North Carolina who, as far we know, only ever succeeded in leading one person to faith in Jesus. However, because that person who came to faith was the stadium evangelist Billy Graham, Albert Makin had over 3,000,000 grandchildren! We can't all be like Billy Graham, but we can all be like Albert McMakin. If you don't believe me, then reflect again on the fact that the 37 trillion cells in your body began as a single cell.[2]

This brings us to 25:5, where the Chronicler is listing the worship leaders in David's Tabernacle. He tells us that *"All these were sons of Heman the king's seer. They were given to him through the promises of God to exalt him. God gave Heman fourteen sons and three daughters."* This little verse tells us that, when God wants to bless a man or woman, he enables them to

---

[2] See Billy Graham's autobiography *Just As I Am* (1997). The disciple Andrew was also like Albert McMakin. We know very little about his own ministry, but he led his brother Peter to Jesus in John 1:40–42.

multiply.[3] He does so to exalt them in his purposes – that is, to increase their influence for the extension of his Kingdom.[4] In a chapter which seems to prize sons more than daughters, this verse also reassures us that the Lord also values daughters.[5] The ancient Hebrews may have thought less of baby girls than baby boys, but the Lord doesn't – which brings us on to a major theme in the Bible: that of infertile women.

Many modern readers skim over these verses because they fail to grasp the importance of reproduction and multiplication. Other readers rush past them because they sense the pain of infertility all too keenly. If you have known this agony first-hand, then please be reassured that the Bible does not emphasise the importance of multiplication in order to rub salt in your wound. Quite the contrary. There is a rich theme that runs throughout the Bible of men and women whose struggle with physical infertility God used to prepare them for greater spiritual fertility than their fertile friends and neighbours. If you are a woman, then the Lord encourages you in Isaiah 54:1 to *"Sing, barren woman, you who never bore a child; burst into song, shout for joy, you who were never in labour; because more are the children of the desolate woman than of her who has a husband."* If you are a man, then the Lord encourages you in Isaiah 56:4–5 that he will give you *"a memorial and a name better than sons and daughters".*

We see this in the book of Genesis, where Sarah, Rebekah and Rachel all struggle to conceive children. The Lord uses this for good, as it provokes them to cry out to him for the spiritual nation that God wants to birth through them. When Rachel cries out, *"Give me children, or I'll die!"*, she becomes the mother of Joseph, the most fruitful of Jacob's sons, who saves the Hebrew

---

[3] We also see this in 26:4–5, where Obed-Edom's eight sons are a mark of God's blessing upon him.

[4] The Hebrew phrase that is used here means literally *"to exalt his horn"*. It is also used to describe the Lord exalting David in Psalm 89:17–24. Heman directs the other two main worship leaders in 6:31–47.

[5] God does not play favourites. See 25:8; Luke 20:21; Acts 10:34; Romans 2:11 and Galatians 3:26–29.

nation from death during a severe famine. When Hannah encounters similar struggles in 1 Samuel, the Lord uses it to stir her to pray, not just that she will have a son, but that her son will play a role in the revival of her backslidden nation. Through her prayers, she gives birth to Samuel, the last great Judge of Israel.[6]

This theme sounds even more loudly as the New Testament begins. John the Baptist is born to an infertile couple named Zechariah and Elizabeth. He prepares the way for Jesus, a childless man who teaches the crowd that his family is anyone who receives his teaching. Jesus ends Matthew's gospel, not with a physical genealogy like the ones in 1 Chronicles, but with a spiritual genealogy. He commands his twelve disciples to go forth, increase and multiply: *"Go and make disciples of all nations".*[7] As a result, the childless Apostle Paul fills his letters with the tender language of a father: *"My dear children"*, *"Timothy my true son in the faith"*, and *"Titus, my true son".*[8]

So, be encouraged. While you have been reading this chapter, your body has been creating 150,000,000 new cells! The same God who has just done that in your body will enable you to multiply disciples as you follow his Great Commission.

---

[6] Genesis 17:15–21; 25:1 and 30:1, and 1 Samuel 1:1–2:11.

[7] Matthew 28:18–20; Mark 3:31–35 and Luke 1:5–25.

[8] 1 Corinthians 4:14–15; Galatians 4:19; 1 Timothy 1:2; 2 Timothy 1:2; Titus 1:4 and Philemon 10.

Enemy at the Gates (1 Chronicles 26:1–32)

"The divisions of the gatekeepers..."

(1 Chronicles 26:1)

Dawson Trotman, who founded the discipleship movement The Navigators, argued that *"Nothing under heaven except sin, immaturity and lack of communion will put you in a position where you cannot reproduce. Wherever you find a Christian who is not leading men and women to Christ, something is wrong."*[1]

I don't know whether you agree with Dawson Trotman, but I have personally found his words to be true. Perhaps the Chronicler has too, because he moves on very swiftly from verses which encourage us to multiply ourselves for God into a chapter which focuses on the gatekeepers of the Lord's Temple. The Jews who returned from the exile in Babylon had appointed trusty gatekeepers to guard their Temple and the city walls of Jerusalem.[2] The Chronicler lists those who guarded those same gates under King David in order to highlight the continuity between Jewish life before and after the exile, but the Holy Spirit who inspired him also wants to use these verses to help us to reflect on why we find it harder to reproduce ourselves today than godly leaders such as Heman found it in the days of King David. We have an enemy at the gates of our lives.

---

[1] Taken from his most famous sermon, entitled "Born to Reproduce", preached in October 1955. By *"lack of communion"*, Trotman means a failure to walk in close friendship with Jesus through his Holy Spirit.

[2] We can read about those gatekeepers in Nehemiah 7:1–3 and 11:19. The detailed list here makes sense if the long-standing Jewish tradition is correct that Ezra wrote all of 1 and 2 Chronicles, Ezra and Nehemiah.

When Dawson Trotman warns us, first, that *sin* can rob us of our God-given ability to multiply disciples, he is echoing what the Bible teaches us about gatekeepers. The Psalmist prays, *"Set a guard over my mouth, Lord; keep watch over the door of my lips. Do not let my heart be drawn to what is evil"*. Job prayed something similar about guarding the gateway of his eyes: *"I made a covenant with my eyes not to look lustfully at a young woman."*[3] It therefore makes sense when Nehemiah 7:2 tells us that after the exile the Jews appointed a chief gatekeeper who *"was a man of integrity and feared God more than most people do."*[4] It is easy to treat spiritual fruitfulness as something random, like being struck by lightning – it either happens to us or it doesn't, and there is very little we can do about it. But in reality, the Scriptures teach us that sin is a crippling disease which renders many would-be fruitful Christians unnecessarily infertile.

When Dawson Trotman warns us, second, that *immaturity* can also rob us of our God-given ability to multiply disciples, he is echoing another aspect of the Bible's teaching about gatekeepers. In the ancient world, elders would hold their meetings at the main gate of their city.[5] These men who guarded the gateways had proved their maturity and wisdom through their leadership of their own families over many years.[6] It therefore makes perfect sense when the Chronicler highlights to us that Obed-Edom's grandsons served as gatekeepers *"because*

---

[3] Psalm 141:3–4 and Job 31:1. See also Psalm 39:1, Matthew 5:29–30 and James 1:26. Only those who have guarded their own senses well can be trusted with guarding the people of God from its bitter enemy.

[4] When the Apostle Paul gives a list of qualifications for church elders – the gatekeepers of the New Jerusalem – he focuses almost entirely on their character. See 1 Timothy 3:1–7 and Titus 1:5–9.

[5] For example, in Genesis 19:1; Deuteronomy 21:19; 22:15 and 25:7; Joshua 20:4 and Ruth 4:11.

[6] Parents are gatekeepers for their families. For example, in Deuteronomy 22:20–21, a daughter who sins is brought to her father's doorstep to be punished, since he ought to have protected her from temptation. Only those who parent their children well ought to be trusted to guard God's family (1 Timothy 3:4–5 and 12).

they were very capable men… with the strength to do the work".[7] In nature, people have to reach a certain age before they become fertile. In God's Kingdom, we come to reproductive age not by the years we chalk up in following Jesus, but by our willingness to take up our cross daily and to yield our entire lives to him.[8]

When Dawson Trotman warns us, third, that a *lack of communion* with God can prevent us from multiplying disciples, he is echoing a third aspect of the Bible's teaching about gatekeepers. It is significant in these verses that King David does not allocate the task of gatekeeping to his bravest warriors, but to the Levites who cherished the Presence of God.[9] In the past, under Moses, the Levites used to carry the furnishings of the Tabernacle through the desert. Now that the mobile Tabernacle is becoming a static Temple, David is able to redeploy many of them, and it is easy to see why he entrusted the task of gatekeeping to many of them.[10] Because Jesus cherished the Presence of God's Spirit within him, he was able to cast out demons with a word.[11] When we cherish the Presence of God's Spirit too, then we are empowered to do as he did.

Don't miss the leading role that Obed-Edom and his sons and grandsons play in this list of gatekeepers. You may remember from chapter 13 that Obed-Edom was a Gittite – that is, a Philistine from the city of Gath. He was not an Israelite, let alone a Levite. However, the three months which the Ark of the Covenant spent at his house was enough to teach him the importance of the Presence of God. In the same way that a human embryo cannot be formed in a mother's womb until a

---

[7] He highlights this three times – in 26:6, 7 and 8. With eight sons and sixty-two grandsons, Obed-Edom epitomises the link between spiritual maturity and spiritual fruitfulness.

[8] Having already emphasised this in 24:31 and 25:8, the Chronicler does so again in 26:13.

[9] *Asaph* in 26:1 is a contraction of *Abiasaph*, one of the three Sons of Korah (Exodus 6:24). This is a different person from the worship leader who is mentioned in chapter 25.

[10] Many of the people listed here had roles in David's Tabernacle until the Temple was completed (15:23–24).

[11] Matthew 8:16. The key to doing this is being filled with the Holy Spirit (1 John 4:4). That's why the Spirit-filled believers of the Early Church could drive out demons, just like Jesus (Acts 8:6–8; 16:16–18 and 19:11–20).

seed fertilises her egg, so the Word of God will not save anyone until it is brought to life deep within a person's heart by the Spirit of God. Obed-Edom is made an honorary Levite because he grasps the importance of God's Presence for the reproduction of God's people right across the Promised Land.[12]

In 26:1–19, the Chronicler focuses on the gatekeepers of the Temple and the wider city. In 26:20–28, he moves on to list the Levites who guarded the holy vessels of the House of God in the Temple treasuries. In 26:29–32, he lists the Levites who went out from the Temple to purify the entire Promised Land by acting as magistrates and missionaries.[13]

God created you to multiply. When his Son Jesus rose victorious from the grave, he commissioned all his followers to go out and make many more disciples.[14] Nothing can stop you from doing so, except for *sin*, *immaturity* or a *lack of close relationship* with him.

So deal with the enemy at your gates, who wants to stop you from multiplying and to render you unfruitful. Hell has its own gates too, so remember that Jesus has promised us: *"I will build my church and the gates of Hades will not overcome it."*[15]

---

[12] The South Gate was the gate which led to the royal palace, so it was the gate used by the king. Obed-Edom is therefore blessed and honoured even further by the Lord in 26:15.

[13] We were told in 23:4 that King David appointed 6,000 Levite magistrates in total so, in addition to the 1,700 and 2,700 who served west and east of the River Jordan, a further 1,600 must have served in the north.

[14] In that sense, Matthew 28:18–20 is the New Testament equivalent of Genesis 1:28. Multiplying disciples isn't just something that keen Christians do. It lies at the heart of what it means for us to walk with God.

[15] Matthew 16:18. Note also the promise of God to you in Isaiah 28:6.

Order
(1 Chronicles 27:1–34)

"This is the list of the Israelites – heads of families, commanders of thousands and commanders of hundreds, and all their officers, who served the king."

(1 Chronicles 27:1)

There's a crazy idea in some Christian circles that church structure is inherently a bad thing. It flows from a fear that rigid structures shut out the working of the Holy Spirit. It is argued that, if we want to experience more of God's Spirit in our church gatherings, then we need to do away with our church structures altogether and become more like the worshippers at David's Tabernacle and at Solomon's Temple.

It doesn't take a lot of insight into these final chapters of 1 Chronicles to realise that this type of thinking is flawed. David's Tabernacle was a place for joyful worship and for freedom in the Holy Spirit, but it wasn't at all disorderly.[1] In chapter 23, David carefully allocates specific leadership roles to each of the Levite families. In chapter 24, he divides the priests into twenty-four divisions so that each can serve in *"their appointed order of ministering"*. In chapter 25, David appoints worship leaders and sets up worship rosters. In chapter 26, he appoints gatekeepers and treasurers and magistrates to enforce godly law and order. While it is true that the wrong type of rigid church structure can stifle the work of the Holy Spirit, these chapters show us that some structure is needed.

---

[1] David danced with careless abandon in chapter 15, but he plans carefully what he will wear, how he will sacrifice, how he will bless the people and everything else that will take place at his new Tabernacle.

In case we haven't learned this from the past four chapters, the Chronicler continues the same lesson here in chapter 27. In 27:1–15, he lists the officers who were appointed by King David to lead the twelve divisions of his citizen militia. While the soldiers in his standing army needed to be ready for action throughout the year, the soldiers in his reserve militia were only expected to leave their lands and families to serve for one month of the year. David entrusts the leadership of each division of this militia to one of the mighty men who are listed in 11:11–47.[2] He tells each of them which month of the year they will be responsible for policing his kingdom and protecting the Tabernacle and Temple.[3] All of this emphasises that clear structure is helpful to God's people.[4]

In 27:16–22, the Chronicler lists the leaders that King David recognised over the twelve tribes of Israel.[5] It doesn't matter to the Chronicler that some of these tribes have not yet returned from the exile at the time of writing. He simply wants to teach his readers that recognising leaders and drawing up rosters is not unspiritual. It was vital for David's Tabernacle and Solomon's Temple, and it was vital for their own Temple too. Until they had a new king, they were to follow the leadership structure that David created for them.

In 27:23–24, the Chronicler addresses our concern that rigid structures can sometimes stifle the work of the Holy Spirit.

---

[2] Benaiah was commander of David's personal bodyguard and became commander-in-chief of the standing army when Joab was executed (11:22–25 and 1 Kings 2:35). As a result, his son Ammizadab did most of the leading of his division of the citizen militia. The same was true of Asahel's son Zebadiah, since Asahel was killed in battle early on in David's reign (11:26 and 2 Samuel 2:18–23).

[3] David included his army officers in many decisions which we might regard as domestic matters. See 11:10; 12:32; 13:1; 15:25; 25:1 and 28:1.

[4] The Chronicler probably wrote during the reign of King Artaxerxes of Persia (465–424 BC), who fought hard to restore law and order to his empire after the assassination of his father Xerxes and an Egyptian rebellion. As a result, law and order is a big theme of Ezra and Nehemiah – and of 1 and 2 Chronicles too.

[5] David doesn't so much appoint tribal leaders as recognise the leaders who have emerged within the tribes. In that sense, nor do we "create" leaders within the Church; we merely recognise leaders who are emerging.

The New Testament teaches us that *"Where the Spirit of the Lord is, there is freedom"*, so whenever our structures tell the Holy Spirit what he can and cannot do, we place a lid on his activity among us.[6] The Chronicler suggests in these verses that this is what David did when he ordered a census of his kingdom. The Lord had to teach him that much of what matters is beyond human control – such as how the twelve tribes of Israel became *"as numerous as the stars in the sky"*.

In 27:25–34, the Chronicler returns to his theme that proper structure can be helpful. He lists a whole host of leaders whose hard work enabled David's kingdom to flourish. He tells us who organised the royal storehouses, the royal farmlands, the royal vineyards, the royal olive groves and the royal fig trees. He says who was in charge of manufacturing the royal wine and olive oil. He lists the names of those who were responsible for the royal herds of cattle, for the royal flocks of sheep and for the royal camels and donkeys.[7] He rounds off the list by telling us the names of those who organised David's sons, David's council chamber, David's social life in the palace and David's standing army in its campaigns.[8] These verses reveal the orderliness of David's kingdom and they insist that proper structures can be helpful for God's people.[9]

We might have spotted this already from creation. In Genesis 1, the Holy Spirit hovers over chaos in order to bring forth godly order. He forms clear boundaries between the light

---

[6] 2 Corinthians 3:17 and 1 Thessalonians 5:19. See also Acts 7:51.

[7] There is no mention in Scripture of David taxing his subjects, so it seems he lived off this royal property.

[8] Ahithophel was the grandfather of Bathsheba. When he turned against David in disgust at his sin, he was replaced as chief advisor by Jehoiada and by the priest Abiathar (2 Samuel 11:3; 15:31 – 17:23 and 23:34).

[9] If anything, David's sons needed greater order than their tutor Jehiel was able to give them. We are told in 3:1–4 that David named them Amnon (*Faithful*), Daniel (*God Is My Judge*), Absalom (*Father Of Peace*), Adonijah (*My Lord Is Yahweh*) and Shephatiah (*The Lord Is My Judge*). However, he needed to follow up these godly names with a father's godly discipline. Tragically, the man who wrote in Psalm 145:4 that *"One generation commends your works to another"* neglected to discipline his own children (1 Kings 1:5–6).

and darkness, between the sky and the sea, between the dry land and the oceans. When the Lord proceeds to create plants and animals, every cell of those organisms proclaims that he is a God of order. Each cell is far more complex in its internal workings than the most sophisticated man-made factory, and all of that complexity is held together by a cell membrane. The larger an organism becomes, the more structured its cell membranes need to be. Trees have to strengthen their cell walls with lignin to grow tall. The right kind of structure supports life, rather than suffocating it.

We might also have spotted this from 1 Corinthians 14. The Apostle Paul encourages us to make room for the work of the Holy Spirit in our church meetings and insists that everybody must find space to operate in their own gifting. Yet he also insists that *"God is not a God of disorder but of peace... everything should be done in a fitting and orderly way."*[10]

But even if we miss it in those two places, at least we have these long chapters at the end of 1 Chronicles. Don't move on from reading about leadership structures and serving rosters without recognising what they wish to teach us. We need to be wary of rigid structures that crowd out the Holy Spirit, but we need to be equally wary of the idea that church structure is, in and of itself, a bad thing. The Lord who helped King David wants to help us to create systems and structures that enable his Church to grow.

[10] 1 Corinthians 14:26, 33 and 39–40. See also what is variously translated as the spiritual gift of "administration" or of "clear guidance" in 1 Corinthians 12:28.

A Simple Plan
(1 Chronicles 28:1–21)

"'All this,' David said, 'I have in writing as a result of the Lord's hand on me, and he enabled me to understand all the details of the plan.'"

(1 Chronicles 28:19)

In May 2013, a teacher at Newmarket College in England hit the news headlines all around the world. Two weeks before her students were due to take their A levels, she confessed to them that she had misread the English syllabus. Although she had spent the past year preparing them to sit an exam on Bram Stoker's *Dracula*, she admitted that their exam in two weeks' time would be on Mary Shelley's *Frankenstein* instead. The teacher was mortified, her students were horrified and their school was utterly vilified.[1]

King David was determined not to commit a blunder like that. He knew that the Lord had chosen his son Solomon to build a Temple, so he prepared him to build the right type of Temple from the very start. You see, there wasn't just one blueprint on the table for him to follow. There were two. He needed to know which of them to follow.

Should Solomon construct a Temple which looked like the Tabernacle of Moses, which now stood on Mount Gibeon as the place where the Israelites offered their blood-sacrifices to the Lord? The design for that Tabernacle had been revealed by God to Moses on Mount Sinai, which is why the repeated refrain of the second half of Exodus is that everything was

---

[1] The teacher's blunder was reported on the BBC News and in every newspaper on 31 May 2013.

built *"as the Lord commanded Moses"*.[2] To what extent should Solomon's Temple follow the Lord's command to Moses, that he must *"set up the tabernacle according to the plan shown you on the mountain"*?[3]

Alternatively, should Solomon construct a Temple which looked like David's Tabernacle on Mount Zion? We saw in chapters 15–16 that King David was a prophet who grasped that Melchizedek was a prophetic picture of the *Messiah*. Based on his insights into the priest–king who ruled over ancient Jerusalem in Genesis 14:18–20, David constructed a radically different Tabernacle as a worship centre for Israel. The only blood-sacrifices that David offered at this new-style Tabernacle were on the day of its dedication. They were slaughtered by King David, not by the high priests descended from Aaron, because they were a prophetic picture of the once-for-all sacrifice by which the *Messiah* would create a New Covenant between the holy God and his sinful people.[4]

If Solomon were to construct a Temple like David's Tabernacle, only to discover later that the Lord wanted it to be like Moses' Tabernacle, then he would feel as foolish as an English teacher who prepared her students for the wrong exam. But if Solomon were to construct a Temple that looked like Moses' Tabernacle, then he would feel even more ashamed if the Lord rebuked him for turning the clock back on his father's revelation.

In 28:1–7, David therefore gathers together all the leaders of Israel who are listed in the previous five chapters. He reminds them that the Temple is to be the throne room from which the Lord rules over the world – the earthly footstool to his heavenly throne.[5] The heart of the new Temple must

---

[2] It does this fifteen times in Exodus 39–40 alone. See Exodus 39:1, 5, 7, 26, 31, 42–43; 40:16, 19, 21, 23, 25, 27, 29 and 32.

[3] Exodus 26:30.

[4] Hebrews 4:14 – 5:10 and 6:13 – 7:28. Peter explains in Acts 2:29–35 that David was a prophet and knew this.

[5] 2 Chronicles 9:18; Psalms 99:5 and 132:7, and Lamentations 2:1.

therefore be the Ark of the Covenant, above the lid of which the Presence of God is said to dwell.[6] David reminds the leaders of Israel that he had it in his own heart to build such a Temple, but that the Lord revealed to him that it must be built by his son Solomon instead.[7] If Solomon obeys the Lord's commands unswervingly, God promises that David's dynasty will prosper and rule forever.[8]

In 28:8–10, David affirms Solomon as the new *messiah* of Israel. He uses "you plural" commands in the Hebrew text of verse 8 to call all of the Israelites to obey the Lord by gladly following the leadership of the young King Solomon. He then uses "you singular" commands in the Hebrew text of verses 9–10 to charge Solomon to obey the Lord gladly too. *"Acknowledge the God of your father, and serve him with wholehearted devotion... for the Lord has chosen you to build a house as the sanctuary."*

In 28:11–19, David reveals that the Lord has given him a precise blueprint for Solomon and his Temple-building team. He has not been like an English teacher who prepares her students for the wrong exam. He has sought the Lord to know how much to follow the design of Moses' Tabernacle and how much to follow the design of his own. In the sight of Israel's leaders, David now entrusts his son with the definitive answer to that question. He gives Solomon the plans that the Holy Spirit has given him for the Temple building, for its sacred furnishings, for its courtyards and for the priests and Levites who minister there.[9] Using one of the Chronicler's favourite names for the Holy Spirit, David declares that *"All this..., I have in writing as a*

---

[6] Exodus 25:16–22 and Numbers 7:89. With this in view, David reveals in 28:18 that from now on the two golden cherubim angels on the lid of the Ark will be overshadowed by the wings of two even larger ones.

[7] The Temple is so important to the Chronicler that he repeats here what he told us in 17:1–27 and 22:6–10.

[8] Solomon is a *messiah* and a *son of God*, but he will fail by falling into sin. God's promise to David's dynasty *"for ever"* in 28:4 will only be fulfilled through the true *Messiah* and the true *Son of God* (Luke 11:31).

[9] That's the irony when we complain about the long lists in chapters 25–29. David received them from God!

result of the Lord's hand on me, and he enabled me to understand all the details of the plan."[10]

The Temple was to be more like the Tabernacle of Moses than that of David. The tent which David erected on Mount Zion was a prophetic picture for his own generation of what the Lord would bring about in the future – a Temple built by God's *Messiah*, in which every worshipper from every nation would have a back-stage pass to enjoy the Presence of God. The Temple which Solomon must build would be a proclamation that this true *Messiah* and true *Son of God* was yet to come. The Ark of the Covenant must be returned to the inner sanctuary as a sign that Israel's Saviour had not yet come.

In 28:20–21, when David issues his final charge to Solomon, it is therefore obvious that the Chronicler has his own readers in mind too. He knows that they are complaining that the Second Temple, built by Zerubbabel, is far smaller than the one destroyed by the Babylonians. He therefore implies that this is a sign from God to them that a Third and Final Temple is on its way. Instead of complaining, they ought to be crying out for the Lord to hurry up and send them his *Messiah*.

It is for those Jews, as much as for Solomon, that the Chronicler records the last words of King David to his son: *"Do not be afraid or discouraged, for the Lord God, my God, is with you. He will not fail you or forsake you until all the work for the service of the temple of the Lord is finished...."*[11]

---

[10] We learn something important here about how the Holy Spirit inspired Scripture. He put thoughts in people's minds (28:12) which they then wrote down for people (28:19; 2 Timothy 3:16–17 and 2 Peter 1:20–21).

[11] 1 Chronicles 28:20.

Stewards for the King (1 Chronicles 29:1–20)

"Everything comes from you, and we have given you only what comes from your hand."

(1 Chronicles 29:14)

In the final volume of the *Lord of the Rings* trilogy, we meet the steward of Gondor. He has been entrusted with ruling and defending humanity until their rightful king returns home. When Aragorn appears as the royal heir of Gondor, however, the steward begins to make excuses. Instead of gladly handing over the kingdom, he fights tooth and nail to keep it as his own. He is a steward by name but a king in his own eyes. He is like many of us when it comes to money.[1]

It ought to be obvious to us that we are nothing more than stewards of our money. We don't bring any of it into the world with us and we leave all of it behind. Even so, the Bible warns us that we can easily forget this. Jesus talks more about money in the gospels than he does about either heaven or hell because how we handle our money is the acid test of our true heart towards the Lord. Jesus warns us that *"No one can serve two masters. Either you will hate the one and love the other, or you will be devoted to the one and despise the other. You cannot serve both God and Money."*[2]

This forms one of the big themes of the final chapter of 1 Chronicles. King Saul consistently forgot that he was just a *nāgīd* – the *viceroy* or *deputy* or *steward* of Israel – for its true King, the Lord. Because of this, the prophet Samuel told him that

---

[1] For more on this, see J.R.R. Tolkien's novel *The Return of the King* (1955).

[2] Matthew 6:24 and Luke 16:13. See also 1 Timothy 6:10.

"Your kingdom will not endure; the Lord has sought out a man after his own heart and appointed him ruler [nāgīd] of his people, because you have not kept the Lord's command."[3] David stands up in 29:1 and proves that he is no King Saul by confessing that although Solomon is *"young and inexperienced"* and *"the task is great"* that lies before him, he must become the new king because he is *"the one whom God has chosen"*.[4] As a steward, David lets the Lord decide.

In 29:2–5, the Chronicler tries to make this a bit more personal. He knows that very few of his readers are kings, but he also knows that money tries to make little kings of us all. He therefore tells us that David proved he was a steward by gladly handing over the riches that the Lord entrusted to him. In chapter 22, David donated massive quantities of gold, silver, bronze, iron, cedarwood, marble and gemstones to enable Solomon to build and beautify the Temple of the Lord. Now he tells us that he is going a step further. He has decided to empty his personal treasury too. He doesn't want to die with anything. He wants the Lord to have it all: 100 tons of gold and 235 tons of silver.[5]

The Hebrew word *segullāh*, which David uses in verse 3, is an important word in the Old Testament. It isn't just used to describe the private treasuries of ancient kings.[6] It is also used by the Lord to describe his people as his *"treasured possession"*.[7] David's logic here appears to be that, if the Lord has made his people his treasured possession, then David cannot allow his

---

[3] 1 Samuel 13:14. The word *nāgīd* is used to describe the new King Solomon in 29:22.

[4] In this sense, Solomon is one of many younger brothers who are chosen by God above their older brothers. For example, Abel, Seth, Shem, Abraham, Isaac, Jacob, Joseph, Ephraim and King David himself.

[5] *"Gold of Ophir"* came from modern-day Yemen and was regarded as the best gold in the world (1 Kings 9:28 and 22:48; Job 28:16; Psalm 45:9 and Isaiah 13:12). Whatever we give to the Lord – whether it is our money or our simple acts of service – we are to give it with excellence, to the very best of our ability.

[6] For example, in Ecclesiastes 2:8.

[7] Exodus 19:5; Deuteronomy 7:6; 14:2 and 26:18; Psalm 135:4 and Malachi 3:17. Equivalent Greek words from the Septuagint translation are also used to refer to the Church as God's *"treasured possession"* in Ephesians 1:14; 1 Peter 2:9 and Titus 2:14.

possessions to possess him. He must steward those possessions in the direction of God's priorities. That's what it means for us to be stewards for the King.

In 29:6–9, we witness the power of a leader's example to stir people into action. When David exhorts the leaders he has appointed to follow his lead, they gladly empty their pockets to the tune of 170 tons of gold, 340 tons of silver, 610 tons of bronze and 3,400 tons of iron, plus a heap of precious gemstones.[8] This is a vast amount of treasure for building the Temple, but the Chronicler is less excited about the amount given than he is about what it proves. Because the leaders gave their treasures *"freely and wholeheartedly to the Lord"*, they revealed that their hearts were undivided. They were not attempting to serve money alongside the Lord. They were truly serving God alone. When the ordinary Israelites see this, they do more than merely rejoice at the generosity of their leaders: they are inspired to give equally generously too.[9]

In 29:10–13, the Chronicler gets even more personal. Music has been called the language of the heart because it can touch us in places left untouched by normal prose. The Chronicler therefore records a psalm for us which David sang amidst the giving. He wants it to stir his readers to reflect on what their own spending reveals about their own devotion to the Lord. There is no statement of faith as accurate as a bank statement.

David praises the Lord as the eternal God who possesses all glory, majesty, greatness and power.[10] He does not ask us to give generously to his work on the earth because he needs our money. David rejoices that *"Everything in heaven and*

---

[8] A *daric* was a Persian coin weighing 8.5 grams of gold. The Jehiel in 29:8 is not the same Jehiel who tutored David's sons in 27:32, but a Levite who served as worship leader and guardian of the Temple treasury (16:5).

[9] The Israelites do more than merely rejoice at the generosity of their leaders (29:9). They are generous too (29:17). Note the echo of Exodus 35:20–29 in these verses.

[10] When the Bible speaks of God being *eternal*, it means both forwards and backwards. He is *"from everlasting to everlasting"*. See also 16:36; Nehemiah 9:5 and Psalms 41:13; 90:2; 93:2, 5; 103:17 and 106:48.

earth is yours". The Lord entrusts us with money as a way of revealing our true heart towards him, like a modern ship which bounces sonar waves off the sea bed to reveal the contours of the rocks which lie hidden beneath the surface of the sea. David is delighted that his generosity has proven that he is nothing like King Saul. He can finally sing with integrity that God is the true King of Israel, because he has held nothing back from him.

In 29:14–19, David returns to prose but keeps on praying. Instead of expecting the Lord to thank him for his generosity towards the Temple, he thanks the Lord for placing him in a position from which he could give![11] He sings that *"Everything comes from you, and we have given you only what comes from your hand... all this abundance that we have provided for building you a temple for your Holy Name comes from your hand, and all of it belongs to you."*

In 29:20, the crowd of Israelites respond with worship of their own. Having been caught up in David's generosity, they are now caught up in his faith and worship too. King David can die happy, since their generosity and worship is a sign that they will follow his son and build the Temple according to the blueprint God has given him.[12]

While the sound of their worship still hangs in the air, take a moment to reflect on your own finances before the Lord. Don't be a King Saul or a steward of Gondor. Be like David, who demonstrated that he was merely stewarding his riches for God as King.[13]

---

[11] This is what David means by *"Wealth and honour come from you"*. It is echoed by Deuteronomy 8:16–18; Ephesians 4:28; Romans 12:8; 1 Corinthians 12:28 and 2 Corinthians 9:10–11.

[12] Abraham, Isaac and Jacob lived almost 1,000 years before there was a king of Judah. David's mention of them encourages the Jews after the exile that God alone is Israel's King. How much more should we celebrate and give generously now that the *Messiah*, the King of Israel, has come!

[13] David's prayer in 29:19 is for Solomon to be as *wholehearted* as the Israelite leaders were *wholehearted* in 29:9. You can pray that as a prayer for yourself too.

What Happens to Heroes (1 Chronicles 29:21–30)

"He died at a good old age, having enjoyed long life, wealth and honour. His son Solomon succeeded him as king."

(1 Chronicles 29:28)

In June 323 BC, Alexander the Great became Alexander the Dead. His death was as unexpected as it was tragic. Aged only thirty-two, he had barely begun to enjoy ruling the largest empire that the world had ever seen. Thirteen years earlier, the Macedonians had only ruled over a small portion of what is Greece today. By the time Alexander died, they ruled from Egypt and the Adriatic Sea in the west all the way to India and the Himalayas in the east. Alexander had become the greatest man in history.

But that is what happens to heroes. Death is the great leveller. No matter how messianic a charismatic leader may appear to be, there comes a moment when they must leave the stage of history and hand their lines over to an understudy who is waiting in the wings.

In 29:21–22, the Chronicler prepares us for the moment when King David does this by focusing our eyes on the Lord as the true King of Israel. He tells us that the day after the Israelites gave generously towards the Temple, they assembled together a second time to offer sacrifices to the Lord.[1] Their high priest

---

[1] David never offered blood-sacrifices at his Tabernacle after the day of its dedication, so this assembly probably took place at Moses' Tabernacle on Mount Gibeon, where Zadok took the lead (16:39 and 29:22). Zadok then went *"from the sacred tent"* to crown Solomon at Gihon, just outside Jerusalem (1 Kings 1:39).

sacrificed 1,000 bulls, 1,000 rams and 1,000 lambs, along with countless drink offerings and other sacrifices. Their eyes were not on King David, but on a greater *Messiah* who was yet to come, as *"they ate and drank with great joy in the presence of the Lord".*[2]

In 29:22–24, the Chronicler records the moment when David finally handed over his kingdom to his son Solomon, as the new *messiah* of Israel. Up until now, he has glossed over David's many weaknesses, since he knows that we can read about them in 2 Samuel. He has bigger fish to fry, since he wants to use the reign of David as a prophetic picture of the coming of a far greater *Messiah* – one who will come proclaiming that *"The time has come. The kingdom of God has come near. Repent and believe the good news!"*[3]

David has already proclaimed Solomon publicly to be the son who will succeed him to the throne of Israel. The twelve tribes of Israel have already ratified Solomon as the Lord's new choice of king, but here they do so a second time through a formal coronation ceremony for Solomon. The Chronicler expects his readers to know all about Adonijah's rebellion at the start of 1 Kings, which provoked David to do this quickly. He focuses instead on the peace which came to Solomon's kingdom when his rebellious older brother was captured and executed.[4] *"Solomon sat on the throne of the Lord as king in place of his father David. He prospered and all Israel obeyed him."*[5] Everybody rallied to the new King Solomon, rejoicing that there was a new *messiah* in town.

---

[2] There is often a link in Scripture between eating and drinking and fellowshipping with the Lord. See Exodus 18:12 and 24:11; Deuteronomy 12:7; 1 Corinthians 10:16–18 and Revelation 3:20.

[3] Mark 1:15. When Jesus talks about the Kingdom of God, he is fulfilling the Chronicler's prophetic picture.

[4] David had two high priests, but Abiathar foolishly sided with Adonijah (15:11 and 18:16, and 1 Kings 1:7–2:35). As a result, Zadok ministers alone in these verses and in the early chapters of 2 Chronicles.

[5] Note the Chronicler's assertion in 29:23 that Israel's throne is *"the throne of the Lord"*. David and his dynasty were only ever *deputies* and *stewards* of that divine throne. The Lord had always been the true King of Israel.

The Chronicler prepares us for this in verse 25 by telling us that Solomon ruled with greater royal splendour than his father. This is what happens to every earthly hero. They quickly die and are forgotten. Only the true *Messiah* can ever truly reign forever. As we reach the end of part two of the Chronicler's story and begin part three, he prepares us for the fact that he will give us an equally selective history of the reign of Solomon. He will not tell us about the new king's many sins and acts of folly. He will not talk about his spiritual backsliding and about the ruin that it brought to Israel. He will present Solomon's reign as a fresh prophetic picture of the coming of the true *Messiah*.[6] Like his father, Solomon will also die and vacate his throne for a better King of Israel. That's what happens to every earthly hero, but the true *Messiah* is on his way.

In 29:26–28, David finally exits the stage of history. He dies at the age of seventy, and his understudy Solomon takes over his role in the play. The Chronicler's admission that David ruled from Hebron for the first seven years of his forty-year reign is the closest he comes to acknowledging that David did not enjoy the support of the northern tribes of Israel from day one.[7] Up until now, he has left us to read about this in 2 Samuel so that David can serve as a prophetic picture of the true *Messiah*, but as David dies he confesses more freely that David is not the King of Israel that we are looking for. Even the greatest earthly heroes pass away. The Lord allows their glory to fade and their lives to end so that, inspired by their example, we will fix our eyes on the true Hero of history.[8]

In 29:29–30, the Chronicler ends part two of his story by encouraging his readers to study the other histories of the reign of David too. He doesn't want to hide the king's shortcomings from us, even though they have not featured in his own account.

---

[6] Zadok means *Righteousness* and Solomon means *Peaceful*. Compare this with Isaiah 9:6–7.

[7] David ruled from 1010 to 1003 BC in Hebron and from 1003 to 970 BC in Jerusalem.

[8] Peter hints at this in Acts 2:25–36 when he preaches that *"David died and was buried, and his tomb is here to this day. But he was a prophet… God has raised this Jesus to life."*

He encourages us to read the records written by the prophet Samuel (presumably the source material for the book which we call 1 Samuel today) and by the prophets Nathan and Gad (presumably the source material for 2 Samuel). That's where we can read all about David's adultery with Bathsheba, about his many run-ins with Joab, and about his struggle to quell rebellions by Absalom, Sheba and Adonijah.

But none of those things are the Chronicler's story. He remains focused on the fact that his original readers are disappointed not to have a new king from David's dynasty ruling over an independent kingdom of Judah. He uses part two of his story to reassure them that King David's legacy lies in something far bigger than a fleshly successor ruling from his throne. He received the blueprint for the Temple and he taught the tribes of Israel that the Presence of God in that Temple was much more important than the presence of a king in the palace. David's throne was *"the throne of the Lord"*.

And so King David died. That's what earthly heroes do. But a better *Messiah* was coming: the true Hero who would come down to earth from heaven and reign for evermore.

Part Three:

Small Things about Solomon (2 Chronicles 1–9)

This is My Son
(2 Chronicles 1:1–17)

"That night God appeared to Solomon and said to him, 'Ask for whatever you want me to give you.'"

(2 Chronicles 1:7)

The Chronicler has a lot of ground to cover in the second half of his scroll.[1] In the first half, he powered his way through the events that are recorded in Genesis and 1 and 2 Samuel. In the second half, he needs to cover the events of 1 and 2 Kings. This will force him to omit a lot of detail from the story and he does so right away. He skirts over the rebellion which marred the early months of Solomon's reign by recording very simply that, once the rebellion was subdued, *"Solomon son of David established himself firmly over his kingdom, for the Lord his God was with him and made him exceedingly great."*[2]

Having hurried through the first two chapters of 1 Kings in a single verse, the Chronicler suddenly slows down the story to add some extra detail of his own. We are told in 1 Kings 3 that, at the start of Solomon's reign, he brought a thousand burnt offerings to Mount Gibeon since *"that was the most important high place"*.[3] The Chronicler expands on this to clarify that this was because Moses' Tabernacle was pitched there. David had constructed a new Tabernacle to house the Ark of the Covenant

---

[1] Although our English Bibles make us think of 2 Chronicles 1 as the start of a new book, remember that the Hebrew text of 1 and 2 Chronicles was originally a single scroll.

[2] That's the whole of 1 Kings 1–2 covered in a single verse! It anticipates the coming of the irresistible rule of Jesus in 2 Thessalonians 2:8.

[3] Solomon could present offerings but they needed to be sacrificed by the high priest Zadok. There remained a strict division at Moses' Tabernacle between the kings and priests of Israel (1 Chronicles 16:39–40).

in Jerusalem, but the bronze altar for blood-sacrifices, built by Bezalel for Moses almost 500 years earlier, remained in front of Moses' Tabernacle.[4] The Chronicler also adds the extra detail that all the leaders of Israel accompanied their new king to Mount Gibeon. It's as if they could sense that something vital for their nation was about to happen there.

In 1:7–10, after Solomon has gone to sleep, the Lord appears to him in a dream and rejoices over him as a delighted Father in his son.[5] In the ancient world, the wealth and power of a king was measured by the size of his flocks and herds, so Solomon throws some of his earthly power away when he offers lavish sacrifices to the Lord. When the Lord responds by making him a fantastic offer – *"Ask for whatever you want me to give you"* – Solomon sacrifices earthly power once again. Instead of using this blank cheque from the Lord to ask for fame or riches or the death of his enemies at home and abroad, he prays very simply that the God who led his father David might now lead him as David's son. Solomon declares himself to be a steward, rather than a king, as he prays, *"Give me wisdom and knowledge, that I may lead this people, for who is able to govern this great people of yours?"*[6]

In 1:11–12, the Lord expresses his delight that Solomon has made such a request. It has proven that he prizes his relationship with God above his possessions, and his inward character above his outward reputation, so he can be entrusted with all those other things too. A thousand years before Jesus taught the crowds to *"Seek first his kingdom and his righteousness, and all these things will be given to you as well"*, the Lord teaches

127

---

[4] Exodus 31:1–11; 35:30 – 36:8 and 38:22–23. Here and 1 Chronicles 2:20 are the only mentions of Bezalel in the Bible outside of Exodus. Like Solomon, he was from the tribe of Judah and chosen by name by the Lord.

[5] 1 Kings 3:5 clarifies that God appeared to him in a dream while he slept, rather than in a waking vision.

[6] Solomon confesses that he is only king because the Lord chose him. Comparing 1:9 with 1 Chronicles 27:23–24, it also appears that he pledges never to conduct a sinful census like his father David.

that same principle to Solomon.[7] Since he has shown that he considers the twelve tribes of Israel to be the Lord's people and his throne to be a gift to steward for the Lord, he can be entrusted with wealth and possessions and honour and peace. The Lord will grant him an incomparable wisdom which will generate all of those other things for him as well.[8]

In 1:13–17, the Chronicler says that Solomon returned from Moses' Tabernacle on Mount Gibeon and ruled over Israel with great wisdom. He leaves out many of the specific details which appear in 1 Kings in order to make the reign of Solomon a general picture of the rule of the *Messiah* who is to come.[9] We might have expected the Chronicler to include the fact that Solomon went straight from Mount Gibeon to David's Tabernacle, where he stood before the Ark of the Covenant and offered fresh sacrifices which signified that his reign was just as much a prophetic picture of the true *Messiah* as was the reign of his father.[10] But he doesn't. Instead, he skips over this detail in order to focus the eyes of his readers on Solomon's Temple.[11]

It's hard to read these verses without wondering whether the Chronicler also abridges his account to prophesy about what would happen to the true and better Son of David. The gospel writers tell us that, when Jesus began to reveal himself to Israel as the *Messiah*, the same voice which spoke to Solomon on Mount Gibeon also boomed out over Jesus at the River Jordan. The same God who delighted over Solomon delighted over Jesus

---

[7] Matthew 6:33 and Luke 12:31.

[8] Solomon says in Proverbs 4:7–10 and 8:10–21 that wisdom often does this.

[9] He omits Solomon's sinful marriages to pagan women (1 Kings 3:1), God's warning that he mustn't abandon the Law (1 Kings 3:14) and many specific details about his wisdom (1 Kings 3:16 – 4:34). Nevertheless, he adds in 1:11 that God called Solomon *"to govern my people over whom I have made you king."*

[10] Solomon's sacrifices in 1 Kings 3:15 were not for the atonement of sin. His thousand burnt offerings at Mount Gibeon had already done that for him! They were to prophesy once more about the true *Messiah*.

[11] The Chronicler copies from 1 Kings 10:26–29 an account of Solomon's arms dealing, as an example of his wealth and power, despite the fact that it was disobedient to Deuteronomy 17:16 and Psalm 20:7. It was also very stupid, since the Arameans who bought his horses and chariots would become great enemies of Israel.

as the true and better Son of David. He beamed with as much pleasure over the insistence of Jesus that John the Baptist must baptise him in the River Jordan as he beamed with pleasure over Solomon's request for wisdom. He caused the same Spirit of Wisdom to descend on Jesus, as he went from the River Jordan to the desert and back to Galilee, that descended on Solomon at the start of his reign. God cried out in pleasure over Jesus: *"This is my Son, whom I love; with him I am well pleased."*[12]

This comparison is not fanciful. It goes to the heart of the Chronicler's story, explaining why he skips over so many details in the story of King Solomon, yet slows down at other times to give us many more. Jesus saw the prophetic picture in this chapter when he taught the crowds that he was its fulfilment: *"Something greater than Solomon is here."*[13]

---

[12] Matthew 3:13–17 and Luke 3:21 – 4:14.
[13] Matthew 12:42 and Luke 11:31.

The Temple-Builder
(2 Chronicles 2:1–18)

"The temple I am going to build will be great, because our God is greater than all other gods."

(2 Chronicles 2:5)

The Chronicler missed out a lot of detail in the last chapter, but that doesn't mean he is in a hurry. He was saving space so that he could slow down to focus on what really matters to his story. Building the Temple takes four chapters in 1 Kings, but here it takes seven. The Chronicler saved space to focus on Solomon as the Temple-Builder.

To do this, he needs to be selective about what he tells us in 2:1–2. He says that Solomon *"gave orders to build a temple for the Name of the Lord and a royal palace for himself"* – but he doesn't say it took him twice as long to build his own elaborate house as it did to build a house for the Lord.[1] He says that Solomon conscripted tens of thousands of foreigners as stonecutters and carriers at his quarries, but doesn't say that Solomon also pressganged people from the northern tribes of Israel, foolishly causing them to resent his evident favouritism towards the tribe of Judah.[2] Nor does he say anything about the fact that Solomon taxed the northern tribes and not Judah.[3] He expects

---

[1] Solomon built his palace concurrently with the Temple yet 3:2 and 8:1–2 reveal that, while it took him seven years to complete the Temple, it took him fourteen years to complete his palace.

[2] Israel had long drafted Canaanite survivors into working as their forced labourers (2:17–18; Deuteronomy 29:11; Joshua 9:21; 2 Samuel 12:31 and 1 Chronicles 22:2). Solomon was wrong to do the same thing with the ten northern tribes of Israel, however, in 1 Kings 5:12–18 and 11:28. "Israel" in 1 Kings 9:22–23 refers to Judah.

[3] The tribe of Judah is not listed among the tribes taxed by Solomon in 1 Kings 4:7–19.

us to know all of this from 1 Kings. His account presents King Solomon as an idealised picture of the righteous reign of the *Messiah*.

In 2:3–10, Solomon sends a letter to King Hiram of Tyre to request more wood from the famous forests of Lebanon.[4] David has already stockpiled large quantities of cedarwood, but Solomon explains that *"The temple I am going to build will be great, because our God is greater than all other gods."* If this seems a rather tactless thing to say to a pagan king, then note his intention in verse 4. Solomon knows that Hiram was friends with his father David, and therefore probably visited David's Tabernacle on Mount Zion.[5] Solomon reminds Hiram that the God of Israel is a forgiving God who loves to build deep friendships with people from every nation. When he describes for Hiram the consecrated bread and fragrant incense and burnt offerings that will be offered to the Lord at his new Temple, it is a not-so-subtle invitation for him to renounce the idols of Tyre and to worship the God of Israel instead.[6]

Solomon continues to commend the Lord to Hiram in verse 5, when he warns Hiram not to be confused that the God of Israel is upgrading his Tabernacle to a Temple. Hiram mustn't imagine that Yahweh is like the Phoenician idols that inhabit the temples in Tyre and Sidon, such as Baal and Astarte. The truth about the Lord is that *"the heavens, even the highest heavens, cannot contain him"*. Solomon is not building a Temple because the God of Israel needs a building he can live in, but because the Israelites need a place where they can gather to worship him. It is a mark of his mercy that he has

---

[4] The Chronicler uses the variant name *Huram* in his Hebrew text, but most English translations render it *Hiram* to be consistent with 1 Kings 5 and to avoid confusion with Huram-Abi in 2:13.

[5] We can tell that Hiram was a peer of David, rather than of Solomon, from 2:3 and 2 Samuel 5:11. This is why Hiram initiated friendly relations with his friend's young son at the start of his reign (1 Kings 5:1).

[6] Solomon says literally at the end of 2:4 that these things will go on being offered *"forever"*. This is to encourage the original readers of Chronicles, and it also prefigures Revelation 5:8 and 8:3–5 for us today.

deigned to allow the Israelites to build a Temple *"as a place to burn sacrifices before him".*[7]

Solomon has been building up to a clear call for action. He tells Hiram that the Lord has made space for the king of Tyre to play a crucial role in building his Temple. Hiram can do more than simply sell the finest timber of Lebanon to Solomon. He can also send him one of the most famous Phoenician craftsmen.[8] When Bezalel built the Tabernacle for Moses, the Lord gave him a man from the tribe of Dan named Oholiab to serve as his skilful assistant.[9] Now that Solomon is playing the role of Bezalel in building the Temple, the Lord wants to give him his own Oholiab. It is therefore significant that Huram-Abi has a Phoenician father but a mother who comes from the tribe of Dan.[10]

In 2:11–16, Hiram responds to Solomon's call for him to serve the Lord. He begins with a bold cry of faith – *"Because the Lord loves his people, he has made you their king"* – which spills over into heartfelt worship: *"Praise be to the Lord, the God of Israel, who made heaven and earth!"*[11] Hiram feels delighted that Solomon has asked him to join his Temple-building team. He will gladly send one of his best craftsmen, Huram-Abi, who knows all the secrets of the Phoenicians. Furthermore, Hiram promises not just to sell timber to Solomon; he will also take care of the logistics of delivering it to him. He will float the wood down the Mediterranean coastline from Tyre to Joppa, the chief port of Israel.

The Chronicler skips over some of Solomon's mistakes here. He records that Solomon agreed to give Hiram an eye-

---

[7] This is such an important point that it is repeated in 6:18; Isaiah 66:1 and Acts 7:48–50.

[8] The Phoenicians were world-famous for their skill at shipbuilding. Solomon requests help from one of their finest craftsmen, as their skills were a closely guarded secret.

[9] Exodus 31:1–11; 35:30 – 36:8 and 38:22–23.

[10] Huram-Abi is not mentioned at all in Solomon and Hiram's letters in 1 Kings 5. He is only mentioned in 1 Kings 7:13–45, where his mother comes from the tribe of Naphtali. She was evidently of mixed parentage too.

[11] The Queen of Sheba makes a similar cry of faith in 9:8. Good leaders are always a blessing from the Lord.

watering 4.4 million litres of wheat, 4.4 million litres of barley, 440 litres of olive oil and 440,000 litres of wine as payment for his timber, but he doesn't reveal that this placed such a burden on Solomon that he was forced to clear his debts by renouncing Israel's claim to part of the Promised Land. Nor does he tell us how the Lord restored that territory to Israel in spite of Solomon. The Chronicler leaves that to 1 Kings 9:10–14. His task is to present Solomon as a picture of the *Messiah* who is to come.

At the start of his public ministry, in John 2:19–21, Jesus reveals himself to be the true Temple-Builder. His teaching on the Holy Spirit in John 14–16 echoes Solomon's insight that the Lord is too great for his presence to be contained in a man-made Temple. He has come to earth to turn God's people into a Living Temple by filling them with the same Holy Spirit that dwelt above the lid of the Ark of the Covenant in Solomon's sanctuary.[12] Rather than pressganging people into building with him, he invites them to volunteer, just as Solomon invites Hiram and Huram-Abi to do so in this chapter.[13] If they were eager to say "yes", then how much more ought we to say "yes" to one greater than Solomon!

The Chronicler ends this chapter by returning to the people of the northern tribes who build with Solomon.[14] It is a small verse which matters greatly. Chronicles is inviting you to add your own name to their number and to help God build his Living Temple today.[15]

---

[12] 1 Corinthians 3:16–17; 2 Corinthians 6:16; Ephesians 2:19–22 and 1 Peter 2:4–6.

[13] Isaiah 60:9–16 suggests that King Hiram of Tyre symbolises any Gentile who builds with Jesus today.

[14] 1 Kings says there were 3,300 foremen and 550 supervisors (5:16 and 9:23), while 2 Chronicles says there were 3,600 foremen and 250 supervisors (2:2, 18 and 8:10). Although they categorise the workers differently, their total number is the same.

[15] Solomon's evangelistic tone is absent from the account of his letter to Hiram in 1 Kings 5. Nor does he make mention of Huram-Abi as a new Oholiab to Solomon's Bezalel. This extra detail is to enlist us to build too.

Bigger and Better
(2 Chronicles 3:1 – 4:22)

"Then Solomon began to build the temple of the Lord in Jerusalem on Mount Moriah."

(2 Chronicles 3:1)

If you have ever come downstairs on Christmas morning to discover that you didn't get the present you were hoping for, then you know how the Jews felt when they returned home from their exile in Babylon. Instead of building them a Temple like Solomon's, Zerubbabel had built them something small and second-rate.[1] Rather than attempt to hide this, the Chronicler tackles their disappointment head on. He emphasises that Solomon's Temple was far bigger and better than Moses' Tabernacle.

In 3:1, he explains that the Temple stood on Mount Moriah, which means *The Lord Will Provide* and which had a history stretching back to the days when the Jebusites controlled Jerusalem. Abraham had almost sacrificed his son on that mountain, until the Lord saved Isaac's life by providing a ram to be sacrificed in his place.[2] The ram was caught by its horns in a thicket as a sign that the *Messiah* would be crucified on that same mountain wearing a crown of thorns. Note the future tense: *The Lord Will Provide*.

In 3:2, the Chronicler highlights that King Solomon did not begin to build the Temple until the second month of the fourth

---

[1] See Ezra 3:12; Haggai 2:3 and Zechariah 4:10.

[2] The Chronicler uses the Hebrew variant name *Ornan* for Araunah the Jebusite in 3:1, just as he did in 1 Chronicles 21. English translations keep to the name Araunah for the sake of consistency with 2 Samuel 24.

year of his reign – that is, until April 966 BC. Despite the massive stockpile of materials that his father stored up for him, Solomon waited for more timber to arrive from King Hiram because he was determined that his new Temple would be bigger and better than the Tabernacle that was built by Moses.

In 3:3–4, the Chronicler omits any description of the courtyards of Solomon's Temple. Instead, he rushes straight up to the Temple building.[3] Whereas the Tabernacle was 5 metres wide and 15 metres long, Solomon's Temple measures 9 metres wide and 27 metres long.[4] Unlike the Tabernacle, it is also fronted by a magnificent porchway. Everything about Solomon's Temple proclaims that it is bigger and better.

In 3:5–9, the Chronicler describes the large room inside the Temple which was known to the Israelites as *the Holy Place*. It is shaped like a cube – 20 metres wide, long and high – and its walls, beams and ceiling are coated with 21 tons of solid gold.[5] Its walls are panelled with juniper wood and overlaid with purest gold so that not a trace is left of its walls of quarried stone.[6] The gold is engraved with palm trees and cherubim angels, reminiscent of the Garden of Eden, as a sign that God wants to dwell once more on earth with people.[7] Even the nails that hold the wood together are gold-plated.[8]

In 3:10–14, the Chronicler describes the smaller, inner room of the Temple, shut off by a thick curtain and known to

---

[3] Strictly speaking, the words *Tabernacle* and *Temple* mean only the tent and building, not their courtyards.

[4] 1 Kings 6:2–3 adds that the Temple stood 13.5 metres high. Its porchway ran the whole width of its façade, standing 9 metres high and jutting 4.5 metres out from the façade.

[5] In the book of Revelation, there is no Temple in the New Jerusalem. Instead, the entire city is shaped like a cube, indicating that the entire city has become *the Holy Place* of God (Revelation 21:16 and 22).

[6] In the same way, although the Church looks very ordinary to outsiders, those on the inside recognise that God has covered its living stones with his own imputed holiness through the wooden cross of his Son.

[7] Nobody quite knows what *Parvaim* means in 3:6, but it was probably another name for Ophir, in modern-day Yemen, where the finest gold in the ancient world was mined. See 1 Chronicles 29:4.

[8] Gold is too soft a metal for the 575 grams mentioned in 3:9 to be nails of solid gold.

the Israelites as *the Most Holy Place* or *the Holy of Holies.*[9] In Moses' Tabernacle, it housed the Ark of the Covenant and the Presence of the Lord dwelt between the golden cherubim on its lid. These were reminiscent of the cherubim which guarded God's holy presence in the Garden of Eden in Genesis 3:24. In Solomon's Temple, those golden cherubim on the lid of the Ark are overshadowed by the wings of two more giant cherubim made of wood and overlaid with gold. Their height and wingspan measures 4.5 metres, so that by touching wings they fill the back wall of the inner sanctuary. Everything here is bigger and better than the Tabernacle.

In 3:15–17, the Chronicler goes back outside the Temple to describe its massive porchway. Two giant pillars of bronze extend 8 metres up to heaven, each topped by a bronze capital which is just over a metre high.[10] The pillars are named Jakin and Boaz, which mean *Stability* and *Strength*. The capitals are covered in pomegranates, which Song of Songs reveals to be an ancient Hebrew symbol of deep friendship and intimacy.[11]

In 4:1–22, the Chronicler tells us about the sacred items in the Temple courtyard. The bronze altar outside Moses' Tabernacle, on which blood-sacrifices were offered, was 2.5 metres long and wide, and it stood 1.5 metres high. The altar which Solomon builds to replace it measures 9 metres long and wide, and 4.5 metres high.[12] The book of Exodus never tells us the measurements of the bronze Laver – the place for the priests to wash and purify their hands and which stood between the altar and the Tabernacle. What we do know is that it was much

[9] The curtain described in 3:14 was the precursor of the one ripped in two in Matthew 27:51.

[10] We can tell from 1 Kings 7:15 and 2 Kings 25:17 that the Chronicler means that the pillars and their capitals were 18 metres in length *put together*. The porchway was only 9 metres high. Galatians 2:9 and Revelation 3:12 explain that God wants to make us human pillars in his Living Temple, each given a new name by him.

[11] Song of Songs 4:3, 13; 6:7, 11; 7:12 and 8:2. See also Exodus 28:31–35.

[12] Exodus 27:1. Solomon's new altar was as large as *the Most Holy Place* in Moses' Tabernacle. It was so high that the priests needed to climb up to it on steps, like the altar described in Ezekiel 43:13–17.

smaller than the Sea of bronze which Solomon builds to replace it. Measuring 4.5 metres in diameter and over 2 metres deep, the Sea can hold a staggering 66,000 litres of water.[13] It stands on the backs of twelve bronze bulls, which represent the twelve tribes of Israel, surrounded by ten smaller bronze washbasins for washing the priests' sacred tools.[14]

In 4:7–22, the Chronicler likens Solomon to Bezalel, the great craftsman of Moses' Tabernacle, as he personally crafts the furniture for *the Holy Place*: ten golden lampstands, ten golden tables and a golden altar for burning incense to the Lord. He also crafts a hundred golden bowls for taking blood from the altar into *the Holy Place*. Bronze will do for the courtyard, but not for places closer to the Presence of the Lord. The Chronicler then likens Huram-Abi to Oholiab, who assisted Bezalel in building the Tabernacle. Huram-Abi helps Solomon by crafting everything that is made from bronze.[15]

There is a lot of detail in these two chapters, but it all amounts to a very simple message. The returning Jewish exiles must not weep with disappointment over Zerubbabel's new Temple, because even Moses' Tabernacle could not compete with it for size. Their Second Temple was unimpressive because, like Moses' Tabernacle, it was meant to fix their eyes on something bigger and better to come. The gulf between the Tabernacle and the First Temple was only a faint shadow of the gulf between their Second Temple and the Living Temple that the *Messiah* would one day come and build.

---

[13] The Laver was made from polished bronze mirrors (Exodus 38:8), because it represents the Word of God convicting and cleansing us (James 1:22–24; Ephesians 5:26–27; John 15:3 and 17:17; and 1 Corinthians 6:11).

[14] These washbasins were 1.8 metres wide, 1.3 metres high and held 800 litres of water (1 Kings 7:27–39).

[15] Archaeologists have confirmed what the Chronicler says in 4:17 by finding clay casts for moulding metal objects at Sukkoth and Zarethan, on the east bank of the River Jordan.

Two Become One
(2 Chronicles 5:1–14)

"They brought up the ark and the tent of meeting and all the sacred furnishings in it."

(2 Chronicles 5:5)

I have been involved in enough business acquisitions and church mergers to know that such things rarely go quite as smoothly as planned. Perhaps that's why Solomon waited for eleven months after the completion of his Temple before he dedicated it to the Lord. He was about to merge two very different things together, so he chose the Festival of Tabernacles, in late September 958 BC, as the time when the two would become one.[1]

After bringing any unused gold and silver from his father's stockpile into the Temple storerooms, Solomon calls the Israelites to gather in its courtyards to celebrate two of the greatest festivals in the Jewish calendar: the Day of Atonement and the Festival of Tabernacles.[2] The first spoke of forgiveness for sin and the second of God's desire to dwell among his people, so it was the perfect moment to bring together the Tabernacle of Moses (Israel's blood-sacrifice centre) and the Tabernacle of David (Israel's worship centre). It was called the Festival of Tabernacles because it recalled the way in which the Israelites dwelt in tents for forty years in the desert, but this year it would

---

[1] 1 Kings 6:38 says that Solomon completed the Temple in October or November 959 BC. The September festivals which were celebrated at its dedication must therefore have been in the following year.

[2] The Chronicler doesn't name these festivals because he expects us to know that they dominate the seventh month of the Jewish calendar (7:8–10; Leviticus 23:34–43 and Deuteronomy 16:13–16). It was on the last and greatest day of the Festival of Tabernacles that Jesus predicted the coming of the Holy Spirit, in John 7:37.

also mark the day on which the two great Tabernacles of Israel merged together into one new Temple.

The Chronicler records that the Levites brought the Ark of the Covenant from David's Tabernacle on Mount Zion into *the Most Holy Place* of the new Temple.[3] He also says that they brought *"the tent of meeting"* – that is, the Tabernacle of Moses – and *"all the sacred furnishings in it"*, carefully stowing them away in the Temple storerooms.[4] Neither Tabernacle is ever erected again, because the two have become one in Solomon's Temple.

This is such a dramatic moment in the story of Israel that the Chronicler lingers on it for a moment longer. When two Tabernacles become one, a lot of things need to change. The urn of manna and the staff of Aaron, kept next to the Ark in Moses' Tabernacle, are now placed in storage too. All that remains with the Ark now are the two stone tablets on which Moses received the Ten Commandments.[5] These represent the Old Covenant which the Lord made with the Israelites at Mount Sinai, as a result of which the Ark now needs to stop being displayed for all to see.[6] It must be hidden away once more in the inner sanctuary, accessed only by the high priest on only one day of the year.[7] The Chronicler makes much of the fact that *"the priests then withdrew from the Holy Place."*[8] For a brief moment,

---

[3] Solomon's procession of the Ark from David's Tabernacle to his new Temple, marked by a bevy of blood-sacrifices, is meant to echo its procession from Obed-Edom's house to Jerusalem in 1 Chronicles 15.

[4] Moses' Tabernacle is called *"the tent of meeting"* three times in 2 Chronicles 1, and 142 times elsewhere in the Old Testament. Meanwhile, David's Tabernacle is never once referred to as *"the tent of meeting"*.

[5] The Greek text of Hebrews 9:4 should be translated that these two sacred objects were laid *by* the Ark, not *in* the Ark. After all, Aaron's staff was bigger than the Ark itself! (Exodus 16:33; Numbers 17:10 and Deuteronomy 31:26.)

[6] Horeb in 5:10 means *Desolate* and was the other name for Mount Sinai, which means *Full-of-Thorns*.

[7] Since that one day was the Day of Atonement, which was celebrated on the tenth day of the seventh month, it is likely that 5:1 – 7:3 took place on the Day of Atonement and 7:4–10 took place at the Festival of Tabernacles.

[8] The Hebrew text of 5:14 says literally that the priests *could not stand to minister*. This probably means they could not enter the Temple, but it may mean that they fell flat on their faces before the Presence of the Lord.

David's Tabernacle predicted a day when all would freely enjoy the Presence of God, but that day is yet to come.[9]

Nevertheless, the worship which marked David's Tabernacle remains a major feature of Solomon's new Temple. Although it may look like a return to the distant days of Moses, this is not a turning back of the clock on the story of salvation. It is simply a recognition that Israel needs to wait for its *Messiah* to come before it can enjoy the intimate friendship with God about which David prophesied. As Asaph, Heman and Jeduthun take up their familiar places as worship leaders and reprise the song which they sang at the dedication of David's Tabernacle, the cloud of the glory of the Presence of God suddenly fills the Temple. Chronicles is inviting us to sing our own praises to God with them: *"He is good; his love endures for ever."*[10]

Because the proper person built the Temple according to the proper blueprint, the Lord now does as he has promised and makes this earthly Temple the footstool to his heavenly throne. In case we miss how important this is, the Chronicler uses a word to describe the inner sanctuary of the Temple, which was never used to describe the Tabernacles of Moses and David. He describes it as the *debīr* – a Hebrew word that means *Oracle* or *the Divine Word*.[11] There is now a sacred place on the earth where the voice of heaven can be heard.

In case we miss this clue, the Chronicler gives us another. Solomon prays a long prayer in chapter 6 which culminates in the great request, *"Arise, Lord God, and come to your resting place, you and the ark of your might."* As he does so, the Chronicler

---

[9] The Chronicler is quoting from one of his primary sources when he says in 5:9 that *"they are still there today"*. Everybody knew that the Ark had been lost or destroyed amid the destruction of Jerusalem in 586 BC.

[10] In other words, God's love is not like an arrow, fired in haste but quickly falling to the ground. It flies on forever; what happened five centuries earlier in Exodus 40:34–35 now happens again. This song which began at David's Tabernacle (1 Chronicles 16:34 and 41) continues in 2 Chronicles 7:3, 6 and 20:21, and Psalm 136.

[11] See John 1:1. The word *debīr* is translated *sanctuary* in 2 Chronicles 3:16; 4:20 and 5:7–9. The only other places it occurs in the Old Testament are once in Psalm 28:2 and eleven times in 1 Kings 6–8.

does something clever to show us that this prayer lies right at the heart of King Solomon's story.

> **A) Solomon's wisdom, wealth and power (1:1–17)**
> **B) A foreign king hails Solomon (2:1–18)**
> **C) Solomon builds the Temple (3:1 – 4:22)**
> **D) The Presence of God fills the Temple (5:1–14)**
> **E) Solomon prays for heaven and earth to become one (6:1–42)**
> **D) The Presence of God fills the Temple (7:1–22)**
> **C) Solomon builds his kingdom (8:1–18)**
> **B) A foreign queen hails Solomon (9:1–12)**
> **A) Solomon's wisdom, wealth and power (9:13–31)**

Theologians have a special name for this symmetrical form of Hebrew storytelling. They call such an *ABCDEDCBA* structure a "chiasmus". But more important than knowing the theological term for such a structure is knowing what the Chronicler seeks to teach us through it. By placing this prayer at the centre of Solomon's reign, he is rejoicing that, as the Tabernacles of Moses and David merge together into a single Temple, they are not the only two things becoming one. Heaven is joining together with the earth, as the Lord declares that this new Temple is the earthly footstool to his heavenly throne.

It is an amazing moment of an amazing merger. It points towards an amazing Gospel.

The Shadow
(2 Chronicles 6:1–42)

"But will God really dwell on earth with humans? The heavens, even the highest heavens, cannot contain you. How much less this temple that I have built!"

(2 Chronicles 6:18)

You may have heard the famous story about a mother who went out shopping for a new dress for her daughter's wedding. After searching all day, she finally found the perfect dress. The only problem was that it was designed by Christian Dior and cost £15,000. Unsure what to do, she messaged her husband, who replied in an instant, *"No price too high!"* Blushing with excitement and a real sense that her husband appreciated her, she bought the dress and quickly hurried home to show him. When she got home, her furious husband demanded that she re-read his message. In her excitement in the shop, she had missed his punctuation. The reply had actually read: *"No – price too high!"*

Little things can make a massive difference, and the Chronicler constantly seeks to teach us that the Lord is the God of such small things. We therefore mustn't miss the small but striking feature of King Solomon's prayer of dedication for his new Temple to the Lord.

In 6:1–2, the king cannot contain his excitement that the Lord is willing to take up residence in his new Temple. He is delighted that the *"dark cloud"* of God's Presence, which descended on Mount Sinai and led the Israelites through the desert, has now descended again to make Jerusalem his permanent home.[1] If you find it surprising that the Chronicler emphasises that Solomon's Temple was God's home *forever*, given that the Presence of God left the Temple on 17 September 592 BC and the Temple was destroyed in 586 BC, then well done – you are picking up on his small clues.[2] As King Solomon prays a prayer of dedication, he emphasises that his new Temple is but a shadow of a far greater Temple which is yet to come.

In 6:3–11, Solomon proclaims a blessing over the people of Israel. It is a blessing, but it feels more like a victory celebration. We can almost picture Solomon punching the air with his fists and shouting out, "Mission accomplished!" Throughout his childhood, his father told him that the Lord had chosen him to build the Temple, and now, through God's faithfulness, he has completed the task allotted to him.

In 6:12–42, Solomon launches into a long prayer. The Chronicler allocates more verses to this prayer than he does to many of the reigns of the kings of Judah, so it clearly contains an important message. As Solomon prays from a bronze platform that has the same dimensions as *the Most Holy Place* at the old Tabernacle of Moses, he gives us several clues that even his own Temple is also a tiny shadow of something greater yet to come. He repeatedly hints that the gulf between the Tabernacle and his Temple is far smaller than the gulf which lies between his Temple and the Living Temple that the true *Messiah* will build after he is gone.[3]

The biggest thing that strikes us in Solomon's prayer is how many times he states that his new Temple is only the

---

[1] Exodus 13:21–22; 19:9; 24:15–18 and 33:9–11. Don't be confused that 1 John 1:5 says, *"God is light; in him there is no darkness at all."* While God's *light* speaks of his holiness, the *cloud* speaks of the mystery of his Presence.

[2] Ezekiel 9:3; 10:4–5, 18–19 and 11:22–23.

[3] It is significant that these verses culminate with a description, in 6:42, of Solomon as the *messiah*, or *anointed one*. These verses follow 1 Kings 8:12–61 quite closely, but the Chronicler adds that Solomon knelt down to pray on the platform. Since it was unthinkable in the ancient world for a king to kneel down in front of his subjects, Solomon is consciously stating that he is merely stewarding the throne for the real *Messiah*.

Lord's dwelling-place in a limited sense of the word.[4] His great confession in verse 18 – *"But will God really dwell on earth with humans? The heavens, even the highest heavens, cannot contain you. How much less this temple that I have built!"* – is followed by eight further frank confessions that God dwells in heaven, not in any man-made building.[5] Solomon rejoices to see the glory of God fill his new Temple, but he knows that it is just his footstool. God's throne room is still in the highest heavens.

Solomon prays about the many different reasons why people might come into the Temple courtyards to meet with God. Some might want justice in a civil lawsuit.[6] Others might want to repent of their sins after defeat in battle or a failed harvest or a terrible pandemic.[7] Foreigners might want to turn to the God of Israel. Exiled Jews might want to pray towards the Temple as a way of renouncing foreign idols.[8] What strikes us most about this list of reasons is that the Temple plays a fairly minor role in the story of Israel after the death of Solomon. His successors come to desecrate it with their idols and to steal its treasures to buy off invading armies, but relatively rarely to pray.[9] The Chronicler knows this. He is reminding his readers

---

[4] Isaiah 6:1 confirms that the Temple could barely contain even the hem of the Lord's royal robes. As God's glory descends, Solomon feels the need to plead with him in 6:20 not to overlook this tiny Temple.

[5] 2 Chronicles 6:21, 23, 25, 27, 30, 33, 35 and 39. If we miss this, we miss the meaning of the prayer. It seeks to correct a false reliance on the Temple, which God has to confront in Jeremiah 7:4–15 and Micah 3:11–12.

[6] Examples of what Solomon describes in 6:22–23 can be found in Exodus 22:10–12 and Numbers 5:11–31.

[7] Solomon's prayer sounds like a long quotation of the blessings and curses in Leviticus 26 and Deuteronomy 28 because he cannot imagine any circumstance under which Israel would be defeated and unfruitful unless it sinned and fell under the Lord's judgment. We need to take this to heart whenever our churches stop advancing; it may well be that God is calling us to repent before he will prosper us further.

[8] Ordinary Israelites were not permitted to enter the Temple building. They could only pray *"towards the Temple"* from its courtyards or – when exiled to Babylon – in the general direction of Mount Moriah (Daniel 6:10). Foreigners could also pray towards Jerusalem to the God of Israel, and it is clear from Solomon's prayer that he wants the evangelistic mandate of David's Tabernacle to be carried over to his new Temple.

[9] The two big exceptions are King Jehoshaphat in 2 Chronicles 20 and King Hezekiah in 2 Kings 19.

that what Solomon built was only ever a shadow of what God intended his Temple to be.

Salvation for Israel was not to be found in a sanctuary made of stone, but in a Saviour made of flesh and blood. Solomon points our gaze towards the coming of that *Messiah* by predicting that David's dynasty will only sit on Israel's throne for as long as it stays faithful to God's Word, and that this will be far shorter than expected (verses 14, 16 and 36).[10] In the New Testament, the writer of Hebrews explains that Solomon's Temple was merely *"a copy and shadow of what is in heaven."* That's why he needed to stick so carefully to the blueprint the Holy Spirit gave to his father. Solomon's Temple and its furnishings were *"only a shadow of the good things that are coming – not the realities themselves."*[11] Even as Solomon dedicates his new Temple, he urges people to look beyond it.

The Chronicler has copied much of Solomon's prayer from 1 Kings 8, but he ends it with two verses from Psalm 132:8–10. This is the psalm which records the shepherd boy David's desire to build a Temple for the Lord and which prophesies about the Lord's *Anointed One* or *Messiah*. It is also a psalm which freely confesses that the Lord's true dwelling-place will remain in heaven, even after the Temple has been completed.

Solomon is excited that the day has finally arrived, but he uses it to proclaim that something even better lies ahead. What he has built is but the shadow of a greater heavenly reality. It points towards a Living Temple that is yet to come.

---

[10] What Solomon states quickly in 6:36, he states more explicitly in Proverbs 20:9 and Ecclesiastes 7:20.

[11] Hebrews 8:5 and 10:1. For example, in Ezekiel 1 we meet the four real-life cherubim angels which are foreshadowed by the four golden cherubim surrounding the Presence of God in *the Holy of Holies*.

Mouth and Hand
(2 Chronicles 6:3, 15)

"You have kept your promise to your servant David my father; with your mouth you have promised and with your hand you have fulfilled it – as it is today."

(2 Chronicles 6:15)

When I was last travelling through Eastern Europe, I bought a Russian doll as a souvenir. Open up the first doll and you find another, smaller doll inside. Open up the second doll and you find a third one. I'm sure you know how it is with Russian dolls.

For worshippers arriving at Solomon's Temple, the experience felt a bit like opening a Russian doll. Pete Greig describes its courtyards as a *"brutal hierarchy of progressive exclusion – on the basis of ethnicity, gender and ordination"*.[1] If you were foreign or disabled, then you might not even make it through the large, bronze-plated double doors that led into the outer courtyard. If you did, you faced a second obstacle. A second set of double doors barred the inner courtyard from everybody but the king, priests and Levites.[2]

Members of that select group who entered the inner courtyard were straightaway confronted by a massive bronze altar.[3] They could not step any closer to the glorious Presence

---

[1] Pete Greig says this in his book *Dirty Glory* (London, Hodder & Stoughton 2016). See Leviticus 21:17–21 and Deuteronomy 23:1–8.

[2] We can tell this from 4:9; 6:3 and 13.

[3] Jeremiah 36:10 says that the priests and Levites needed to climb a flight of stairs from the outer into the inner courtyard. This warned of their increasing nearness to the holy Presence of God.

of the Lord without atoning for their sins by slaughtering an innocent animal. Once they made it past the altar, their path was blocked by a giant washbasin made from polished mirrors. They couldn't help but see their reflection as they approached it, which was God's way of inviting them to own up to their shortcomings and to wash them away with water before venturing any further.[4]

Beyond the Sea of water lay further obstacles. Only the priests could enter through the great bronze pillars into the porchway of the Temple building. The other Levites were excluded, as was any priest whose turn had yet to come up on David's roster of the twenty-four priestly families, which is carefully listed for us in 1 Chronicles 24.[5]

Inside the porchway were more double doors, overlaid with purest gold, which barred the entrance to *the Holy Place*.[6] Engraved on those doors were pictures of the cherubim angels whose flaming sword drove Adam and Eve away from the Garden of Eden after they sinned. Those engravings warned any priest who was concealing secret sin that they dare not step any further. The eyes of any priest who dared to do so were dazzled in the half-light by floor-to-ceiling gold and precious jewels. A thick curtain fenced off *the Most Holy Place* from them. The Temple was obstacle after obstacle, just like the opening of a Russian doll.

Only the high priest was permitted to enter *the Most Holy Place*, and even he was only permitted to enter on one day of the year. On the Day of Atonement, he could enter carrying blood from the altar – trembling as he remembered what happened to two of Aaron's sons when they disrespected the inner sanctuary

---

[4] We can deduce this from Exodus 38:8, and it prefigures Acts 22:16 and James 1:22–24. Whatever else the Sea of cast metal signifies, it encourages us to get busy baptising people today!

[5] Even the king was excluded from the Temple building. When King Uzziah defies this in 26:16–21, he is immediately struck down with leprosy.

[6] 2 Chronicles 3:4–7 indicates that, while burnished bronze was acceptable for the Temple courtyard, nothing but the purest gold and finest jewels were good enough for a room so close to the holy Presence of the Lord.

of the Tabernacle.[7] On the other 364 days of the year, God's holy Presence above the Ark was fenced off from all human eyes, protected by the four cherubim of gold.

We are told in Hebrews 9:1–12 that the Lord designed the Temple this way, like a Russian doll, to teach the Israelites that the Old Covenant he made with their nation at Mount Sinai was insufficient and must soon pass away. The architecture of Solomon's Temple proclaimed that David's Tabernacle had been right – a New Covenant was coming, in which God's people would be granted far more access to his Presence.

In 6:3, Solomon blesses the people based on his certainty that this New Covenant is coming. The Israelites might need to wait a few more centuries to enjoy what was prefigured by David's Tabernacle, but they could draw hope from the fact that the Temple had been completed in precise accordance with David's blueprint from the Lord. *"Praise be to the Lord, the God of Israel, who with his hands has fulfilled what he promised with his mouth to my father David."* In 6:15, Solomon repeats this: whatever the Lord's mouth promises, his hand delivers. *"You have kept your promise to your servant David my father; with your mouth you have promised and with your hand you have fulfilled it – as it is today."* Solomon's Temple was like a Russian doll; it excluded people at every turn. But every inch of its architecture looked forward to a day when every worshipper would be granted an "Access All Areas" pass to enjoy the Presence of the Lord.

Solomon invites the Israelites to worship God for this, even before it happens. Their Hebrew ancestors worshipped the Lord in Egypt when he promised to deliver them from slavery, long before any of the Ten Plagues fell on their slave masters.[8] In the same way, Solomon calls the worshippers at his new Temple to praise the Lord ahead of time. If he has promised with his mouth that the days of Russian dolls will soon be over, then they can trust him to fulfil that great promise. We live on the other

---

[7] Leviticus 10:1–3.

[8] Exodus 4:31.

side of the coming of the true *Messiah*, yet we still need to walk in faith that everything he has promised us is true. The message of the Bible is that God has *"provided proof to everyone"* and that he wants us to worship him as people *"sure of what we hope for and certain of what we do not see."*[9]

Maybe you can spot it a few more times than I can, but I counted at least eighteen references in Solomon's blessing and prayer to God's covenant faithfulness to Israel.[10] They can trust him to upgrade Solomon's Russian doll Temple into a living, New Covenant Temple when the *Messiah* comes.

What God spoke with his mouth, he fulfilled with his hand for David and Solomon. What he speaks with his mouth, he will fulfil for us too. However exciting the day of dedication was to Solomon, we have far greater promises from God ourselves.

---

[9] Acts 17:31 (NET) and Hebrews 11:1 (NIVUK, 1984).

[10] 2 Chronicles 6:4, 6, 10, 11, 14, 15, 16, 17, 20, 27, 29, 31, 33, 34, 38, 39, 41 and 42. The Lord is always faithful to his covenants – but don't miss Solomon's reminder in 6:14 and 16 that this includes his covenant promises to judge and discipline his people if they refuse to carry on wholeheartedly in his way.

If and When
(2 Chronicles 7:1–22)

"If my people, who are called by my name, will humble themselves and pray and seek my face and turn from their wicked ways, then I will hear from heaven."

(2 Chronicles 7:14)

Italian diplomats felt that they had scored a major victory in Africa when they signed the Treaty of Wuchale with Ethiopia in 1889. Not only did the treaty grant them rule of Eritrea, but they also believed that King Menelik II had agreed to the annexation of Ethiopia too. In the Italian version of the treaty, Article 17 proclaimed that *"His Majesty the King of Kings of Ethiopia must go through the government of His Majesty the King of Italy whenever doing business with any other power or government."* Because the negotiators did not understand Amharic, the language of Ethiopia, they did not notice that the Amharic version merely stated that he was ***"permitted** to go through the government of His Majesty the King of Italy."* We know by now that such small things make a major difference. In this case, it led to a war in which Italy was routed on the battlefield by the Ethiopians.[1]

With that in mind, did you notice something small but startling about King Solomon's prayer in chapter 6? As he listed the many ways in which the Israelites might sin and the many reasons why they might need to repent in the Temple courtyards, he didn't say *"if"*. He said *"when"*. He predicted that the Israelites would not remain faithful to the Lord beyond his own lifetime.

---

[1] Ironically, Article 19 of the treaty stated that *"This treaty is drafted in Italian and Amharic and the two versions agree with each other perfectly"*. The small differences between 2 Chronicles 1–9 and 1 Kings 1–11 matter deeply.

*When anyone wrongs their neighbour... **When** your people Israel have been defeated by an enemy because they have sinned against you... **When** the heavens are shut up and there is no rain because your people have sinned against you ... **When** famine or plague comes to the land... **When** enemies besiege them... **When** they sin against you.*[2]

This repeated "when" in King Solomon's prayer begins to form an "if" in our own minds at the start of chapter 7. If the Israelites are this sinful, will the Lord truly come and make Solomon's new Temple the earthly footstool to his heavenly throne? Having filled the Temple with the cloud of his glorious Presence at the end of chapter 5, will he now change his mind at the beginning of chapter 7? Perhaps that's why the Chronicler adds some detail that is missing from the parallel account in 1 Kings. He tells us in 7:1–3 that, as soon as Solomon finished praying, *"fire came down from heaven and consumed the burnt offering and the sacrifices, and the glory of the Lord filled the temple."* The Lord had done this twice before – once to signify his acceptance of the sacrifices at Moses' Tabernacle (Leviticus 9:23–24), and once to signify his acceptance of David's sacrifice at the threshing-floor of Araunah (1 Chronicles 21:26). The Lord does it for a third time here to reassure the Israelites that he will also accept blood-sacrifices at their new Temple. The "when" of human sin is swallowed up by the greater "when" of his salvation.

The priests back away in fear as the Presence of God fills the Temple.[3] The Israelites fall down in worship and reprise their chorus from 1 Chronicles 16 and 2 Chronicles 5: *"He is good; his love endures forever."* Their song is a mighty proclamation that, when it comes to the Lord's love towards his people, it is never a case of *if*. It is always a case of *when*.

---

[2] It must have been comforting for the returning Jewish exiles to be reminded that Solomon prayed about God "bringing back" his people from a land of exile (6:25 and 36–39). The sin and failure which led to the destruction of Jerusalem in 586 BC had not been a surprise to the Lord.

[3] The Chronicler tells us that the Israelites worshipped when they saw the glory of the Lord *"above"* the Temple because they could not see inside it, but the Temple was filled too.

In 7:4–10, Solomon leads the Israelites in celebrating the certainty of God's grace towards them. He ends his dedication of the Temple by sacrificing so many bulls, sheep and goats that the priests need to set up an overflow altar behind the bronze altar in the Temple courtyard.[4] Sacrificing these animals takes two whole weeks – from the Day of Atonement until the last and greatest day of the Festival of Tabernacles.[5] After two weeks of rejoicing, the crowds go back to their homes across the length and breadth of Israel, assured that God's grace is powerful enough to overcome their nation's sin.[6]

After the crowds have gone, in 7:11–22, the Lord appears to Solomon in a dream. We are meant to see this as part two of the dream he had at Moses' Tabernacle, but twenty years later.[7] Solomon does not know it yet, but this dream will mark the turning-point of his reign.[8] The Lord reassures him that, when it comes to his faithfulness towards his people, it is never a case of *if*; it is always a case of *when*. He will indeed answer Solomon's prayer in chapter 6, despite Israel's future unfaithfulness towards him. *When* there is drought, *when* there is famine and *when* there is pandemic, he will hear the prayers they pray towards his Temple and remember his covenant of mercy towards them.

The only question is whether the Israelites will ever actually pray such prayers towards his Temple. Will such disasters humble

---

[4] Solomon's new altar was 21m² in size (4:1), yet even two weeks was insufficient time for it to accommodate such a vast number of sacrifices. It is likely that the overflow altar was the one from Moses' Tabernacle.

[5] The Day of Atonement was 10th Ethanim, the seventh month in the Jewish calendar. The Festival of Tabernacles ran from 15th to 23rd Ethanim (Leviticus 23:27–43).

[6] The stock phrase in the Old Testament for referring to the whole land of Israel is *"from Dan down to Beersheba"*. The Chronicler deliberately extends this in 7:8 to include Syria and Egypt, as an indication that the news about Solomon's Temple had begun to spread beyond the borders of Israel.

[7] In 8:1, we learn that Solomon finished building the Temple and palace twenty years into his reign. Be patient, therefore – it took eight years for his prayer in 958 BC to be answered in 950 BC!

[8] Solomon's first dream was mainly promises, with just a hint of warning. His second dream is still rich in promises, but the Lord warns him more urgently, knowing that he is about to backslide into sin.

them into repentance, or will they persist stubbornly in their sin? The Lord promises that *"If my people, who are called by my name, will humble themselves and pray and seek my face and turn from their wicked ways, then I will hear from heaven, and I will forgive their sin and will heal their land."* But that is a big "if".[9]

The Lord asks the same question of Solomon and of his dynasty.[10]

> *As for you, if you walk before me faithfully as David your father did, and do all I command, and observe my decrees and laws, I will establish your royal throne, as I covenanted with David your father when I said, "You shall never fail to have a successor to rule over Israel." But if you turn away and forsake the decrees and commands I have given you and go off to serve other gods and worship them...*

Well, in that case, you should expect a different story.

The Lord is explaining to Solomon that his Plan A is to convince the pagan nations that he is the only true God by blessing the Israelites and their kings. If they refuse to follow him, he has a Plan B up his sleeve. He will convince the pagan nations that he is the only true God by judging the Israelites and their kings and their polluted Temple. This is why the returning Jewish exiles have no king from David's dynasty on the throne. From this point on, the Chronicler starts repeating that it is a direct result of their sin.[11]

These verses are much more than ancient history, however. They were also written for you and me. The Lord's promise towards you and your church and your nation remains a "when". How you respond to that promise remains an "if" for you to clarify today.

---

[9] 2 Chronicles 7:14 is one of the greatest revival promises in the Bible. So, what will you do with God's *if?*

[10] The Hebrew word for "you" is singular in 7:17 and plural in 7:19, meaning both Solomon and the future kings of Judah. God makes a "forever" promise in 7:16 because a better *Messiah* will come to David's dynasty.

[11] 2 Chronicles 12:5; 15:2, 7; 16:7, 9; 19:2–3; 21:12–15; 24:20; 25:15–16; 28:9; 34:24–28 and 36:11–21.

So Close and Yet So Far
(2 Chronicles 8:1–18)

*"At the end of twenty years, during which Solomon
built the temple of the Lord and his own palace..."*

(2 Chronicles 8:1)

I once took a wrong turn on the motorway and ended up arriving almost two hours late to meet a friend. The Lord presents Solomon with a similar, decisive fork in the road in his second dream. He calls him to resolve firmly that he and his dynasty will always follow the Lord's commands. Tragically, Solomon decides to take a big wrong turn. He is so close and yet so far from being the *Messiah* that all Israel is waiting for.

The Chronicler says far less about Solomon's backsliding than the parallel account in 1 Kings does. He hints at it repeatedly, but he never states it openly, expecting his readers to know enough about what happened to grieve with him over Solomon's wrong turn.

In 8:1–2, the Chronicler hints that wrong priorities crept into the latter years of Solomon's reign.[1] He says it took him twenty years to build a Temple for the Lord and a palace for himself. Since we know that it took Solomon three years to stockpile building materials and seven years to build the Temple, this means that he took considerably longer to build his own house than he did the house of the Lord. David had been embarrassed by the splendour of his palace, so there was

---

[1] Saul, David and Solomon all reigned for forty years (1 Chronicles 29:27; 2 Chronicles 9:30 and Acts 13:21). Each of them drifted away from the Lord halfway through their reign.

no need for such extravagance by his son.[2] It made Solomon so heavily indebted to King Hiram of Tyre that he was forced to clear his debts by ceding to him a section of the Promised Land around Lake Galilee. This probably included Nazareth, Capernaum, Cana and Nain, the villages where Jesus called his disciples, so what Solomon jeopardises by his greed is far more serious than he knows. The writer of 1 Kings explains what the Chronicler merely hints at when he tells us that Hiram "gave" those villages to Solomon. By God's grace, Hiram despised Nazareth and its surrounding villages, throwing them back in Solomon's face. The crisis was averted, but the foolish Solomon blundered on.[3]

In 8:3–6, the Chronicler hints that King Solomon became increasingly self-reliant in the second half of his reign. He does not condemn outright the fact that Solomon built "store cities" to accommodate large numbers of horses and chariots, because he expects us to know that God forbade the kings of Israel from doing this in Deuteronomy 17:16. It expressed the opposite of David's faith in Psalm 20:7: *"Some trust in chariots and some in horses, but we trust in the name of the Lord our God."*[4] Solomon hedged his bets instead.

In 8:7–10, the Chronicler hints that King Solomon began to pressgang people from the northern tribes of Israel into his army of forced labourers. We will miss this if we forget that throughout 1 and 2 Chronicles he regularly refers to Judah as "Israel".[5] Since we know from 1 Kings 5:13–14, 11:28, 12:3–4

---

[2] 1 Kings 6:38; 1 Chronicles 17:1 and 2 Chronicles 3:2. Solomon began building what became known as "the Palace of the Forest of Lebanon" concurrently with the Temple, so it took him twice as long to complete it.

[3] 1 Kings 9:10–13. We can tell how repugnant this was to the Lord by contrasting Solomon's attitude towards the Promised Land with that of godly Naboth in 1 Kings 21:3. The Lord would turn those worthless villages into something worthy by making them the centre of his true *Messiah*'s ministry (Isaiah 9:1 and John 1:46).

[4] Solomon's self-reliance stands in stark contrast to his father David, who hamstrung captured horses on the battlefield to stop them from tempting him towards self-reliance (1 Chronicles 18:4).

[5] The Chronicler quotes the words *"to this day"* from one of his primary sources in 8:8, just as he did in 5:9.

and 12:18 that Solomon conscripted forced labourers from the ten northern tribes which had initially rejected his father's rule, the Chronicler's statement that *"Solomon did not make slaves of the Israelites for his work"* must mean that he saw those northern tribes as less *bona fide* Israelites than the tribe of Judah. In the second half of his reign, he stopped trying to hide his favouritism for his own tribe.

In 8:11, the Chronicler hints that King Solomon married many foreign women. We are told all about this in 1 Kings, where his royal harem swells like a festering boil into 700 wives and 300 concubines. The Chronicler merely hints at this by telling us that Solomon's chief wife was a daughter of Pharaoh. Solomon therefore reversed the Exodus by going back to Egypt and welcoming its pagan pantheon into God's holy city. He piously recognised that *"My wife must not live in the palace of David king of Israel, because the places the ark of the Lord has entered are holy."* But this is an admission that he has sinned by marrying an idolater. In a shockingly short period of time, 1 Kings informs us, the builder of God's Temple in Jerusalem became the builder of pagan temples on the Mount of Olives.[6]

In 8:12–16, the Chronicler says that Solomon continued to worship the Lord, sticking closely to the blueprint his father had given him for the Temple.[7] Even this, however, hints at the shortcomings of the second half of his reign. Solomon was good at sticking to the spiritual goals his father set for him,

---

[6] 1 Kings 3:1; 9:16, 24 and 11:1–13, and 2 Kings 23:13. There is surely no greater picture of the gulf between Solomon and Jesus than the fact that Solomon built pagan temples on the mount where Jesus would sweat blood for us in the Garden of Gethsemane and from which he would ascend back to heaven. Exodus 1:11 suggests that he got the idea of building self-reliant "store cities" from his pagan father-in-law Pharaoh.

[7] It isn't clear whether the Chronicler is saying that Solomon asked the priests to offer sacrifices, or if he offered them himself three times a year as a prophetic picture of the King-Priest who was coming in the order of Melchizedek. What is clear, however, is that he was becoming less and less like that true *Messiah*.

but he failed to set fresh spiritual goals of his own.[8] As soon as his building work was over, he allowed the Devil to find new work for his idle hands to do. Rather than planning how to make his Temple a place where many pagans would come and worship the Lord, he busied himself building pagan temples where many Israelites would come and worship foreign idols. The Lord's "forever" promises to David's dynasty would never be fulfilled through such a son as Solomon. They would only be fulfilled through a better Son of David, when the true *Messiah* came.

In 8:17–18, the Chronicler hints that Solomon became wealthier than he was wise. He cut a deal with King Hiram of Tyre to construct a Red Sea fleet of Phoenician merchant ships in order to bring back the finest gold from Arabia.[9] This was disobedient to the Lord's command in Deuteronomy 17:17 that no king of Israel must foster a spirit of self-reliance by accumulating large quantities of silver and gold, but note also what the Chronicler doesn't say. There is no trace in these verses of the young King Solomon's fervour in his letter in chapter 2 to commend the God of Israel to King Hiram.

Solomon came so close to being the Son of David about whom the Lord prophesied in his covenant with David in 1 Chronicles 17. So close and yet so far. In the second half of his reign, the Chronicler hints that he took a big wrong turn. The wise King Solomon became a fool.

---

[8] Is the Chronicler hinting at this in 8:14 when he refers to Solomon observing *"each day's requirement"* for the Temple? It hardly expresses a deep enjoyment of the Temple worship which had meant so much to David.

[9] In the Hebrew text of 9:21, Solomon's ships are twice called *"ships of Tarshish"*. This was a Phoenician colony in Spain, not on the Red Sea, but it was a generic term for any ship crafted in the Phoenician way.

What Might Have Been
(2 Chronicles 9:1–31)

"All the kings of the earth sought audience with Solomon to hear the wisdom God had put in his heart."

(2 Chronicles 9:23)

In the Charles Dickens novel *A Christmas Carol* the miser Ebenezer Scrooge is granted a vision of what might have been. He sees his life as it is now and as it will be in the future, while also catching glimpses from his past of how much better his life might have been. At the end of the novel, he pleads with the Ghost of Christmas Future, *"Answer me one question. Are these shadows of the things that **will** be, or are they shadows of things that **may** be, only?... Why show me this if I am past all hope?... Assure me that I yet may change these shadows you have shown me!"*[1]

In the last of the nine chapters which the Chronicler devotes to the reign of King Solomon, we catch a glimpse of what might have been had he remained faithful to the Lord. The Chronicler uses this chapter to provoke his readers to ask the same question as Ebenezer Scrooge, because their future need not echo the tragic fate of ancient Israel.

In 9:1, we see a picture of the *blessing* which Israel might have enjoyed had King Solomon remained faithful to the Lord. The Queen of Sheba comes to Jerusalem, having heard about his new Temple and palace. This dates her visit to shortly after Solomon's second dream – late enough for him to have finished

---

[1] Charles Dickens published *A Christmas Carol* in 1843.

his building work but early enough for him still to appear wise. The Chronicler copies down much of this chapter from 1 Kings 10, so don't miss a deliberate change that he makes as he does so. He omits the reference from verse 1 to the Queen of Sheba coming to find out about *"his relationship to the Lord"*. Solomon is already starting to drift away from God, so this visit from the Queen of Sheba and her royal retinue is a taste of the blessings that might have been.

In 9:2–8, we see a picture of the *missionary breakthrough* that the Israelites might have seen had King Solomon remained faithful to the Lord. They had prayed at David's Tabernacle that their pagan neighbours might come to Jerusalem in search of the Lord. Solomon voiced this same prayer at the dedication of his Temple in 6:32–33. Their prayer is finally answered when the Queen of Sheba arrives in Jerusalem, from what must have felt like the ends of the earth, to share her deepest yearnings and to ask her toughest questions of King Solomon. Here we see what might have happened had he persisted in calling the pagans to exchange their worthless idols for the Lord, instead of deciding to run after pagan idols too. The Hebrew word *rūach* in verse 5 either expresses that the queen was *breathless* with astonishment or that there was *no spirit left* within her. Either way, what she sees in Jerusalem makes room for God's Spirit to move within her.

Jewish tradition and the words of Jesus in Matthew 12:42 and Luke 11:31 suggest that the Queen of Sheba came to believe in the God of Israel through her visit to Jerusalem. Before she returns home, she hints at the missionary breakthrough that might have been.[2] Many other foreigners would have echoed her confession of faith too:

Praise be to the Lord your God, who has delighted in you
and placed you on his throne as king to rule for the Lord

---

[2] We have already noted that 2 Chronicles 1–9 is structured as a symmetrical "chiasmus". It is therefore deliberate that the Queen of Sheba's words in 9:8 echo King Hiram's words in 2:11–12.

your God. Because of the love of your God for Israel and his desire to uphold them for ever, he has made you king over them, to maintain justice and righteousness.[3]

In 9:9–16, we see a picture of the *prosperity* which Israel might have enjoyed had King Solomon remained faithful to the Lord. At the end of chapter 8, the Chronicler told us that Solomon built a fleet of ships to sail the Red Sea in search of treasures from the land of Ophir, in what is modern-day Yemen, famous for its purest gold and priceless jewels. King Hiram of Tyre helped him because Solomon needed to find a way to pay off his debts to Hiram after borrowing so much to build his palace. Since the Queen of Sheba ruled the region of Ophir, it is significant that she gave Solomon four tons of gold – the exact amount of gold that 1 Kings 9:14 tells us Solomon owed to Hiram![4] Had Solomon taken the road of obedience, the Lord would have sorted out his money problems for him. Solomon's sailboats on the sea in search of treasure looked impressive, but they were in fact a tragic picture of his self-reliance and of his loss of what might have been.

The Chronicler hints at Solomon's backsliding, rather than stating it openly, because he expects his readers to know the rest of the story from 1 Kings. He chooses what he says here very carefully because he wants to present Solomon as a picture of the perfect *Messiah*. In case we are slow on the uptake, he records the annual income from Solomon's Red Sea fleet as *"666 talents"* of gold. In Hebrew thought, the number seven represented God's perfection, so the number 777 spoke of total perfection (as in *"holy, holy, holy"* in Isaiah 6:3). These *"666*

---

[3] In quoting from 1 Kings 10:9, the Chronicler changes the queen's words to state more clearly that she recognised Solomon as a mere steward of his throne for the Lord, the true King of Israel. Her words remain true for us today: whenever God wants to bless us, he gives us good leaders, and whenever he wants to curse us, he takes them away. See Isaiah 3:1–7 and Ephesians 4:7–13.

[4] The name Yemen comes from a Semitic word meaning *South*, because it sits at the far south of the Arabian Peninsula. That's why Jesus refers to her as *"the Queen of the South"* in Matthew 12:42 and Luke 11:31.

talents" therefore hint that, for all Solomon's great riches, he fell short of God's desire to entrust Israel with the true riches of heaven.[5]

In 9:17–28, we see a picture of the *power* which Israel might have wielded had King Solomon remained faithful to the Lord. The Chronicler notes that his throne exceeded that of any other kingdom and that it included a great footstool of gold.[6] This is significant, since the Temple was meant to be the earthly footstool of God's heavenly throne. The Chronicler laments instead that *"King Solomon was greater in riches and wisdom than all the other kings of the earth."* Note the order: riches and wisdom. In the second half of his reign, the once-wise Solomon began to have more money than sense.

In 9:29–31, King Solomon finally dies. The book of Ecclesiastes seems to indicate that he repented of his backsliding and returned to the Lord before he died, but he did so too late to restore Israel to what might have been. Tragically, instead of promoting the God of Israel to his foreign visitors, he had promoted trade deals with them. Rather than enlisting them to worship the Lord with him, he had enlisted their help to break the Lord's command in Deuteronomy 17:16 by striking deals with them to bolster the number of chariots and horses that he amassed, in self-reliance, in his "chariot cities".

So don't miss the little details in this chapter through which the Chronicler hints to his readers that they need a better Son of David. Jesus is looking back to this chapter when he tells the crowd in Matthew 12:42 that *"The Queen of the South... came from the ends of the earth to listen to Solomon's wisdom, and now something greater than Solomon is here."*

---

[5] 666 talents is 23 tons of gold, and Solomon added to it further by taxing the busy trade routes which passed through his kingdom and demanding tribute from his vassal territories. He looked like a successful ruler but Revelation 13:18 looks back to this verse with disapproval and grief over what might have been.

[6] Ivory was very costly, yet Solomon had so much wealth that he covered over much of his ivory with gold!

Part Four:

Small Things about Judah (2 Chronicles 10–36)

Not the Man You're Looking for (2 Chronicles 10:1)

"Rehoboam went to Shechem, for all Israel had gone there to make him king."

(2 Chronicles 10:1)

The fourth and final section of 1 and 2 Chronicles is very different from the first three sections. Parts one to three are optimistic. They talk about God's plans for Israel, and they depict David and Solomon as prophetic pictures of the *Messiah* who is coming to achieve those plans by conquering Israel's enemies. Part four, on the other hand, reveals how far the kings from David's dynasty fell short of God's plans for them. It looks at nineteen kings and concludes about each one of them: *this is not the man you're looking for*.

The Chronicler starts to pick up speed as he enters the final section of his story. He devoted twenty chapters to the events of David's reign, and nine chapters to the events of Solomon's. In the final twenty-seven chapters, he gallops through the reigns of nineteen kings of Judah, giving us a highlights reel from each of their reigns, rather than an exhaustive record of 344 years of Jewish history.

At the beginning of this final section of the story, the nation of Israel is torn in two. The ten northern tribes become the "kingdom of Israel". They reject the dynasty of David and, with it, the idea that the Lord is the true King of Israel. The two southern tribes become the "kingdom of Judah".[1] They continue to be ruled by David's dynasty but they sway back and forth between David's devotion to the Lord and Solomon's backsliding and idolatry. The Chronicler focuses his story on the southern kingdom, only mentioning the northern kings when their actions reverberate across the border. He never forgets that he is writing for Jews who have come back home from Babylon and who are longing to be ruled by a new king from David's dynasty. He uses the nineteen rulers of Judah to warn them that they need to place their hope in something better than a merely human king.

The Chronicler presents the first few decades of the southern kingdom of Judah as a story of "six plus one". Six kings rule from David's dynasty. They are either "bad" or "good". The Chronicler is deliberately simplistic in his account because he either wants to contrast or to liken each of them to the true *Messiah*. After six kings comes a usurper named Athaliah, who does not belong to David's dynasty. She is a false *messiah* – an antichrist – whose reign is meant to make us cry out for the real *Messiah* yet to come.

Rehoboam (930–913 BC) – "bad"
Abijah (913–910 BC) – "bad"
Asa (910–869 BC) – "good"
Jehoshaphat (872–848 BC) – "good"
Jehoram (853–841 BC) – "bad"[2]
Ahaziah (841 BC) – "bad"
[Athaliah (841–835 BC) – "antichrist"]

---

[1] The Chronicler sees the two southern tribes as *"Judah and Benjamin"* (11:1, 3, 10, 12 and 23), although much of Benjamin became part of the northern kingdom. This was offset by the fact that Simeon, whose territory was within the land of Judah, was gradually absorbed into Judah. This maintained a split of ten tribes to two.

[2] Jehoshaphat and Jehoram are crowned king before their father dies, just like Solomon, reigning at first as co-rulers alongside their father.

The Chronicler presents the next few decades as another story of "six plus one". David's dynasty is restored, but its rulers remain compromised in sin. Three kings begin well but turn bad in the end. Two kings remain faithful to the Lord throughout their reigns, but one makes no effort to follow him at all. The seventh king, Manasseh, is like Athaliah. Although he belongs to David's dynasty, he becomes as much a murderer as she was. He too is an antichrist, whose reign is meant to make us cry out for a better *Messiah*.

> **Joash (835–796 BC) – "good" then "bad"**
> **Amaziah (796–767 BC) – "good" then "bad"**
> **Uzziah (792–740 BC) – "good" then "bad"**
> **Jotham (750–732 BC) – "good"**
> **Ahaz (735–715 BC) – "bad"**
> **Hezekiah (715–686 BC) – "good"**
> **Manasseh (697–642 BC) – "antichrist"**[3]

The Chronicler also presents the final few decades of the southern kingdom as a story of "six plus one". Only one of the last six kings of Judah is faithful to the Lord. The rest – as before – merely serve to make us cry out for a better Son of David. The sin and failures of the kings of Judah lead directly to the Jewish exile in Babylon. With that, their throne passes to King Nebuchadnezzar of Babylon, another antichrist, who destroys the Lord's Temple and who slaughters the Lord's people. The Chronicler uses this to warn his readers that salvation will not come to the Jews through the mere restoration of David's dynasty. They need an altogether different Son of David, one who will succeed where every other king of Judah failed. They need a very different *Messiah*.

> **Amon (642–640 BC) – "bad"**
> **Josiah (640–609 BC) – "good"**
> **Jehoahaz (609 BC) – "bad"**

---

[3] Uzziah, Jotham, Ahaz and Manasseh all begin their reigns as co-rulers alongside their fathers too.

Jehoiakim (609–598 BC) – "bad"
Jehoiachin (598–597 BC) – "bad"
Zedekiah (597–586 BC) – "bad"
[Nebuchadnezzar – "antichrist"]

One of the most famous lines in the original *Star Wars* movie is the moment when Obi-Wan Kenobi persuades a stormtrooper that R2-D2 and C-3PO are not the droids they've been searching for. The Chronicler says something similar to his readers throughout the final twenty-seven chapters of his story. His account of the reigns of these nineteen kings of Judah teaches us over and over again: *This is not the Messiah you're looking for.*

The first verses of the New Testament pick up on this. Matthew deliberately echoes these chapters by starting his gospel with the family tree of Jesus, which includes the kings who are listed here. He informs us that *"There were fourteen generations in all from Abraham to David, fourteen from David to the exile to Babylon, and fourteen from the exile to the Messiah."* Like the Chronicler, Matthew gives us a selective history of Judah so that his gospel closely parallels these chapters.[4] If the story of David's dynasty was "six plus one" three times over and it ended in abject failure, then the story of Jesus is "six plus one times two" three times over, and it ends in matchless victory. He is the *Messiah* we're looking for.

---

[4] Matthew 1:17. In order to make it three times "six plus one times two", Matthew leaves out several people from the genealogy of Jesus. For example, Ahaziah, Joash, Amaziah and Jehoiakim are all missing.

Soft Southerner
(2 Chronicles 10:1 – 11:4)

"So Israel has been in rebellion against the house of David to this day."

(2 Chronicles 10:19)

David and Solomon had something in common. They were both soft when it came to training up their sons to rule as king. David spent the final few years of his reign fighting off insurrections from one son after another. The writer of 1 and 2 Kings records the last of them and lays the blame squarely on the fact that *"His father had never rebuked him by asking, 'Why do you behave as you do?'"*[1] Tragically, as Rehoboam becomes the new king of Israel, we discover that Solomon followed the parenting failures of his father.

King Rehoboam was the son of the richest man in the world. Solomon found it difficult enough to remember the names of his 700 wives and 300 concubines, let alone to discipline their sons. As a result, the crown prince learned to strut around the palace and to ask his father's servants to give him anything he wanted. Instead of giving him the hands-on parenting that he needed to steward such power and privilege, Solomon wrote a book for him to read instead. We still have it in our Bibles. The book of Proverbs reaches out to Rehoboam, as a pampered prince, and its pages seek to parent him from afar: *"My son, do not forget my teaching."*[2]

---

[1] 1 Kings 1:6. See also 2 Samuel 13:21 and 14:23–24, where David fumes with anger on the inside but says nothing to discipline his sons that might have delivered them from a tragic end.

[2] Proverbs 1–9 consists of twelve fatherly talks, the first eleven of which begin with a passionate appeal to *"my son"*.

Rehoboam needed more than a book to prepare him to rule over the twelve tribes of Israel. His name means *The People Have Grown Bigger*, because Israel had prospered greatly under his father, but something he did in the first year of his reign would make his kingdom grow a whole lot smaller. In 10:1, Rehoboam travels to Shechem for his coronation. Since neither David nor Solomon had been crowned king in that city (only the usurper Abimelek, in Judges 9:6), the fact that Rehoboam agrees to travel north for his coronation is an indication of the growing power of the northern tribes. Shechem was on the border of Ephraim and Manasseh, so Rehoboam is venturing into the heartland of the ten tribes that his father taxed and conscripted into his labour gangs, treating them as second-class citizens compared to people from the tribe of Judah.

In 10:2–4, Rehoboam discovers that his father's enemy Jeroboam has returned from Egypt to head up the ancient equivalent of a trades union delegation. The ten northern tribes inform him that they will only crown him as their new king if he agrees to end his father's unfair taxes and his labour gangs. If he refuses, then they will form a breakaway kingdom instead. In Jeroboam, they have a rival *messiah* ready and waiting in the wings.[3]

In 10:5–11, Rehoboam dismisses the trades union delegation. He says he needs three days to consult the wise men who served his father. After all, it says somewhere in the book his father gave him that *"For lack of guidance a nation falls, but victory is won through many advisors."*[4] The wise men give him a very simple answer: Become a servant-leader and the northern tribes will gladly serve you.[5] He gets

SOFT SOUTHERNER (2 CHRONICLES 10:1 – 11:4)

169

---

[3] David and Solomon ruled the ten northern tribes on a different basis to the southern tribes (2 Samuel 2:4 and 5:1–5, and 1 Kings 1:35 and 4:20). This unusual arrangement worked for seventy-three years due to much wisdom and kindness. However, 1 Kings 11:26–40 records how Solomon's sins turned the northern tribes against him.

[4] Proverbs 11:14. Rehoboam would also have done well to remember Proverbs 20:29.

[5] This is wise advice for any leader. See Mark 10:42–45 and 1 Peter 5:1–6.

a very different answer, however, from his boyhood friends as a pampered prince in the palace.[6] They warn that giving a soft answer will make the northern tribes believe that he is soft as a leader. He needs to show them that he's a tough guy by standing up to the bully Jeroboam. If he acts like a soft southerner, then he will never convince the northern tribes that he is a real *messiah*.

Rehoboam's fear that he will be seen as soft reveals the flimsiness of his faith in the God of Israel. He consults the elders who served his father and the boys who grew up with him in the palace, but at no point does he go to the Temple to seek guidance from the Lord. He was the son of an Ammonite woman, so he was probably as familiar with the pagan temple which his father built for the baby-burning worshippers of Molek on the Mount of Olives as he was with the Temple which his father built for the Lord on Mount Moriah.[7] His actions reveal that he has very little sense that he is merely stewarding the throne for the Lord, who is the true King of Israel. Instead of following the advice that his father gave him in the book of Proverbs – *"A soft answer turns away wrath, but a harsh word stirs up anger"* – he imitates his father's worst moments of folly.[8]

In 10:12–15, Rehoboam gives his answer to the trades union delegation. Believing that the advice of his father's wise men is too soft, he delivers the harsh answer of his boyhood friends. If Solomon taxed the ten northern tribes unfairly, then Rehoboam has a few extra taxes in mind. If Solomon pressganged them into his labour gangs, making them feel the sting of his whip on their shoulders, then Rehoboam has so many plans to make them work for him that his whip on their backs will feel like the sting of a scorpion.

---

[6] Rehoboam was forty-one when he became king (12:13), but three times the Hebrew text of 10:8–14 refers to his immature friends as mere *boys*.

[7] 1 Kings 11:1–8 and 2 Chronicles 12:13. It is foolish to marry a nonbeliever yet to expect believing children.

[8] Proverbs 15:1 (ESV).

In 10:16–17, Rehoboam's fear of seeming soft results in the breakup of his father's kingdom. Spurred on by the words of Ahijah's prophecy to Jeroboam, the ten northern tribes renounce all loyalty to the kings of Judah. *"What share do we have in David, what part in Jesse's son? To your tents, Israel! Look after your own house, David!"*[9] The writer explains to us in 10:15 that the Lord's hand of judgment is behind this, but it nevertheless feels tragic. One minute, a united Israel is winning the world to the Lord through its God-given wisdom. The next, it self-destructs as a result of its idolatry.[10]

In 10:18 – 11:4, Rehoboam refuses to face up to what has happened. He sends out Adoniram, the manager of his forced labour gangs, to prove that he will not be soft in his response to their sedition.[11] It is only when a lynch mob of irate northerners stone Adoniram to death that he grasps the seriousness of the situation. He flees by chariot to Jerusalem, where he has himself crowned king of Judah and musters 180,000 soldiers to force the northern tribes to receive him as their king. A prophet named Shemaiah intervenes to stop the bloodshed. His name means *Hears The Lord* and he declares that this northern rebellion is the Lord's doing. Since Rehoboam has refused to rule as a steward of the throne of Israel for the Lord, he will not rule the northern tribes at all.[12]

---

[9] We can tell from 9:29 that the Chronicler expects us to know about Ahijah of Shiloh's prophecy in 1 Kings 11:26–40. He also expects us to spot that the northern tribes are echoing the war-cry of Sheba's rebellion against David, determined to succeed where their grandparents failed (2 Samuel 20:1–2).

[10] Students of Church history discover that this same tragedy has been repeated many times by God's people. Whenever we seek to serve God *and* public opinion, the Church loses its influence with startling speed.

[11] 1 Kings 4:6 and 5:14 identify him as the leader of the labour gangs. The Chronicler uses the Hebrew variant name *Hadoram*.

[12] We are told in 10:19 that *"Israel has been in rebellion against the house of David to this day"*, so note that Shemaiah refers in 11:3 to *"all Israel in Judah and Benjamin"*. In other words, Rehoboam and his men are also in rebellion against what David's dynasty is meant to symbolise.

Here we have in miniature the message of this entire fourth section of 1 and 2 Chronicles. The dynasty of David is softening its devotion to the Lord, and it will ultimately fall. The twelve tribes of Israel will never be reunited under a *messiah* like Rehoboam. That will only happen when the true *Messiah* finally comes and sits on David's throne.

Two Faces of
David's Dynasty
(2 Chronicles 11:5 – 12:16)

*"After Rehoboam's position as king was established
and he had become strong, he and all Israel with him
abandoned the law of the Lord."*

(2 Chronicles 12:1)

The Chronicler is like my grandmother's TV when I was a child –
everything is in black and white. Instead of the more nuanced
history that we find in 1 and 2 Kings, the Chronicler prefers to
present the kings of Judah as either "good" or "bad". The reign of
Rehoboam is unusual in that it swings back and forth between
the two. The Chronicler uses it to introduce his readers to the
two conflicting faces of David's dynasty.[1]

In 11:5–12, Rehoboam reveals himself to be as self-reliant
as Solomon. He is taking a page out of his father's playbook
when he constructs "store cities" on his borders – as if amassing
shields and spears and stockpiles of food is sufficient to protect
his kingdom. Worse than that, the fifteen cities listed defend only
the western, southern and eastern borders of Judah. Rehoboam
does not fortify the border between Judah and Israel because,
deep down, he refuses to believe God's word to him that the
ten northern tribes are lost for good. His wilful self-reliance in
these verses is a denial of the central faith of Israel, which is
celebrated by his grandfather David in Psalm 20:7 – *"Some trust*

---

[1] The account of Rehoboam's reign in 2 Chronicles 11:1 – 12:16 is much more detailed
than in 1 Kings 14:21–31.

in chariots and some in horses, but we trust in the name of the Lord our God."

In 11:13–17, we are reminded that David's dynasty has a more pleasant face. For all his faults, Rehoboam remains the *messiah* that God has chosen to steward the throne of Israel for him. Jeroboam is a false *messiah*. Like Aaron in the desert, he persuades the northerners to worship golden calves, fearing that if they travel south to worship the Lord at his Temple then they will be won back to supporting David's dynasty.[2] The priests from Aaron's family and the other Levites are furious, but he responds by accepting anyone from any tribe to become a priest at his pagan shrines. As a result of Jeroboam's sinfulness, even the self-reliant Rehoboam appears godly. Repulsed by Jeroboam's idolatry and desiring to remain faithful to the Lord, large numbers of northerners travel south across the border into Judah. Many of the priests and Levites abandon their share of the Promised Land, preferring to be homeless in the southern kingdom than godless in the northern kingdom. By God's grace and in spite of his own folly, Rehoboam finds his kingdom being strengthened spiritually and militarily.

In 11:18–23, we return to the other face of David's dynasty. Rehoboam imitates his father's folly by taking eighteen wives and sixty concubines. Two of them are royal cousins – both granddaughters of David – but one is the daughter of Absalom, the rebel son who soured David's reign. Our hearts sink when we are told that she is his favourite wife and that her son is the next king of Judah. Sure enough, the toxic influence of Absalom's daughter causes great trouble for David's dynasty in 15:16.[3]

In 12:1, David's dynasty descends even further into sin. *"After Rehoboam's position as king was established and he had*

---

[2] We are told more about this in 1 Kings 12:26–33, where the writer notes scathingly that Jeroboam appointed priests, literally *"from the lowest of people"* (verse 31). Don't be confused when the Chronicler refers to the golden calves as "goats". It is a Hebrew way of stating that evil spirits are at work behind them (Leviticus 17:7).

[3] The Hebrew text should be translated that she was the *granddaughter* of Absalom, not his daughter. We are told in 13:2 that her father was a man named Uriel and, besides, a daughter would be past child-bearing age.

become strong, he and all Israel with him abandoned the law of the Lord." Rehoboam felt very vulnerable during the first three years of his reign, so it was pragmatic for him to unite his subjects under a pretence of piety.[4] After three years, he feels secure enough to do away with the Jewish Law and to serve the pagan idols of his foreign mother.[5] Even now, all is not lost, however. Note how the Chronicler refers to the southern kingdom of Judah as "Israel" – something he will do continually throughout this final section of his story. It signifies his refusal to acknowledge the legitimacy of the northern kingdom or of any royal dynasty other than that of David. He longs for the day when the twelve tribes will be reunited under a true and better Son of David. Until then, not everything that calls itself Israel is truly Israel. The real Israel is Judah.[6]

In 12:2–4, we witness the consequences of Rehoboam's sin. Solomon had brokered an alliance with Egypt by marrying one of Pharaoh's daughters. His folly was revealed a few years later, when her father was deposed by Shishak, better known to historians as Pharaoh Shoshenq I, the founder of the Twenty-Second Dynasty. Judah therefore became an enemy of Egypt, since it had allied itself with the old regime. Shishak offered sanctuary to Judah's enemies for many years, and now he invades its territory.[7] The chain of fortress cities which Rehoboam built along his western border quickly falls to the Egyptian army. Within two years of the people of Judah backsliding into sin, their capital city is surrounded by the enemy.[8] In case we

---

[4] People always follow their leaders, for good or ill. Note how happily the people of Judah flip-flop with him.

[5] The Chronicler spares us the details of Rehoboam's backsliding, but 1 Kings 14:22–24 says that Judah was filled with idols, gay shrine prostitutes and the other *"detestable practices"* of the Canaanites.

[6] The New Testament picks up on this in John 1:47 and 8:39, Romans 9:6–9, and Revelation 2:9 and 3:9. The Chronicler wants to teach the Jews after the exile that their nation is for "true Jews" from all twelve tribes of Israel.

[7] 1 Kings 11:14–22; 11:40 – 12:2, and 2 Chronicles 10:2.

[8] Shoshenq ruled from about 945 to 924 BC. One of the walls of the temple of Amun at Karnak, near Luxor in Egypt, depicts his campaign against Judah. He advanced as far north as Megiddo to fight the kingdom of Israel too.

are unsure as to why, the Chronicler spells it out for us. It was *"because they had been unfaithful to the Lord"*.

In 12:5–8, we return to the brighter face of David's dynasty. The prophet Shemaiah appears a second time and informs Rehoboam and his leaders that the Lord plans to use this Egyptian invasion to judge the kingdom of Judah for its rebellion against him. They immediately humble themselves and repent of their sin, confessing freely that *"The Lord is just"* in judging their idolatry.[9] God can see that they truly mean it, so he commutes their punishment into a suspended sentence. He will teach Judah a lesson through Pharaoh Shishak, but he will not destroy it. Again the Chronicler spells out for us why. He tells us in 12:12 that it was because the Lord saw two faces to David's dynasty. *"Indeed, there was some good in Judah."*

In 12:9–14, we see its ugly face again. In order to persuade Pharaoh Shishak to withdraw his army from Jerusalem, Rehoboam plunders gold from the Lord's Temple and from the royal palace. As part of this, he surrenders the 500 magnificent gold shields which his father Solomon constructed in 9:15–16. The Lord intends this major blow to Judah's prestige to be a lesson for the pampered prince in long-term humility. Sadly, Rehoboam merely replaces those shields of gold with shields of bronze, then carries on in his idolatry precisely as before.

As a result, in 12:15–16, Rehoboam dies aged only fifty-eight, which is the same age as his father Solomon. His kingdom remains split in two and seemingly beyond repair. Since his heart is divided towards the Lord, occasionally repentant but largely rebellious, his kingdom is divided too. It is a tragic reflection of the two faces of David's dynasty.

---

[9] The Hebrew word which they use in 12:6 for *"just"* is *tsaddīq*, which literally means *righteous*.

Ready, Get Set, Go! (2 Chronicles 12:13–14)

"He did evil because he had not set his heart on seeking the Lord."

(2 Chronicles 12:14)

Every child knows how a race begins: *Ready, get set, go!* Not everybody grasps, however, that the race of life begins the same way. That's why the Chronicler makes several throwaway comments throughout this final section of his story which repeatedly warn us that how we set our hearts dictates our actions, which in turn dictates our destiny in God.[1] Read too quickly and you may miss what he is trying to teach us about the God of such small things.

In 11:16, the Chronicler explained why many people from the northern tribes of Israel were willing to give up their properties and travel south over the border to become part of the kingdom of Judah. He told us that they were *"those from every tribe of Israel* **who set their hearts on seeking the Lord, *the God of Israel"*.** They had set their hearts to live their lives as a sacrifice to the Lord, and as a result they were ready to go. They quickly saw through the false name of the northern kingdom and recognised that Judah had become the real Israel. By way of contrast, the Chronicler uses the same phrase in 12:14 to inform us sadly that Rehoboam *"did evil because* **he had not set his heart on seeking the Lord."**

This is important because we tend to view our sins as spontaneous. We claim that we were "caught up in the moment"

---

[1] The Apostle Paul describes the destiny of each of our lives as a race in Acts 20:24; 1 Corinthians 9:24; Philippians 3:13–14 and 2 Timothy 4:6–8.

and that what happened "was not like us at all". The Chronicler doesn't buy that for a moment. He has read too much of the wisdom of Rehoboam's father Solomon: *"Above all else, guard your heart, for everything you do flows from it."*[2] He has also read the Old Testament Prophets, who teach us that the Exodus generation of Israelites forfeited the Promised Land because *"their hearts were devoted to their idols."*[3] He is convinced that our daily actions are forged by our heart decisions, way ahead of time. If we want to act well in the future, then we need to set our hearts in the right direction now. The battle against sin is not a series of isolated skirmishes, but the daily outworking of an internal battle that we have already won or lost in our hearts.

The Chronicler is concerned that we might dismiss this as a small thing. To avoid this, he keeps repeating it throughout the final section of his story. Why was Asa such a godly king of Judah? Because *"Asa's heart was fully committed to the Lord"* (15:17). Why was his son Jehoshaphat also a godly king? Because *"his heart was devoted to the ways of the Lord"* (17:6), such that one of the prophets of the Lord could commend him: *"You... have set your heart on seeking God"* (19:3). Why did the people of Judah backslide into sin and idolatry after Jehoshaphat died? The answer is just the same: *"The people still had not set their hearts on the God of their ancestors"* (20:33).

Why did the Lord forgive and rescue the people of Judah under Hezekiah? Because it is his nature to forgive anyone *"who sets their heart on seeking God"* (30:19). Why did the Lord destroy Jerusalem under Zedekiah? For the exact same reason. It was because the king *"became stiff-necked and hardened his heart"* (36:13). Had he set his heart towards repentance, the kingdom of Judah would have been spared exile, because *"the eyes of the Lord range throughout the earth to strengthen those whose hearts are fully committed to him"* (16:9). Each of these verses on their own might be dismissed

---

[2] Proverbs 4:23.
[3] Ezekiel 20:16.

as a throwaway comment, but put together these small things become a big thing.[4]

The Devil loves to tempt people from the outside in. He targets our eyes to inflame our bodies, so that our flesh attempts to dominate our inner being, instead of being governed by it.[5] When we are born again, the Lord begins to restore our lives to his proper order. He unites our spirit with his Holy Spirit so that we become one with him. Then his Spirit starts to flow out from our inner being to grant us mastery over our thoughts, our emotions and our bodies.[6] He enables us to follow the example of Asa and Jehoshaphat by setting our hearts towards godly actions every day. When it comes to sanctification (the daily struggle to live more and more like Jesus) the battlefield lies within us. Our actions are merely the evidence of whether or not we have won.[7]

The best time for us to learn to set our hearts towards godliness is as children, under the direction of our parents. Solomon may not have practised what he preached with Rehoboam, but he speaks wisdom when he urges parents in Proverbs 22:6 to *"Start children off on the way they should go, and even when they are old they will not turn from it."* One of the duties of a parent is to furnish self-control for their children until such a time as their children are wise enough to develop self-control for themselves. Tragically, the Chronicler tells us in 12:13 that the primary influence over Rehoboam's childhood was his mother Naamah – an Ammonite woman, who was one of the pagan princesses that Solomon married in order to

---

[4] If you are not convinced of this principle from 2 Chronicles alone, then you can find similar resolutions of the heart which lead to godly action in Job 31:1; Psalm 17:3; Daniel 1:8; Luke 21:14 and Acts 11:23.

[5] For example, in Genesis 3:6 and 6:2; Joshua 7:21; 2 Samuel 11:2–4; Psalm 119:37; Matthew 5:28 and 6:22–23; James 1:14–15 and 1 John 2:16. Our hearts are our steering wheel, and what we see affects how we drive.

[6] The New Testament explains that when God's Spirit unites himself with our spirit (1 Corinthians 6:17), his holiness flows out from within us – from *spirit* to *soul* and to *body* (note the order in 1 Thessalonians 5:23).

[7] Jesus teaches this in Matthew 12:34–35; Mark 7:14–23 and Luke 6:45.

broker peace with his foreign neighbours. Even when his harem began to resemble the United Nations, Solomon never stopped to ask himself how a baby-burning worshipper of Molek could be expected to train his son in godliness.

Thankfully, the Lord is faithful to us, even when our parents aren't. The Chronicler reassures us in 12:13 that, despite the sins of David's dynasty, Jerusalem remained *"the city the Lord had chosen out of all the tribes of Israel in which to put his Name."* Even as the people of Judah descended deeper into sin, the Presence of the Lord continued to dwell in his Temple in Jerusalem. Whenever we are unfaithful, the Lord remains faithful, because his faithfulness depends on who he is, and not on who we are.[8] If you feel horrified by the sin that you see lurking within you, and if you feel that you are losing your daily struggle against sin, then take heart from these verses. The Lord promises to fill you with his Spirit and to empower you to reset your heart towards him. He is a good Father, who loves to help his children to run well, saying to them: *Ready, get set, go!*

So take a moment to make these little verses in 2 Chronicles a big topic of your prayers. By the Holy Spirit's help, reset your heart to run well after God. To encourage you, the nineteenth-century preacher Charles Spurgeon explains what resetting your heart means:

> The Christian is no more a common man... If you and I are tempted to sin, we must reply, "No, let another man do that, but I cannot. I am God's man; I am set apart for him; how shall I do this great wickedness and sin against God?" Let dedication enforce sanctification.[9]

---

[8] This is the glorious promise of 2 Timothy 2:13.

[9] From a sermon entitled "Threefold Sanctification", preached at the Metropolitan Tabernacle in London on 9 February 1862. The reference is to a similar heart resolution made by Joseph in Genesis 39:9–10.

Manifesto
(2 Chronicles 13:1–22)

"Don't you know that the Lord, the God of Israel, has given the kingship of Israel to David and his descendants for ever?"

(2 Chronicles 13:5)

After the Nazi invasion of Russia, Winston Churchill was criticised for supporting Joseph Stalin and the cruel Soviet regime. He was pragmatic in his reply. *"I have only one purpose, the destruction of Hitler, and my life is much simplified thereby. If Hitler invaded Hell I would make at least a favourable reference to the Devil in the House of Commons."*[1]

The Chronicler takes the same approach when it comes to the reign of Rehoboam's son Abijah. The writer of 1 and 2 Kings makes short shrift of him, dismissing his reign in eight verses that tell us *"He committed all the sins his father had done before him; his heart was not fully devoted to the Lord his God, as the heart of David his forefather had been."*[2] The Chronicler is a lot more generous towards Abijah. He devotes three times as many verses to his reign and he chooses to focus on what was good. Abijah preached a manifesto on the battlefield which summarises God's plan for the people of Israel.

The Chronicler does not pretend that Abijah was a good king of Judah. Joseph Stalin was still Joseph Stalin, even when he needed to become an ally for a while. Abijah only ruled

---

[1] Churchill recounts this in the third volume of his World War Two memoirs, entitled *The Grand Alliance* (1950).

[2] The events of Abijah's reign, from 913 to 910 BC, are recorded in 1 Kings 15:1–8.

for three years, which is a sign of God's displeasure with his regime. We are also told that he was born into a marriage alliance between David's sinful son Absalom and the sinful family of King Saul.[3] We are also told that he shared his father's refusal to accept the Lord's decree that the ten northern tribes would never be reconquered through force of war. Rehoboam built fortress cities on every border except the one between Judah and Israel because he stubbornly insisted that the division of his kingdom was temporary. Abijah goes a step further by invading Israel as the major objective of his short reign.

The Chronicler deals with these matters quickly because he wants to tell us all about Abijah's appeal to the ten northern tribes before he defeats them on the battlefield. Campaigning his way deep into the heartland of Israel, he climbs a mountain in the hill country of Ephraim, where he can stand at a safe distance and still be heard.[4] Abijah didn't walk his talk in these verses, but the Chronicler wants us to listen to what he said. It is a fantastic summary of God's purposes for Israel, a manifesto for God's people.

Abijah's name means *My Father Is The Lord*. Based on the words of his manifesto alone, we would certainly believe it. He declares to the ten northern tribes that the battle they are about to fight together is a contest that will prove which of their kingdoms is the true Israel. Is it the southern kingdom, which serves the God of Israel, or is it the northern kingdom, which has turned against him to worship false idols instead? Abijah reminds the northern tribes that *"the Lord, the God of Israel, has*

---

[3] The Hebrew text should be translated that Maakah was the *granddaughter* of Absalom, through the marriage of his daughter Tamar to Uriel of Gibeah (2 Samuel 14:27). Gibeah was King Saul's home town and a very sinful city in the territory of Benjamin (1 Samuel 15:34; Judges 19:11–30).

[4] Zemaraim means *Two Fleeces of Wool*, so it may have been the same location in the hill country of Ephraim where Gideon laid down his two fleeces before battle. See Judges 6:34–40 and 7:24.

given the kingship of Israel to David and his descendants forever".[5] By rejecting David's dynasty and running after Jeroboam, they have rejected God himself. They are no more "Israel" than the Gentiles.[6]

Abijah depicts Jeroboam as a rebellious servant, who nursed an ambition above his station and who took advantage of Rehoboam's youthful folly.[7] This is a bit rich, given that Rehoboam was aged forty-one when he came to the throne! It also fails to mention that the Lord stirred that ambition in Jeroboam's heart by sending Ahijah of Shiloh to prophesy that he would become king of the ten northern tribes as a result of Solomon's sin. Nevertheless, what Abijah says here is largely true. By rejecting David's dynasty, the northern tribes rejected the idea that the throne of Israel belonged to the Lord and that only he could decide who ought to steward it for him. By rejecting David's dynasty, the northern tribes had also turned their back on the Lord's Temple. That's why the northern kingdom was ruled by nine different dynasties in just 208 years, before it fell in 722 BC, well over a century before the southern kingdom. The kings of Judah had their failings, but the northern kingdom never had a single godly king.[8]

Abijah points out to the northern tribes that their rejection of David's dynasty has quickly led to their rejection of the God of Israel. Their vast army might outnumber Judah's two to one, but it is accompanied by golden calf idols and by priests who cannot

[5] In 13:5, Abijah calls God's covenant with David in 1 Chronicles 17 *"a covenant of salt"* because costly salt accompanied the sacrifices by which it was sealed (Leviticus 2:13 and Mark 9:49). The Lord says something similar in Numbers 18:19. Salt is a preservative, so a covenant sealed by salt-sacrifice was seen as irrevocable.

[6] This theme of *"the true Israel"* is picked up by John 1:47 and 8:39; Romans 9:6–9, and Revelation 2:9 and 3:9.

[7] The Hebrew phrase *"sons of Belial"*, which Abijah uses in 13:7, occurs over twenty times in the Old Testament. It means literally *"sons of yokelessness"* and it refers to anyone who refuses outright to submit to the Lord.

[8] This is a warning against any church split which the Lord has not expressly commanded. Invariably, the leaders of the new regime turn out to be even less godly than the leaders of the old regime.

trace their ancestry back to Aaron and Levi.[9] All those who can do so have emigrated south to become part of the real Israel. *"Didn't you drive out the priests of the Lord, the sons of Aaron, and the Levites, and make priests of your own as the peoples of other lands do?"*[10]

In other words, the northern kingdom has become a pagan nation, while the kingdom of Judah remains the true *"kingdom of the Lord"*. It is ruled by God's chosen royal dynasty. It is home to God's chosen Temple, where each day God's chosen priests offer sacrifices, present sacred bread, burn incense and light the lamps in his sanctuary.

> *The Lord is our God, and we have not forsaken him... We are observing the requirements of the Lord our God. But you have forsaken him. God is with us; he is our leader... People of Israel, do not fight against the Lord, the God of your ancestors, for you will not succeed.*

The fact that Abijah failed to practise what he preaches here does not make it untrue. This is a magnificent marching manifesto for God's people. In order to prove it, the Lord allows the army of Israel to spring an ambush on the army of Judah. This scares them into acting as the people that their king has just declared them to be. The priests blow their trumpets, the soldiers cry out to the Lord in prayer, and the Lord enables them to rout the soldiers of the northern kingdom. This is so important to the Chronicler that he ignores the subtle art of storytelling to explain bluntly that *"God routed Jeroboam and all Israel... God delivered them into their hands... The people of Judah were victorious because they*

---

[9] Two armies of 400,000 and 800,000 men fighting in a single battle, with 500,000 casualties, makes this one of the largest battles in ancient history. Such numbers fit with 1 Chronicles 21:5, yet it must have been a day of unprecedented carnage. Even so, Jehoshaphat refused to repent and was struck down in 909 BC.

[10] Before we criticise this, let's consider whether every church leader today has truly been called and appointed by the Lord. It is possible that we have our own systems for self-appointment and self-promotion.

relied on the Lord... Jeroboam did not regain power... The Lord struck him down and he died."[11]

The chapter ends with honesty that Abijah didn't practise all he preached. He ignored the Lord's command in Deuteronomy 17:17 not to marry many wives, just like Solomon and Rehoboam. As a result of his sin, he died young like Jeroboam, but as he died he bequeathed this marvellous marching manifesto to God's people.

---

[11] Abijah captured Bethel, where Jeroboam's golden calves had their shrine (1 Kings 12:26–33). Sadly, he soon lost it and the shrines were quickly repaired and restored to their idolatry (2 Kings 10:29 and 23:15).

Son of David
(2 Chronicles 14:1 – 15:19)

"Asa did what was good and right in the eyes of the Lord his God."

(2 Chronicles 14:2)

I love to take my son to watch West Ham United play football. When our team is losing, and one of our star substitutes comes on to play, there is nothing like the roar of hope that reverberates around the stadium. That's how I feel when I read about the reign of King Asa of Judah. Here at last we have somebody who looks like a real Son of David.

King Asa ruled from 910 to 869 BC. That's one year longer than either David or Solomon, and his reign harks back to theirs. We are told that *"in his days the country was at peace for ten years"* – something which has not been true since the heady days of Solomon. It is a sign that things are getting back on track under a new and better Son of David. The Chronicler devotes forty-seven verses to his reign, compared with only sixteen verses in 1 Kings, because Asa serves as a picture of the true *Messiah*. The Chronicler rejoices that *"Asa did what was good and right in the eyes of the Lord his God."*[1]

---

[1] Careful readers will spot that the Chronicler makes an important change here in copying from 1 Kings 15:11. He omits the second half of the statement that *"Asa did what was right in the eyes of the Lord, **as his father David had done**."* This serves as an early warning that Asa is going to disappoint us in chapter 16.

In 14:1–5, Asa leads Judah in a spiritual revival. He destroys all of their *"high places"*.[2] He demolishes their foreign altars and destroys their foreign idols. From now on, everybody in his kingdom must worship the Lord alone and obey every commandment in his Law.[3]

In 14:6–16, Asa strengthens the network of fortified cities which Rehoboam built on the borders of Judah. If this sets our alarm bells ringing, given that those fortress cities were a symbol of Rehoboam's self-reliance, then the Chronicler quickly allays our fears by assuring us that his grandson knew full well that the Lord was the true Protector of his kingdom. Asa knew that all of his peace and prosperity flowed from the fact that *"we have sought the Lord our God; we sought him and he has given us rest on every side."*

This becomes apparent when Zerah the Cushite marches out to invade Judah with an army of 300 chariots and countless thousands of foot soldiers. This may be another name for Pharaoh Osorkon I, the son of Shishak, who ruled from 922 to 887 BC, or it may be the name of his top general. Either way, Asa is in trouble, and he knows precisely where to turn.[4] He cries out to the God of Israel, *"Lord, there is no one like you to help the powerless against the mighty. Help us, Lord our God, for we rely on you... Lord, you are our God; do not let mere mortals prevail against you."* Asa believes the manifesto that his father preached but failed to follow, and the Lord responds with delight to this

---

[2] There were two types of "high place" – those where idols were worshipped and those where the Lord was worshipped away from the Temple and contrary to his Law (Leviticus 17:1–9). Since Asa both removed them (14:5) and failed to remove them (15:17), it seems he removed the first type of "high place" but not the second.

[3] Asherah means *Happiness* in Hebrew, and she was a Canaanite fertility goddess. An Asherah *pole* was a sacred pillar erected next to an altar of Baal in order to worship both deities together. The Chronicler does not mention their shrine prostitutes, but we are told about them in 1 Kings 14:23–24 and 15:12.

[4] The Valley of Zephathah controlled the road from Egypt into Judah, so if Asa lost this battle he would lose his entire kingdom. Asa takes a stand near one of the fortified cities his father built to guard the valley (11:8).

better Son of David.[5] He routs the Egyptian army so completely that it never quite recovers. *"The Lord and his forces"* bring back great quantities of plunder to Jerusalem.[6]

In 15:1–7, the Lord sends his prophet Azariah to meet Asa on his way home from victory on the battlefield.[7] He brings encouragement from the Holy Spirit that Asa needs to keep on acting as a true Son of David. Azariah prophesies that the people of the southern kingdom are the true Israel and that they are worshipping the true God, led by the true priests and in possession of the true Law.[8] This is not a moment for Asa to go back home to relax in his palace. His spiritual revival of Judah must be completed.[9] *"The Lord is with you when you are with him. If you seek him, he will be found by you, but if you forsake him, he will forsake you... Be strong and do not give up, for your work will be rewarded."*[10]

In 15:8–19, Asa responds to this prophecy by finishing the work that he has started. Having already demolished the *"high places"* of Judah, he now roots out any foreign idols lurking elsewhere in his territory. When he captures some border towns from the northern kingdom of Israel, he extends his

---

[5] Asa's prayer presents this battle between Egypt and Judah as a contest between the Name of the Lord and the names of mortal men. Because he sees his army as the army of the Lord, he is granted a stunning victory.

[6] Cush refers to Upper Egypt, so this event echoes Exodus 12:36. It is also a reversal of what happened to the sinful Rehoboam in 12:9–11. Chronicles is inviting us to choose the path of obedience ourselves.

[7] We know nothing more about this Azariah, except that his name means *The Lord Has Helped Me*.

[8] Note the Devil's three-step strategy in 15:3. He seeks to deprive God's people of their confidence in his Word, which destroys their confidence in his leaders and ultimately destroys their confidence in God himself.

[9] The Chronicler continues to describe the southern kingdom as *"Judah and Benjamin"*, despite the fact that most Benjaminites joined the northern kingdom. This is because the ones who went south flourished and came back in large numbers from the exile (Ezra 1:5; 4:1 and 10:9; Nehemiah 11:3–8 and Philippians 3:5).

[10] The Chronicler wants to speak these words to the Jews after the exile, and his words apply to modern readers too. The success of our churches does not depend on our seeking out new methods, but on our seeking out the Lord. Note that, in 15:2 and 15, it's not our seeking that finds God, but God who graciously permits us to find him.

revival into that new territory. He captures those border towns in response to King Baasha of Israel sealing off his border in a vain attempt to stop large numbers of northerners from emigrating south to become part of Asa's godly kingdom.[11] Their new king assembles them at the Temple in Jerusalem and welcomes their participation in the lavish sacrifices which celebrate Judah's great victory over Egypt. What matters now is not which tribe of Israel a person is from, but whether or not that person is part of the "true Israel". To emphasise this, Asa commands his subjects to surrender their whole lives to the pursuit of the true God of Israel. Anybody who refuses will be executed – the spiritual stakes are simply that high.[12] The southern kingdom must respond to Azariah's prophecy. They must seek the Lord and find him.

The great crescendo of these verses is the moment when King Asa deposes his own grandmother from her position of power in the palace as the widow of Rehoboam. She has been worshipping the pagan goddess Asherah, which reveals her to be a true granddaughter of Absalom and a true descendant of King Saul, who has wormed her wicked way into the royal house of David. When Asa burns her foul idol in the Kidron Valley, which lies between the Temple Solomon built for the Lord on Mount Moriah and the temples Solomon built for pagan idols on the Mount of Olives, it is an action that reveals him to be a true Son of David.

David's dynasty has finally produced another man after God's own heart. The throne of Judah has finally come to a new ruler who has firmly set his heart to seek the Lord.[13]

---

[11] We are told more about this tussle in 16:1–6. Church leaders do not have to worry about how to grow their congregations. If they preach God's Word faithfully, then people will come and join them.

[12] Don't be too shocked by this. It was commanded by the Law, in Deuteronomy 13:6–9 and 17:2–7.

[13] 2 Chronicles 15:12–15 echoes 12:14 and precedes 16:9. The Lord is serious when he tells us: *Get set, go!*

Get Set Again
(2 Chronicles 16:1–14)

"For the eyes of the Lord range throughout the earth to strengthen those whose hearts are fully committed to him."

(2 Chronicles 16:9)

Asa is a good king, but even good kings can turn bad. In chapters 14–15, the Chronicler presents him as a true Son of David, but he is honest in chapter 16 that Asa had his own Bathsheba moment. Out of the blue, this good king set his heart on evil instead.

King Asa was a poster boy for the Chronicler's assertion that godly action flows from a firm decision to set our hearts to seek the Lord. He is the man about whom the Chronicler said in 15:17, *"Asa's heart was fully committed to the Lord"*. But then suddenly, Asa allows his heart to be drawn away to other things. He needs to get set all over again.

It all begins with trouble across the border with the northern kingdom of Israel. One of Jeroboam's generals has overthrown and slaughtered his dynasty. Baasha's major worry for his new dynasty is that large numbers of Israelites are fleeing south over the border to become part of the spiritual revival which is taking place in Judah.[1] He therefore fortifies the border to prevent anyone from crossing it, determined that the northern tribes will either worship his golden calves

---

[1] There is a copying error in the text of 16:1. Baasha ruled from 908 to 886 BC, so he was no longer alive in the thirty-sixth year of Asa's reign. The original Hebrew text probably said *"the sixteenth year"*, rather than *"the thirty-sixth year"*. Alternatively, the scribe may have written *"Baasha"* instead of *"Omri"*, who ruled from 885 to 874 BC.

or not worship at all. Asa cannot permit this blockade of his kingdom, but instead of turning to the God who gave him victory over the Egyptian army, he directs his gaze towards an earthly helper.

There is a new power arising in the north. King Ben-Hadad of Aram is expanding his empire from his capital in Damascus. Asa therefore spots an opportunity for the two of them to work together in a pincer movement against Baasha. The only problem is that Ben-Hadad already has a military alliance with the kingdom of Israel, which is why Baasha is able to concentrate all of his forces on blockading his southern border. Asa knows that, if he can persuade Ben-Hadad to exchange an alliance with Israel for an alliance with Judah, then Baasha will be unable to fight a war on two fronts, but tempting Ben-Hadad into betraying his present ally will require a lot of money.

Asa hurries to the Temple courtyard, but not to do what Solomon expected the kings of Judah to do when foreign kings amassed troops on their border. In the prayer that he prayed at the dedication of his Temple, Solomon imagined his successors coming to its courtyards in order to lay national crises at the feet of the Lord. The young King Asa might have done this, since he was painfully aware of his dependence on the Lord. The older and more experienced King Asa, however, has become self-reliant. He has begun to believe his own court propaganda about the role he played in routing the Egyptian army. He thinks that he knows how to solve his problems without enlisting the intervention of the Lord. At first, he appears to be right. The army of Aram and the army of Judah make gains in the north and south of Israel.[2]

But suddenly a prophet named Hanani appears and delivers the Lord's verdict on Asa's actions. What he says

---

[2] The two centres for golden calf worship in the northern kingdom were Bethel and Dan. God judged one of those cities in 13:19, and now he judges the other in 16:4. The Arameans target cities in the north which control the trade route from Damascus to the Mediterranean. The Assyrians do the same in 2 Kings 15:29.

stands in contrast to Azariah's encouragement in chapter 15. He declares that Asa's actions are proof he has no longer set his heart to serve the Lord. He is no longer like the northerners who are streaming over the border because they have "**set their hearts** on seeking the Lord" (11:16). He has become like his grandfather Rehoboam, whose sins stemmed from the fact that "**he had not set his heart** on seeking the Lord" (12:14). Asa has forgotten the discipleship lesson that we learned together a few chapters ago. He needs to relearn the lesson and to say afresh to himself: *Ready, get set, go!*

The heart of Hanani's prophecy lies in verse 9. King Asa has been foolish, because if he had relied on the Lord then he would not just have resisted Israel – he would have been empowered to conquer Aram too.[3] His man-made solution has granted him a reprieve, but God's solution would have granted him a mighty victory, like the one he enjoyed over the Egyptian army. Hanani therefore calls the foolish king of Judah to set his heart afresh to follow the Lord by encouraging him in verse 9 that *"The eyes of the Lord range throughout the earth to strengthen those whose hearts are fully committed to him."*[4]

At this point, Asa reveals that he is not a true Son of David at all. Rather than repent, he rages. He throws Hanani into prison for daring to prophesy words that he would prefer not to hear.[5] When some of his godly subjects rise up as advocates for Hanani, he brutally oppresses them. The Lord needs to teach Asa the hard way what he tried to teach him gently in 15:6. When troubles befall God's people, it is never a sign of God's

---

[3] The gold and silver that Asa gives to Aram enables it to grow into a regional superpower. When the Arameans threaten to destroy Judah several times in the rest of 2 Chronicles, it is a result of Asa's folly.

[4] We can tell from Zechariah 4:10 and Revelation 5:6 that *"the eyes of the Lord"* is a reference to the Holy Spirit. He is eager to strengthen God's people, so he seeks out hearts that are set towards faith and obedience.

[5] True prophets of God must be prepared to be unpopular. For every Azariah who is received with open arms, there is a Hanani who is received with anger. Hanani appears to have seen this coming, since he has already trained up his son Jehu to carry on prophesying without him (19:2 and 20:34, and 1 Kings 16:1–7).

weakness, but only ever of his strength. He permits those he loves to suffer when it is the only way to reset their hard hearts towards repentance.[6]

The Lord strikes Asa down with a *"disease in his feet"* (verse 12). We do not know what this disease was, but we do know that the Hebrew word for *feet* is sometimes used in the Old Testament as a euphemism for *genitals*.[7] The Lord hits Asa where it hurts to help him set his heart afresh for holiness. And here's what's really ironic: the name Asa means *Healer*.

There is a lesson for each of us here. Setting our hearts to serve the Lord while we are young is only half the battle. We need to keep resetting them to serve the Lord with each new season of our lives.[8] Asa is willing to pay money for doctors to heal him, but he is unwilling to accept heart surgery from the Lord. The bonfire that burns at his funeral is a sober warning that the fires of hell await those who refuse to set their hearts on God.[9]

There is also a more general lesson for us in these verses. In chapters 14–15, we dared to dream that Asa might prove to be a true Son of David. The Chronicler uses Asa's folly in chapter 16 to disabuse us of that false hope. This is not the *Messiah* we are looking for.

---

[6] This is why we must never regard church setbacks as satanic victories over an enfeebled God. We will see in 18:12–27 that the Devil is like a dog on a leash to God. God only permits him to appear victorious when he wants to use him to discipline his sinful people. As soon as a church repents, it finds that 16:9 is true.

[7] For example, in Isaiah 7:20.

[8] Ecclesiastes 7:8 warns us that how we end our lives is even more important than how we begin them.

[9] This bonfire does not refer to cremation, since that was not a Hebrew tradition. Nor does it indicate with any certainty Asa's eternal destiny. Even in his unfaithfulness to God, God was faithful to him.

False Unity
(2 Chronicles 17:1 – 19:3)

"Jehoshaphat… allied himself with Ahab by marriage… 'I am as you are, and my people as your people; we will join you in the war.'"

(2 Chronicles 18:1, 3)

King Jehoshaphat of Judah believed passionately in the unity of God's people. From the very outset of his reign, he dreamed about reunifying the twelve tribes of Israel as one nation. The Chronicler gives us several clues that it filled his thoughts night and day.

In 17:1-2, we are told that the new king of Judah *"strengthened himself against Israel"*. He stationed soldiers in the towns his father Asa had captured from Baasha, hoping to use them as a springboard for the total reunification of the northern and southern kingdoms.

In 17:3-6, we are told that *"The Lord was with Jehoshaphat because he followed the ways of his father David"*. This is the first time that the Chronicler has compared any of the kings of the divided kingdom of Judah to the united rule of David. It signifies that Jehoshaphat has rejected the sins of Solomon, which divided the twelve tribes. Because he has set his heart on seeking the Lord, he removes the *"high places"* that were rebuilt during the final years of his father.[1] He destroys any

---

[1] As with King Asa in 14:5 and 15:17, the Chronicler says that Jehoshaphat both removed the *"high places"* (17:6) and didn't remove the *"high places"* (20:33). That's confusing! There were two types of "high place" – those where idols were worshipped and those where the Lord was worshipped away from the Temple and contrary to his Law (Leviticus 17:1–9). Jehoshaphat removed the first type of "high place" but not the second.

images of Baal and Asherah that have crept over the border from the increasingly backslidden northern kingdom.[2]

In 17:7–11, Jehoshaphat launches a missionary campaign to reunify God's people under God.[3] He commissions priests and Levites and other royal officials to preach throughout the kingdom of Judah from what are now the first five books of our Bibles.[4] A fresh fear of God begins to fall on the southern kingdom, and very soon those missionaries are also preaching God's Word to people across the border. Sadly, there is no record here of people from the ten northern tribes repenting of Baal-worship and returning to the Lord. The Philistines come to see Jehoshaphat with gifts of silver. The Arabs come to see him with sacrifices of sheep and goats. But we are not told about any similar response from the northern tribes of Israel to this preaching of faith in the Lord.

In 17:12–19, it starts to look as though Jehoshaphat may succeed in reunifying the twelve tribes of Israel. Because he sets his heart to serve the Lord, he is blessed by the Lord.[5] He becomes more and more powerful and builds more and more fortress cities. He raises a mighty army of over a million men. Suddenly, his dream of unity seems achievable.

The Devil loves disunity. He hates it when God's people bury their differences and come together under a united banner. He has a favourite tactic to stop it, which he uses here: *false unity*. In 18:1, he tempts Jehoshaphat into thinking that he can reunify God's people by fleshly means. Before we know it, Jehoshaphat has joined the kingdom of Judah to the

[2] By now, Baal had become the principal idol of the northern kingdom, due to the influence of King Ahab's new wife Jezebel. She was a Phoenician princess, whose father's name was Ethbaal (1 Kings 16:30–33).

[3] Jehoshaphat ruled alongside his sick and dying father for the first three years of his reign. He could only begin his missionary campaign once the stubborn King Asa was out of the way.

[4] Spiritual revival and the preaching of God's Word invariably go hand in hand. To pray for revival without planning for Gospel preaching is to live in a state of spiritual unreality.

[5] These verses illustrate the message of 15:2: seek the Lord and be blessed, or forsake the Lord and be cursed.

kingdom of Israel by the marriage of his son Jehoram to Ahab's daughter Athaliah.

At a moment when Christians in Victorian Britain were calling for unity at any price, Charles Spurgeon spoke out against the Devil's temptation to foster false unity.

> *A new religion has been initiated, which is no more Christianity than chalk is cheese... The atonement is rejected, the inspiration of Scripture is derided, the Holy Spirit is degraded into an influence, the punishment of sin is turned into fiction, and the resurrection into a myth, and yet these enemies of our faith expect us to call them brethren, and maintain a confederacy with them!*[6]

Spurgeon was criticised for being divisive, but he pointed people to the foolishness of Jehoshaphat and insisted that false unity is even more dangerous than false doctrine:

> *A chasm is opening between the men who believe their Bibles and the men who are prepared for an advance upon Scripture... We cannot hold the inspiration of the Word, and yet reject it; we cannot believe in the atonement and deny it; we cannot hold the doctrine of the Fall and yet talk of the evolution of spiritual life from human nature; we cannot recognise the punishment of the impenitent and yet indulge the "larger hope". One way or the other we must go... With steadfast faith let us take our places; not in anger, not in the spirit of suspicion or division, but in watchfulness and resolve. Let us not pretend to a fellowship which we do not feel.*[7]

---

[6] Charles Spurgeon wrote this in his *Sword and Trowel* magazine (August 1887).
[7] Also from *The Sword and Trowel* magazine (September 1887).

In 18:2–34, we discover the foul fruit of false unity. King Ahab of Israel loves the idea of unity, just so long as it is a unity based around his own sinful aims. He has made Baal the new national god of Israel, so the Lord has sent the Arameans to conquer some of his territory east of the River Jordan in order to humble him into repentance. Ahab asks Jehoshaphat to put his talk of unity into action by sending the army of Judah onto the battlefield alongside the army of Israel. Jehoshaphat's response in 18:3 serves as a mantra for his reign: *"I am as you are, and my people as your people; we will join you in the war."*[8]

Jehoshaphat should have noticed that the bulls and sheep Ahab slaughtered were not sacrificed to the Lord. He should have run a mile when he requested to hear from a prophet of the Lord and Ahab responded by summoning 400 prophets of Baal. Jehoshaphat should have grown suspicious when Ahab disguised himself before the battle but insisted that Jehoshaphat wear his royal robes, making him the primary target for the Aramean archers. But that's what false unity does. It blinds us to the truth, it exposes us to dangers and it wastes our strength on projects which are not blessed by God. Ahab's talk of unity was simply a smokescreen to hide his own sinful schemes.

In 19:1–3, the Lord sends the prophet Jehu to expose the foolishness of Jehoshaphat's false unity. Jehu is the son of the prophet who was imprisoned by Jehoshaphat's father Asa, so he is very brave when he asks the king, *"Should you help the wicked and love those who hate the Lord? Because of this, the wrath of the Lord is on you."* The Hebrew word here for *love* is *'ahab*, which is deliberately ironic. In pursuing a fleshly form of unity through a man-made marriage alliance, Jehoshaphat has brought great trouble on David's dynasty.

Real unity amongst God's people can never come about by wishful thinking and fleshly initiatives. It can only come through

---

8 Jehoshaphat is far too hasty in his reply. He takes no time to pray before saying "yes" to Ahab. What is worse, he does this at a *threshing floor* (18:9), the very place where wheat and chaff are meant to be divided!

preaching God's Word, as Jehoshaphat initially sets out to do. It is only when God's people surrender the whole of their lives to God that they are able to surrender to one another whatever it is that divides them. Jehoshaphat began his reign like David, but he finished it like Solomon by trying to forge false unity.

Let Off the Leash
(2 Chronicles 18:18–34)

"Now the Lord has put a deceiving spirit in the mouths of these prophets of yours. The Lord has decreed disaster for you."

(2 Chronicles 18:22)

In the movie *The Usual Suspects*, Verbal uses a well-known argument that the greatest trick that Satan ever pulled was fooling the world that he doesn't exist. The Bible would suggest that this is true. Most of the time, Satan lurks in the shadows, preferring to do his work undetected and unopposed, but every once in a while, he is tempted out of hiding by a larger-than-usual opportunity to oppose God's purposes for his people. We saw him do so in 1 Chronicles 21, where he enticed David to conduct a sinful census of Israel. Now he does so again on the eve of the great battle between Israel and Judah and the Arameans.[1]

King Ahab has been heavily influenced by his wife Jezebel, the daughter of a priest of Baal who killed his master to become the new king of Tyre. She has persuaded Ahab to make the Phoenician idol Baal the new national god of Israel.[2] When Jehoshaphat asks to hear advice from a prophet of the Lord before engaging in battle with the Arameans, Ahab therefore

199

---

[1] Other than in the book of Job, Satan is only mentioned by name four times in the entire Old Testament – once in 1 Chronicles and three times in Zechariah. The description of demonic activity in this chapter is also unusual.

[2] Jezebel is not mentioned by name in 1 and 2 Chronicles, but she is mentioned twenty-one times in 1 and 2 Kings. Revelation 2:20 suggests that a powerful demon was at work within her, and we are told in 1 Kings 21:25 that Ahab sinned because he was *"urged on by Jezebel his wife"*.

summons 400 prophets of Baal instead.[3] One of them is named Zedekiah, which means *The Lord Is Righteous*, and he prophesies in the name of the Lord, but Jehoshaphat sees through his pretence of piety. Jehoshaphat demands, *"Is there no longer a prophet of the Lord here whom we can enquire of?"*[4]

There is one named Micaiah, which means *Who Is Like The Lord?*[5] At first, he mimics the prophets of Baal by encouraging Ahab to *"Attack and be victorious… for they will be given into your hand."* Spotting at once that Micaiah is being sarcastic, Ahab commands him to confess what he has really heard spoken in the Lord's heavenly throne room about the forthcoming battle. When Micaiah predicts that the king of Israel will be killed in battle and that his army will be scattered, the king dismisses him in anger. He refuses to believe that the Devil is at work in the prophets of Baal, attempting to lure the joint armies of Israel and Judah to their destruction at the hands of the Arameans.

Micaiah refuses to be dismissed so easily. The king has asked to hear what he has seen in the throne room of heaven, so hear he shall. The Devil is lurking in the shadows but this prophet of the Lord is determined to expose his tactics to the leaders of the twelve tribes of Israel. Micaiah declares that he has seen a war council in heaven. Multitudes of angels and demons have assembled before God's throne to enforce the day of his great judgment on a nation that has turned away to worship Baal. The Lord has decreed that Ahab must die on the battlefield of Ramoth Gilead. A demon has offered to achieve that goal by speaking lies through his false prophets in the name of Lord. Perhaps surprisingly, the Lord has granted it permission to go

---

[3] A few years earlier, the prophet Elijah had slaughtered Ahab's 450 prophets of Baal and 400 prophets of Asherah (1 Kings 18:19 and 40). These prophets therefore represent the resurrection of a slaughtered order.

[4] Zedekiah's prophecy sounds convincing because it echoes Deuteronomy 33:13–17. Nevertheless, it is utter fabrication. Those who pursue false unity easily fall prey to false prophets (2 Corinthians 11:14).

[5] Elijah is mentioned seventy-nine times in 1 and 2 Kings, but only once in 1 and 2 Chronicles. He was evidently elsewhere on the eve of this battle, since 1 Kings 22 agrees that they were forced to consult Micaiah instead.

out and deceive. The demon which is at work in Zedekiah and his friends has been sent by the Lord![6]

Many readers get confused here. A few get so offended that they stop reading, but most merely shrug their shoulders, ignore what they have read and quickly move on. But we have learned to look for God in such small details in 1 and 2 Chronicles. You see, this isn't an isolated incident in Scripture. It summarises what the Bible says about the Devil.

In Chronicles 21:1, you will remember that the Chronicler altered some of the words that he was copying from 2 Samuel 24:1. The earlier writer stated that *the Lord* exposed David's pride by inciting him to take a census of Israel, yet the Chronicler states that it was *Satan* who incited him to do so. We must not rush to smooth over this discrepancy, because the Devil really is in the detail. Martin Luther referred to him as *"God's Satan"* because he can only act on the Lord's say-so. The Bible depicts him as a fierce dog on a tight leash. God only lets him off the leash to act within some very strict parameters whenever he sees a way to use Satan's evil schemes to promote an even greater good.

In Job 1:6–12 and 2:1–7, we are given a similar picture to the one which is witnessed by the prophet Micaiah. Satan needs to seek permission from the Lord in the heavenly realm before he can cause any trouble for Job. The Lord permits it, under strict conditions, because he can accomplish his Kingdom purposes more completely if Satan is made to step out of the shadows and work in the open. We see something similar in Judges 9:23 and 1 Samuel 16:14, where *"an evil spirit from the Lord"* afflicts two men who see themselves as the true kings of Israel, rather than as stewards of God's throne.

In Matthew 8:29–32 and Luke 8:28–33, we discover again that demons need to seek permission from Jesus before they can wreak any of their havoc in the world. They beg him, like

---

[6] Don't be surprised by this. It happens in Isaiah 19:14 and John 13:27. The Apostle Paul warns us in Romans 1:21–28 and 2 Thessalonians 2:11 that it also happens all around us today.

little dogs begging to be let off the leash, before they are able to enter a herd of pigs on a mountainside. They have no idea that Jesus only consents because he is far wiser than they are. He has seen a way that he can use the maddening power of demons to rid the region of a meat forbidden by the Jewish Law. In the same way, we are told in Luke 22:31 that Satan needed to ask permission from God before he could tempt Peter to deny Jesus three times on the eve of his crucifixion. God permitted it so that he could expose Peter's pride and prepare him to lead the Church after the ascension of Jesus back into heaven. God knows how to use the Devil's work for good.[7]

That is what happens here. King Ahab of Israel refuses to listen to Micaiah's warning. He throws him into prison and hurries to his death on the battlefield. Jehoshaphat persists in his false unity but, when the battle turns against him, he finally comes to his senses. Ahab enters battle in disguise so that he will not be targeted by the Aramean archers, yet the Lord ensures that he is fatally wounded *"at random"* all the same.[8] Jehoshaphat foolishly agrees to make himself the primary target for the Aramean archers, yet when his folly dawns on him, *"Jehoshaphat cried out, and the Lord helped him."*

So be encouraged. If you suspect the Devil is at work around you, then it can only be because the Lord has permitted it for your greater good. "God's Satan" may have been let off the leash for a moment, but the Lord will help you if you cry out to him.

---

[7] The crucifixion is the greatest example of this. Satan caused it (John 13:27), but God was behind it (Acts 2:23), allowing Satan to crucify his Son so that the whole world could be saved.

[8] The Chronicler expects us to see through this ironic statement in verse 33. God used Satan's evil for his greater good.

"Our God, will you not judge them? For we have no power to face this vast army that is attacking us. We do not know what to do, but our eyes are on you."

(2 Chronicles 20:12)

The name Jehoshaphat means *The Lord Judges*. After his shameful defeat at the Battle of Ramoth Gilead, he reset his heart towards God and resolved to live up to his name.

In 19:1–3, the prophet Jehu tells him two things.[1] First, that the Lord is angry with him for pursuing false unity with the idolatrous northern kingdom. Second, that the Lord has delivered him from the Arameans because *"you... have set your heart on seeking God."*

In 19:4–11, Jehoshaphat demonstrates this by renewing his missionary campaign to reunify God's people through a shared repentance towards the Lord. He again sends out his touring team of priests and Levites and royal officials to preach from what we now know as the first five books of our Bibles. Having attempted to reunify the twelve tribes by fleshly means and failed, he now returns to the means that the Lord has given us: the preaching of God's Word by the power of God's Spirit. The Chronicler emphasises that Jehoshaphat goes out with them personally, not just to Judah but also to the places that his

---

[1] Jehu means *The Lord Is He* – in other words, *The Lord Is The True God*. He warns us that God regards false unity with nominal believers as a way for Christians to *"help the wicked and love those who hate the Lord"*.

father captured across the border in the northern kingdom of Israel.[2]

To bolster this spiritual revival, and to help it spread to the neighbouring nations, Jehoshaphat appoints some of his missionary team to serve as judges in Jerusalem and in the fortified cities which defend the border crossings in and out of Judah.[3] In ancient Israel, judges did more than merely issue rulings in court cases. They were teachers of God's Law and rulers of God's people, as can be seen by what they get up to in the book of Judges. The man whose name means *The Lord Judges* or *The Lord Rules* is therefore setting up a network of judges to rule his kingdom for the Lord. They are accountable to the high priest and to the leader of the tribe of Judah for how well they steward the revival, helping it to spread across the border.[4]

In 20:1–2, the Devil launches a counterattack to this renewed spiritual revival.[5] He entices a large Moabite and Ammonite army to invade the land.[6] It breaches Jehoshaphat's network of border fortresses and reaches the oasis of En Gedi, on the western shores of the Dead Sea. This is where David hid in caves from King Saul, so it reveals to us whether or not Jehoshaphat is truly a Son of David.[7] Will he panic, like his

---

[2] *"The hill country of Ephraim"* was the southernmost region of the northern kingdom of Israel.

[3] The Chronicler probably devotes a whole chapter to this because the Jews had managed to restore a similar system of judges after the exile, even if they had failed to restore their king. They had also restored the division between the rule of the high priest and the rule of tribal elders that is described in 19:11.

[4] Ultimately, they are accountable to the Lord (19:6). So are we in our workplaces today (Colossians 3:23–24). The Chronicler insists in 19:7 that it is healthy for us to fear the Lord as the Judge of how we work for him.

[5] Demonic counterattack is part and parcel of revival. See Exodus 17:5–16 and 1 Samuel 7:1–7. The Chronicler gives us his number one principle for how to fight off such spiritual warfare in 20:15.

[6] Edomites were in this army too (*Mount Seir* in 20:10), but the Hebrew text of 20:2 says it came from *Aram* – in other words, these were allies of the Arameans who were following up their victory at Ramoth Gilead. Since the Hebrew words for Aram and Edom look similar, the word is mistranslated by some English Bibles.

[7] 1 Samuel 23:29 and 24:1.

father Asa, and plunder the Temple treasuries, or will he put his trust in the Lord?

In 20:3–19, Jehoshaphat lives up to his name by hurrying to the Temple, not to steal its gold and silver to buy off the invader, but to do what Solomon envisaged the kings of Judah would do in his prayer of dedication. The Hebrew text of 20:3 says literally that *"Jehoshaphat set his face to seek the Lord"*. He calls his nation to fast from food and to assemble in the Temple courtyard to plead with God to deliver them.[8] Hezekiah does something similar in 2 Kings 19, but this is the only time in the pages of 2 Chronicles that any king of Judah ever does this. Jehoshaphat leads the people in a prayer which proclaims that the Lord is the true Ruler of Judah and of every other foreign nation too. The only reason why God's people dwell in the Promised Land is that he gave it to them. The only reason why the Moabites and Ammonites and Edomites are able to invade it is that the Lord forbade Moses from pouring out his judgment on them when he poured it out on the sinful Canaanites. The Lord must therefore do as Solomon envisaged. He must display his righteousness by proving himself to be the Judge of all the world.[9] *"Our God, will you not judge them? For we have no power to face this vast army that is attacking us. We do not know what to do, but our eyes are on you."*

Suddenly, the Holy Spirit falls on one of the Temple worship leaders, just as David hoped he would. Jahaziel is a Levite from the family of Asaph, so he embodies what David planned for the Lord's Temple in 1 Chronicles 25.[10] He proclaims to Jehoshaphat and the people of Judah that *"The battle is not yours, but God's."* He pinpoints the exact location where they will find the enemy, but he reassures them that *"You will not have to fight this battle. Take up your positions; stand firm and see the deliverance the*

---

[8] The reference to a *"new"* courtyard in 20:5 suggests that Jehoshaphat enlarged it for this occasion.

[9] The reference in 20:13 to *"wives and children and little ones"* emphasises how much hangs in the balance.

[10] Even the name Jahaziel means *He Prophesies For God.*

Lord will give you". Jehoshaphat has no proof that this prophecy is anything more than wishful thinking on the part of Jahaziel, yet he decides to receive it by faith as a word from the Lord. He and the Levites lead the people of Judah in spontaneous faith-filled worship.

In 20:20–30, Jehoshaphat leads out what is left of his army to battle, believing that the outcome will be very different to what happened at Ramoth Gilead. He urges his troops to *"Have faith in the Lord your God and... have faith in his prophets".* Meanwhile the Levites lead the troops in the marching song of David's Tabernacle and Solomon's Temple: *"Give thanks to the Lord, for his love endures forever".* While the soldiers are still singing, the Lord throws the invading army into confusion. The Ammonites and Moabites and Edomites turn on one another and start slaughtering each other.[11] By the time the army of Judah reaches the battlefield, the invading army has become a pile of corpses. It takes them three days to carry off the plunder, and a fourth day to worship the Lord – both on the battlefield and back home in the Temple courtyard – for such a stunning victory.[12]

In 20:31–37, the Chronicler comes back to Jehoshaphat's great dream of reunifying the twelve tribes of Israel. You may have noticed that the Chronicler described the Moabites and Ammonites in 20:29 as *"the enemies of Israel"*, rather than the enemies of Judah, because this is the perfect moment for Jehoshaphat to redouble his missionary effort to convert the northern tribes of Israel back to God. Tragically, he returns instead to his former folly by forging a fresh alliance with the son of Ahab, who has inherited both his father's throne and his father's love of the false god Baal. Helped by his mother Jezebel's friends, Ahaziah builds a new Red Sea fleet of trading ships for Jehoshaphat so that they can restart Solomon's search

---

[11] The Chronicler uses a play on words here in the Hebrew text. Because they *stand* in God's Presence (20:9) and *stand* firm in their faith (20:17), the Lord causes their enemies to *stand* and destroy each other (20:23).

[12] The Valley of Berakah means the Valley of *Praise*. It was evidently renamed in honour of their victory.

for foreign gold together.[13] The prophet Eliezer is forced to confront Jehoshaphat for pursuing false unity yet again: *"Because you have made an alliance with Ahaziah, the Lord will destroy what you have made."*[14]

Jehoshaphat's godly reign therefore ends on a note of failure. He is the closest we have come to finding the true Son of David, but even he is not the *Messiah* we are looking for.[15]

---

[13] That's why the Hebrew text of 20:36–37 describes them as *"ships of Tarshish"* (a Phoenician colony in southern Spain) despite the fact that Ezion Geber was the southernmost port of Judah, on the Red Sea.

[14] We know nothing else about Eliezer, other than that his name means *My God Helps*. Jehu reappears in 20:34 to write a history of the reign of Jehoshaphat, which the Chronicler used as one of his primary sources.

[15] The Chronicler actually understates this. In 2 Kings 3, we read about another near-fatal battle that he fought alongside Ahaziah's younger brother, King Joram of Israel. Note what he says in 2 Kings 3:7!

How God Judges
(2 Chronicles 19:7)

"For with the Lord our God there is no injustice or partiality or bribery."

(2 Chronicles 19:7)

Before we move on from the reign of the man whose name means *The Lord Judges*, let's take a moment to reflect on what he teaches us about how the Lord judges. He makes an important little comment in 19:7, and we have learned to find God in such small things.

Jehoshaphat was eager to bring the twelve tribes of Israel back to a proper understanding of the nature of God. Whenever we neglect the revelation that he has given us through the Scriptures, we end up with a false view of him, so Jehoshaphat sent out missionaries to preach God's Word to his people. In 19:7, he urges them not to forget what the Lord is like and what it truly means for him to be the Judge of all the world: *"Judge carefully, for with the Lord our God there is no injustice or partiality or bribery."*

Jehoshaphat wouldn't want God's people to regard him in the same way as Catherine the Great. The Russian ruler famously boasted that *"I am a dictator: that's my job. And the good Lord will forgive me: that's his job."* Catherine the Great was convinced that God would overlook the fact that she despised the Christian faith and merely used it as a means of manipulating her peasant subjects. She felt no fear of God for having usurped the throne as part of a violent coup against her husband, or for having taken a long string of sordid lovers. She mistook her own low standards and short memory for a clear conscience. She convinced herself that Judgment Day was for other people and not for her.

That's why the first thing Jehoshaphat highlights in this verse is that *the Lord judges people without injustice*. It doesn't matter to him whether they are the lowliest serf in a rural Russian farmhouse or the mightiest Empress in a royal Russian palace. His holy character demands that he will administer equal justice for all. In the words of Hebrews 6:10, *"God is not unjust; he will not forget"*. In the words of Proverbs 17:15, *"Acquitting the guilty and condemning the innocent – the Lord detests them both."*[1] The Bible is very clear. God doesn't just hate it when bad things happen to good people who don't deserve it. He also hates it when bad things don't happen to bad people who do deserve it!

Jehoshaphat is also concerned that God's people should not regard him in the same way as Heinrich Heine. The German poet boasted with his final breath on his deathbed in 1856 that *"Of course God will forgive me: that's his job."*[2] His logic was that he was not a heathen from sub-Saharan Africa, or even a Muslim from its Mediterranean shores. He was a European, and an educated one at that. It seemed unthinkable to Heinrich Heine that the God of heaven would dare to shut the doors of heaven in the face of a wealthy white man whose poems were the praise of every European salon.

That's why the second thing that Jehoshaphat highlights in this verse is that *the Lord judges people without partiality*. He isn't swayed by our appearances – by our ethnicity or by our place in society or by our contribution to the arts. To put it in more modern terms, he pays no attention to our bank balance or to what our friends think of us or to how many followers we

---

[1] The Hebrew word *tō'ēbah* indicates that the idea of allowing unrepentant sinners to go unpunished is an *abomination* to God. Proverbs 18:5 explains why – it would be to defraud of justice those they have sinned against. To gamble on God turning a blind eye to our sin, like an indulgent old uncle, is utter, utter folly.

[2] Quoted by Sigmund Freud in his book *The Joke and Its Relation to the Unconscious* (1905).

have on social media. Jehoshaphat knows how easy it is for us to fool ourselves that God's Judgment Day is not coming, because he himself made that mistake at the Battle of Ramoth Gilead. When the Lord granted him a reprieve, he became determined not to waste it. He would never fool himself about God's justice again.

Jehoshaphat is also concerned that God's people should not regard him in the same way as the American stand-up comedian Emo Philips, who famously joked that he used to pray every night for a bicycle and, when his prayers were not answered, decided to steal a bicycle and pray every night for forgiveness instead! Beneath his joke lay something serious. He was poking fun at the way that many modern Christians behave, as if cheap confession of sin were the same thing as real repentance.

Jehoshaphat addresses this when he states that *the Lord judges people without bribery*. We can't buy off God with sham words of sorrow or with a pledge of better behaviour in the future or with a promise that we will give him a gift on Sunday. If a human judge caught taking bribes can expect to be sacked, then how much more *"Will not the Judge of all the earth do right?"*[3] There is no buying off the God of justice.

With one exception. The first five books of the Bible, which Jehoshaphat commanded should be preached throughout his kingdom, rejoice that God has provided one thing for us that is able to placate his implacable justice. He tells the Israelites in Leviticus 17:11 that *"The life of a creature is in the blood, and I have given it to you to make atonement for yourselves on the altar; it is the blood that makes atonement for one's life."* Although they did not grasp it fully at the time, the innocent animals that they sacrificed on the bronze altar at Moses' Tabernacle and at Solomon's Temple were prophetic pictures of the death of the *Messiah*, who would be nailed to a cross as the Lamb of God –

---

[3] Note that this prayer of Abraham in Genesis 18:25 does not save Sodom. It hastens Sodom's destruction.

the only sacrifice for sin, whose blood alone delivers people from God's judgment.[4]

We need to respond to this personally. Let's not fool ourselves, like Catherine the Great and Heinrich Heine and Emo Philips, that God's love for us means that he will set aside his perfect justice for our benefit. Let's take to heart the warning of Jesus in Matthew 7:21–23:

> *Not everyone who says to me, "Lord, Lord," will enter the kingdom of heaven, but only the one who does the will of my Father who is in heaven. Many will say to me on that day, "Lord, Lord," ... I will tell them plainly, "I never knew you. Away from me, you evildoers!"*

Let's also face up to what this means for those around us. Jehoshaphat issues us with a warning in 19:10, which echoes similar warnings in Ezekiel and Acts. If we keep the message of God's judgment to ourselves, then he will hold us guilty of the sin of bloodshed.[5] He will consider people's fatal complacency to be the fruit of our cowardly refusal to be as truthful with them as Jehoshaphat's missionaries were with Judah. If we reassure people that worshipping the wrong god or paying lip service to the real God might be enough to save them, then the Lord will regard us as having murdered them.

It couldn't be more serious. The man whose name means *The Lord Judges* explains exactly how he judges, then he invites us to become part of the Lord's great missionary team.

---

[4] Matthew 1:21; John 1:29, 36; Romans 5:9; 1 Thessalonians 1:10, and Revelation 1:5 and 5:9. God never ignores sin. He always punishes it in the sinner or in the *Messiah*'s sacrifice for sin. The choice is ours.

[5] Ezekiel 3:16–21 and 33:1–9, and Acts 18:6 and 20:26–27.

Christ and Antichrist
(2 Chronicles 21:1 – 22:12)

"When Athaliah the mother of Ahaziah saw that her son was dead, she proceeded to destroy the whole royal family of the house of Judah."

(2 Chronicles 22:10)

It should be pretty obvious to you by now that 1 and 2 Chronicles are books about the *Messiah*. That's the Hebrew word which the Israelites used to describe their kings, and it means *The Chosen One* or *The Anointed One*.[1] What you may not have noticed is that they are also books about *false messiahs*. They are about both Christ and Antichrist.

The Chronicler depicts the kings from David's dynasty as prophetic pictures of the true *Messiah* who is yet to come, so don't miss the fact that Jesus warned his followers that *"False messiahs and false prophets will appear and perform great signs and wonders to deceive."* The Apostle John issued this same warning, using the word *Christ*, the Greek translation of the Hebrew word *Messiah*. He warned that *"As you have heard that the antichrist is coming, even now many antichrists have come. This is how we know it is the last hour."*[2] In English the prefix *anti-* means "opposed to" (as in antiseptic, antisocial, anti-ageing and anti-aircraft), but in Greek the prefix *anti-*

---

[1] In the Hebrew text of 1 Samuel, Saul is described as the Lord's *messiah* in 12:3, 5; 24:6, 10; 26:9, 11, 16 and 23. David is described as the Lord's *messiah* in 16:6 and throughout 2 Samuel.

[2] In Matthew 24:24 and Mark 13:22, Jesus uses the word Greek *pseudochristos*, meaning *false Christ*. John uses the word *antichristos*, meaning *alternative Christ*, in 1 John 2:18 (twice), 2:22 and 4:3, and in 2 John 7.

also means "instead of".[3] John is therefore telling us to expect the Devil to distract people from Jesus by raising up his own counterfeit *messiahs*.

John doesn't specify how his readers may have heard that such antichrists are coming, but it is possible that he is looking back to the message of 1 and 2 Chronicles. The Chronicler begins by comparing the godly King David with the rebellious King Saul. He then proceeds to paint King David and King Solomon in their best possible colours, as prophetic pictures of the true *Messiah* who is to come. In the fourth and final section of his story, the Chronicler records the failures of the kings of Judah to show that they are not the King of Judah we are looking for. We need an altogether better type of *Messiah*.

Which brings us onto what takes place in chapters 21–23. These are important chapters in the story, because the Chronicler groups the kings of Judah three times over into "six plus one". Jehoram and Ahaziah are the last of the first six, and Athaliah is the "plus one".

Rehoboam (930–913 BC) – "bad"
Abijah (913–910 BC) – "bad"
Asa (910–869 BC) – "good"
Jehoshaphat (872–848 BC) – "good"
Jehoram (853–841 BC) – "bad"[4]
Ahaziah (841 BC) – "bad"
[Athaliah (841–835 BC) – "antichrist"]

In 21:1–20, we witness the toxic fruit of Jehoshaphat's foolish attempt to forge false unity with the northern kingdom. Ahab was heavily influenced by his wife Jezebel, whose Phoenician name means *No Cohabitation*. She is a power-hungry manipulator, and their daughter Athaliah is the same. Jehoshaphat had no

---

[3] For example, in the Greek text of Matthew 20:28, Jesus says that his death is a death *"anti"* many.
[4] Like Solomon, Jehoshaphat and Jehoram are crowned king before their father dies, reigning at first as co-rulers alongside their father.

idea what he was doing when he arranged for his son Jehoram to marry her because, after his death, she becomes the *de facto* ruler of the southern kingdom by manipulating her weak husband.[5]

Jehoshaphat had seven sons, but Athaliah persuades her husband to consolidate his reign by murdering his six brothers. He also murders the officials who helped Jehoshaphat to bring about the spiritual revival of Judah. The Chronicler is in no doubt as to why: *"He followed the ways of the kings of Israel, as the house of Ahab had done, for he married a daughter of Ahab."* The Lord calls him to repent by making him forfeit the empire that his father extended into Edom through his great victory in chapter 20.[6] Jehoram also receives a letter which the prophet Elijah wrote before ascending to heaven in a chariot of fire, in which he prophesies that God will judge Jehoram for killing his brothers and for building "high places" to Baal all across the southern kingdom.[7] When Jehoram stubbornly refuses to repent, the Lord brings Philistine and Arab raiders against him.[8] They carry off all of his wives except for Athaliah and all of his sons except for Ahaziah. Jehoram dies of an excruciating disease of the bowels, aged less than forty, to nobody's regret and without any state funeral.[9] He is not even buried in the royal tombs of David's dynasty, signifying that he was an utter failure as *messiah*.

In 22:1–9, things get even worse for David's dynasty. Ahaziah is young and is easily manipulated by his mother

---

[5] This is also what Jezebel does in 1 Kings 21:25. Athaliah becomes the Lady Macbeth of 2 Chronicles.

[6] This fulfils a prophecy which Isaac gave to Esau many centuries earlier, in Genesis 27:40. *"To this day"* in 21:10 shows that the Chronicler collated much of his material from contemporary sources.

[7] The events of 2 Kings 2 take place just before Jehoram became king. Elijah is mentioned seventy-nine times in 1 and 2 Kings, but only once in 1 and 2 Chronicles, which focuses its attention on the southern kingdom of Judah.

[8] Note the deliberate contrast between the fruit of sinfulness here and the fruit of godliness in 17:11.

[9] God was merciful to Jehoram and gave him time to repent before he contracted the disease he prophesied.

Athaliah.[10] If you are surprised that he would be so stupid as to join forces with the king of Israel to fight the Arameans a second time at Ramoth Gilead, then bear in mind that the king was his uncle and that *"his mother encouraged him to act wickedly."* While Ahaziah is pursuing false unity with the northern tribes of Israel, he gets caught up in the violent coup by which Jehu overthrew the house of Ahab and installed himself as the new ruler of the northern kingdom.[11] Ahaziah is killed, leaving no adult heir to David's dynasty.[12] It appears to have been extinguished. Athaliah is finally able to get her hands on the throne of Judah. Due to Jehoshaphat's foolish false unity, even as Jezebel dies in the north, her daughter becomes queen of the south.

In 22:10–12, Athaliah finally fulfils her long-term strategy. Her name means *Afflicted By The Lord* and, like her mother, she cannot abide his favour towards David's dynasty. She kills off her own grandchildren so that she alone will be the undisputed ruler of Judah.[13]

Nobody spots that Athaliah has failed to slaughter Ahaziah's baby son. Everyone believes that the throne of Judah now belongs securely to her. The Lord allows this to happen to warn us not to pursue a false unity between believers and nonbelievers.

---

[10] The Chronicler uses the Hebrew variant name Jehoahaz. Like Ahaziah, it means *The Lord Is The True Owner.* English translations stick to his name in 2 Kings to avoid confusing him with King Jehoahaz of Israel.

[11] You can read about this coup in 2 Kings 9–10. Jehu's was the fifth dynasty of Israel in less than a century.

[12] Ahaziah's brothers were merely taken captive in 21:17. By 22:1, they have been executed.

[13] Don't be surprised by this. The same spirit at work in Athaliah, which stops at nothing to wipe out the *Messiah*, will be ready to murder again in order to do so in Matthew 2:13–20 and Revelation 12:1–17.

Because there can be no unity between the Lord and Baal. There can be no unity between David's dynasty and Ahab's dynasty. And as Queen Athaliah takes her place on the throne of Judah, as a false *messiah*, we are reminded that the Chronicler and the Apostle John are right: there can be no unity between Christ and Antichrist.

When God Seems to Fail (2 Chronicles 23:1 – 24:27)

"In the seventh year Jehoiada showed his strength."

(2 Chronicles 23:1)

For a God who is going to be eternally victorious, he seems remarkably content for everyone to think that he has failed. The greatest example of this is the cross of Jesus. Even his closest disciples were disappointed, disillusioned and depressed beyond words when they watched the *Messiah* being murdered by his enemies.[1] The Devil and his demons must have danced with delirious delight, believing that they had finally succeeded where Queen Athaliah failed.

But the Lord is the God of death and resurrection. He is content to let our hopes sink down to the grave in order to be able to lead us out on the other side into a new life that can never die. That's what he did to David's dynasty. He took it down to the grave and brought it back again to grant it a fresh start at the heart of his salvation story.

In 23:1, it looks as though God's promises have failed. For six long years, people assume that David's dynasty has died out and that Ahab's dynasty has won. I wonder how I might have responded had I been alive in those days. Would I have walked by faith and not by sight when the Lord's promises appeared to have failed? Or would I have grown bitter? Would I have walked away from faith in God? It's difficult not to do so when the promises of God seem to fail.

217

---

[1] See Luke 24:13–31. The Greek word *skuthrōpos* in Luke 24:17 conveys that they were *gloomy looking*.

Nobody knows that Ahaziah's sister managed to smuggle the one-year-old son of Ahaziah out of the palace before Athaliah's bloodbath started.[2] Nobody knows that her husband, the high priest Jehoiada, is hiding a son of David in the Temple courtyards – the one place where Athaliah is the least likely to go. Jehosheba's name means *The Lord Has Made An Oath* and Jehoiada means *The Lord Knows*, but nobody else knows that the Lord has remained faithful to his oath to David that one of his sons will never cease to reign over God's people. It is like Easter Saturday. The son of David is hidden in a tomb.

In 23:1–11, God begins revealing to his disillusioned people what he has been doing behind the scenes. Jehoiada summons the leaders of Judah to the Temple courtyard and shocks them with the news that a son of David has survived. The Lord still has a *messiah*! Together, they crown him king, anointing him with the same sacred oil as Solomon and presenting him with a copy of the Law of Moses, as commanded in Deuteronomy 17.[3]

In 23:12–21, Athaliah discovers what happens to the Devil's false *messiahs*. When she hears cries of *"Long live the king!"* and sees the seven-year-old Joash standing by one of the pillars of the Temple porchway, we are reminded of how the Devil must have felt on Easter Sunday, when he suddenly realised that crucifying Jesus hadn't thwarted God's plan of salvation – it had hastened it![4] Like the Devil, Athaliah resorts to doublespeak, but no longer is anybody fooled by her cries of *"Treason! Treason!"* Her reign crumbles in a moment before the sudden resurrection of David's dynasty. After killing her the people of Judah also kill the priests of Baal. They demolish

---

[2] Jehoram had wives other than Athaliah (21:17) so Jehosheba was probably one of their daughters. Even so, it would appear that Ahab and Jezebel were ancestors of Jesus via Ahaziah. Such amazing grace.

[3] 1 Kings 1:39. This coronation service for Joash recognises afresh that the Lord is the true King of Judah.

[4] The two tall bronze pillars of the Temple porchway represented the joining of heaven and earth through the Temple. We can surmise from 23:13 and 34:31 that it became a tradition for the king to stand next to one of the pillars and for the high priest to stand next to the other.

every temple, every altar and every idol. Then Jehoiada leads the boy-king Joash and his subjects in a renewal of their nation's covenant with the Lord. They restore to the Temple the sacrifices listed in the Law of Moses and the worship rosters that God's Spirit gave to David.[5]

The Lord's covenant with David, which seemed for six years to have failed, has now been revealed again in triumph for everyone to see. *"All the people of the land rejoiced, and the city was calm, because Athaliah had been slain with the sword."* This ought to encourage us whenever any of God's promises seem to have failed. On the day when Jesus returns from heaven, all of God's secret workings will be revealed. Until then, even if our own lives appear to fail and our churches appear to flounder, let's trust that God is faithful to every promise that he has given to his people.[6]

In 24:1–16, we start to see why the Lord needed to lead David's dynasty along this death-and-resurrection pathway. Had Joash been brought up in the palace under the influence of his grandmother, he would probably have persisted in her policy of promoting Baal. Instead, because David's dynasty "died", it springs back to life with fresh vigour. Joash hates everything about Athaliah and her idols. He is committed to serving the Lord. He even rebukes Jehoiada and the other priests and Levites for not restoring the Temple fast enough after its years of desecration.[7] At long last, Judah seems to have a true *messiah*.[8]

---

[5] The Chronicler highlights the importance of the Temple in the restoration of David's dynasty. He is urging his readers to devote themselves to the Lord's Temple until the day when his *Messiah* is finally revealed.

[6] David died in 970 BC, 135 years before the coronation of Joash. Yet such is God's faithfulness that his promises to David are mentioned and reaffirmed in 21:7, 12; 23:3, 9.

[7] Athaliah's sons are long since dead (22:1), so the *"sons"* mentioned in 24:7 must be her evil order of priests of Baal (1 Kings 18:19).

[8] The Chronicler emphasises that Joash restored the Temple to its God-given design via Moses and David. Even without a king from David's dynasty, the returning Jewish exiles could find continuity in their Temple.

In 24:17–27, we discover that this sadly isn't quite true. After the death of Jehoiada, Joash begins to drift away from his earlier devotion to the Lord. Despite what Athaliah did to his family, Joash reintroduces Phoenician idols to his kingdom and abandons the Temple of the Lord. When the Holy Spirit inspires Jehoiada's son Zechariah to prophesy to Joash, *"Because you have forsaken the Lord, he has forsaken you"*, Joash sins even further.[9] He stones to death his own cousin, the son of the man who rescued him from Athaliah. This is awful, but the Chronicler seems equally appalled that Joash does so in the sacred courtyard of the Temple.[10]

As a result, the Lord uses the Aramean army to discipline Joash for his sin. For once, the army of Judah outnumbers that of its enemies, yet it is routed on the battlefield. The Temple is plundered of its gold and silver. Before Joash can recover from his injuries in battle, he is assassinated by two of his own courtiers. Like Jehoram, he is not buried with the other kings of David's dynasty, signifying his eventual failure as *messiah*.[11]

These two chapters therefore begin and end with disappointment and confusion. God's promises appear to fail, both at the start and the end of the life of Joash. Chronicles teaches that we too will experience many such moments, both personally and as part of the Church. Through these chapters, we are encouraged to trust that God often leads his people to victory along a death-and-resurrection pathway. We will experience many Easter Saturdays, but take courage – Easter Sunday is always on its way![12]

[9] The Hebrew metaphor that is used in 24:20 tells us literally that the Spirit of the Lord *"clothed"* Zechariah. See 1 Chronicles 12:18; Judges 6:34 and Luke 24:49. Zechariah's prayer in 24:22 echoes the fact that his name means *The Lord Remembers*.

[10] Jehoiada was keen to avoid this in 23:14–15. Athaliah dies instead at the Horse Gate, reminding us of her mother Jezebel's death, in 2 Kings 9:33.

[11] Jehoiada was not part of David's dynasty by birth, yet he died aged 130 and was buried in the royal tomb of the kings. Joash, on the other hand, died aged only forty-seven and was not granted burial in the royal tomb.

[12] This was vital for the returning Jewish exiles, disillusioned that Judea remained a province of the Persian Empire. Whatever your own confusion, God is calling you to trust him to be faithful to his Word.

Run to the Finishing Line (2 Chronicles 25:1 – 26:23)

"But after Uzziah became powerful, his pride led to his downfall."

(2 Chronicles 26:16)

I will never forget the time I tried to win the cross-country race at school. The moment that the starting pistol fired, I was off like a bullet. I sprinted my way to the front of the field and for the first five minutes I ran faster than any of my friends. Then I discovered why the proverb says: *life is a marathon, not a sprint.* I had used up all my energy in the first five minutes of the race. My legs were exhausted and I began to slow down. One by one, every other boy in the school overtook me. Having begun the cross-country race at the front of the pack, I was the very last to cross the finishing line.

The same thing happens with the next two kings of Judah. Amaziah and Uzziah both begin their reigns well, only to stumble and fall at the end of the race.[1]

In 25:1–4, Amaziah starts running well. His mother is from Jerusalem, which suggests that David's dynasty has finally learned its lesson not to marry sinful foreigners. When he executes the Ammonite and Moabite who assassinated his father, Amaziah remembers the Lord's command in

---

[1] The sins of the latter half of these two reigns are not recorded in 2 Kings 14–15. The Chronicler adds that extra detail in order to teach us a lesson about crossing the finishing line of our own races well.

Deuteronomy 24:16 not to execute their children.[2] The start of his race looks promising. This new king of Judah runs like a real *messiah*.[3]

In 25:5–12, Amaziah continues to run well. His great-grandfather Jehoram lost control of the wealthy vassal kingdom of Edom in 21:8–10, but now the Lord enables Amaziah to reassert his rule. He re-enacts David's famous victory over the Edomite army in the Valley of Salt, just south of the Dead Sea, slaughtering 10,000 soldiers on the battlefield and 10,000 more after the battle.[4] When a prophet challenges him for recruiting 100,000 mercenaries from the northern kingdom into his army, Amaziah repents of having pursued the same false unity which almost destroyed David's dynasty in the days of Athaliah. Amaziah continues running his race well by sending the Israelite mercenaries home, putting his trust in the Lord alone for victory.

In 25:13–16, however, Amaziah begins to tire of running fast after the Lord. When he hears that the Israelite mercenaries have raided his kingdom on their way home, killing 3,000 of his subjects and carrying off large quantities of plunder, he is furious.[5] He brings back Edomite idols and begins to worship them in Jerusalem instead of the Lord.[6] When a prophet points out the stupidity of offering sacrifices to idols that were powerless to save their former owners from God's judgment,

---

[2] When 2 Chronicles 24:26 quotes the names of the assassins of Joash from 2 Kings 12:21, it adds the extra detail that they were an Ammonite and Moabite. This ties in with 20:1, since the Moabites and Ammonites were bitter enemies of the Jews after the exile. See Nehemiah 2:10, 19; 4:3–8; 13:1–9 and 13:23.

[3] Here we see God's severe mercy to Judah. It was only because the Arameans killed the evil advisers of Joash in 24:23 that Amaziah was able to reign without their malign influence in his royal council.

[4] See 1 Chronicles 18:11–13 and the title of Psalm 60. The word for *cliff* in 25:12 is *Sela*, the name of the Edomite capital, known to tourists today as *Petra*. Both names mean *Rock* in Hebrew and in Greek.

[5] The Lord urged Amaziah not to renege on his promise to pay these mercenaries 3.5 tons of silver. However, their fury on their way back home suggests that he did so.

[6] This did not come out of the blue. We are told in 25:2 that he never fully set his heart on following the Lord.

Amaziah responds with pride and anger. He threatens to strike down the prophet, in the same way that his father Joash struck down Zechariah. Suddenly, Amaziah's race is as good as over.[7]

In 25:17–28, the Chronicler describes how the Lord judged Amaziah for his idolatry. Puffed up with pride after conquering Edom, Amaziah picks a fight with King Jehoash of Israel. He is probably seeking the extradition of the mercenaries who plundered Judah, but the king of Israel will not be lectured like the vassal ruler of Edom.[8] He responds rudely, describing the kings of Judah as mere thistles compared to the mighty cedarwood kings of Israel.[9] He makes good on this boast by routing Amaziah's army, taking hostage the king and many of his senior leaders. He demolishes a 180-metre-long section of the northern city wall of Jerusalem, making it impossible to defend the city against future Israelite invasion. Before returning home, he plunders the Lord's Temple of its treasures.[10] Having started his race well, Amaziah therefore ends it in disgrace and failure. Like his father Joash, he is assassinated by his courtiers. He goes down in history as yet another failed *messiah*.

In 26:1–15, Uzziah begins running well in place of his father.[11] He listens to his Jewish mother and to the godly Zechariah, and so he prospers under the Lord.[12] He rebuilds

[7] Amaziah's courtiers begin their conspiracy against him in about 784 BC, as soon as he starts worshipping idols (25:27). The Lord gives him plenty of time to repent, since they do not follow through on it until 767 BC.

[8] Amaziah reigned from 796 to 767 BC and defeated Edom in about 784 BC. Since Jehoash reigned 798–782 BC, this quarrel must have broken out as a result of the actions of the mercenaries in 25:6–13.

[9] It was quintessentially Hebrew to quarrel via the telling of parables. See Judges 9:7–15.

[10] The Chronicler mentions *Obed-Edom* in 25:24 to lament that what David orchestrated is being dismantled.

[11] Uzziah is named Azariah in 2 Kings 15:1–7. The one name means *My Strength Is The Lord* and the other *My Help Is The Lord*. The Chronicler appears to use this alternative name to avoid confusing him with the high priest Azariah in 26:20. Since he began to rule alongside his father in 792 BC, twenty-five years before Amaziah died, 26:1 is best translated that Uzziah was aged sixteen when the people made him king *"under his father Amaziah"*.

[12] This is the Chronicler's repeated lesson for his readers: fear the Lord and prosper, or defy the Lord and fail. We do not know anything more about this Zechariah, except that his name means *The Lord Remembers*.

the Red Sea port city of Elath, which his father won back from the Edomites. He fortifies Jerusalem and strengthens the network of fortress cities along the borders of Judah. He strengthens his army so that it defeats the Philistines, the Arabs and the Ammonites.[13] After the disappointment and failure of his father's reign, the start of Uzziah's race is thrilling. Here at last we have a king of Judah who knows how to run like a real *messiah*.

In 26:16–23, however, Uzziah encounters the same problem as his father. After running fast in his early years, midway through his reign he starts to tire of worshipping the Lord. He becomes so proud of his military victories that he begins to believe that the Law of Moses does not apply to him. He defies its stipulation that only priests can enter the *Holy Place* of the Temple to offer incense to the Lord.[14] When the high priest Azariah and eighty other priests courageously confront him with his sin, he sins even further by losing his temper and shouting at them angrily in the *Holy Place*. Suddenly, the hideous symptoms of leprosy begin to break out on his forehead. It is a warning from the Lord that he must repent of his sin, but sadly Uzziah refuses. He spends the final ten years of his reign in enforced quarantine as a leper, far from the royal palace where he should have reigned as king.[15] He too goes down in history as a failed *messiah*.

Amaziah and Uzziah both started out well, yet both ended up limping across the finishing line. They let the blessing of the Lord go to their heads instead of to their hearts. The American

---

[13] The Meunites mentioned in 26:7 were an Arab tribe to the south of Judah (20:1 and 1 Chronicles 4:41)

[14] The Lord wants our obedience, not our self-initiated sacrifices (1 Samuel 15:22). When Uzziah refuses to accept this, he is struck down by the same disease as Miriam when she opposed Moses in Numbers 12:1–15.

[15] The prophet Isaiah, who is mentioned in 26:22, began prophesying in the year Uzziah died (Isaiah 6:1) and he appears to have written a history of Uzziah's reign (now lost to us). Although Isaiah leads Hezekiah to repentance in 2 Kings 20:1–11, Uzziah evidently refused. Jotham was forced to rule as regent for his final ten years. Uzziah was buried in a field *near* to the royal tombs, excluded by his leprosy even in death.

president Abraham Lincoln claimed that *"Any man can stand adversity – only a great man can stand prosperity"*, and both these kings of Judah prove that this is true.[16] It is good to run hard after God, but the lives of these two kings warn us to keep on running. How we begin the race of life matters a lot less than how we cross the finishing line.

---

[16] Quoted by Horatio Alger in his biography *Abraham Lincoln: The Backwoods Boy* (1883).

Love Where You Are
(2 Chronicles 26:10)

*"He had people working his fields and vineyards in
the hills and in the fertile lands, for he loved the soil."*

(2 Chronicles 26:10)

Nobody seemed to know how to reach the poor of Victorian London. Nobody, that is, except for William and Catherine Booth. When a former prostitute was asked at William's funeral why so many tens of thousands of Londoners had been converted to Jesus through his ministry, she simply replied: *"You see, he cared for the likes of us."*

The Chronicler is passionate about proclaiming the Good News of the *Messiah* to those who do not yet believe in him. He does so throughout his retelling of Jewish history, and it includes several great examples of effective Gospel proclamation.[1] Perhaps best of all is this throwaway statement, in 26:10, about Uzziah's fruitfulness as a farmer. It is very similar to the former prostitute's conclusion about William Booth. The Chronicler teaches us that King Uzziah was extremely fruitful as a farmer because *"he loved the soil"*.

Jesus echoes this verse when he declares in John 13:35 that the secret of fruitful evangelistic ministry is to love the people to whom God has sent us. Sadly, when nonbelievers are asked to describe the Christians in their lives, love isn't very often the first word that springs to mind. William Booth addressed this problem when he tried to teach the respectable men and women of London how to reach the poor and unevangelised within their

---

[1] For example, in 2 Chronicles 2:3–10; 13:4–12 and 30:6–11.

city. *"It will be a happy day for England when Christian ladies transfer their sympathies from poodles and terriers to destitute and starving children."*[2]

The Chronicler records that Uzziah became famous for the way he made the most of his royal farms and vineyards and flocks and herds. He dug many new wells and turned many wildernesses into fertile farmlands because *"he loved the soil"*. Jesus did the same when he came as the true *Messiah* to sow Gospel seed among the lost sheep of Israel. Even as a twelve-year-old, his parents found him sitting with the teachers of the Law, honouring them by asking questions and by listening to their replies. When he grew older, he infuriated those self-same teachers of the Law by sitting down with tax collectors and prostitutes, honouring them and winning their hearts back to God through his evident love towards them. When Lazarus died and Jesus wept at his tomb, the crowds exclaimed, *"See how he loved him!"*[3] Jesus was a true son and heir to Uzziah.

The Apostle Paul was just the same. If you are unsure how he succeeded in winning so many Jews and Gentiles to faith in Jesus, just take a look at his letters. He speaks to people as *"you whom I love and long for"*. He treats his co-worker as a *"son whom I love"*. When people say "yes" to his message about the *Messiah*, he exclaims, *"How can we thank God enough for you in return for all the joy we have in the presence of our God because of you?"* He conveys to them so strongly that they are his *"glory and joy"* that when he leaves them they weep, not just because they will miss his brilliant teaching ministry, but because they will miss his deep love towards them. We are told that *"What grieved them most was his statement that they would never see his face again."*[4]

---

[2] Helen K. Hosier's *William and Catherine Booth: Founders of The Salvation Army* (1999).

[3] Luke 2:42–47; 7:34, 39; and 15:1–2, and John 11:36.

[4] Acts 20:37–38; 1 Corinthians 4:17; Philippians 4:1, and 1 Thessalonians 2:20 and 3:9.

Can it truly be that simple? Is the secret to evangelistic fruitfulness as straightforward as truly loving those around us? William Booth was certainly convinced that it is.

> *What is a mission station?... Not a building... but a band of people... To successfully manage a station you must love it with a love that never falters, never swerves, never dies. You must have the same burning, unquenchable flame that Jesus had, or you cannot – will not – succeed; and your success will be just according to the measure of your affection for your people and for the perishing people around you. This love – this passion for souls – is the mainspring of all true religious activity and the principle which governs all real and lasting work for God. Love, rightly directed, makes a good parent, a good husband, a good workman; and nothing short of love, and a great deal of it, will make a good evangelist. The secret of success is often inquired for; here it is: It is not in natural gifts, or human bearing, or exceptional opportunities, or earthly advantages, but in a heart consumed with the flame of ardent, holy, heavenly love.*[5]

I don't claim to be anything of an expert when it comes to evangelism, but my own experience would bear out those stirring words of William Booth. If we want to see people respond with faith to the Gospel seed we sow, then we need to love the soil.

In my own attempts to share the message of the *Messiah* with people, I have often noticed that a greater intensity of desire doesn't make me any more fruitful, but a greater intensity of love towards them often does. I tried for years to convince a work colleague to come to church with me, until I was convicted that I didn't really love her. Within a few days of consciously channelling God's love towards her, she shocked me by asking

---

[5] Booth said this in an address to The Salvation Army Annual Conference, Whitechapel, in June 1876.

if I would mind her coming to church with me. I nearly fell off my chair!

I have also seen this principle at work among my Christian friends. One good friend complained to me that his work colleagues were forever swearing and telling dirty jokes. He said he couldn't bear to be around them. In all the years before he lost his job, he never saw a single one of those work colleagues saved. At the same time, another friend shared with me that he was struggling to work in a very tricky industry, but that he had set his heart to stay there because the Lord had given him a real love for his work colleagues. A few weeks after our conversation, one of those work colleagues was diagnosed with cancer. My friend was able to be there for him throughout his treatment. He was able to share the Good News of Jesus with him and to lead him to salvation a few weeks before he died. As his colleague's only Christian friend, he was invited by the family to speak at the funeral. That's what happens when we truly care for people.

I have also seen this principle at work at a church level. The seasons when I have led churches in evangelistic breakthrough have, without exception, been the seasons when we have loved the community around us. The seasons when we have been unfruitful have always been the seasons when we were distracted by other things. That's why Solomon warns that *"Those who work their land will have abundant food, but those who chase fantasies have no sense."*[6] One of my friends who is a church leader agrees. While he and his wife kept on complaining about the place where God had called them, their church plant floundered, but after they began to speak well of their community and to truly love the people in it, their church plant grew to well over a thousand people.

If that sounds a bit too simple then why not give it a go? Don't despise the Lord when he says that big changes can occur through such small things. King Uzziah became fruitful as a

---

[6] This is such an important principle that he teaches it to us twice, in Proverbs 12:11 and 28:19.

farmer because *"he loved the soil"*. That's still the secret to your fruitfulness today.

The Choice
(2 Chronicles 27:1 – 28:27)

"Jotham grew powerful because he walked steadfastly before the Lord his God... Ahaz... did not do what was right in the eyes of the Lord."

(2 Chronicles 27:6, 28:1)

The southern kingdom of Judah is at a crossroads. It has had too many false starts and too many failed *messiahs*. The Lord is about to destroy the northern kingdom of Israel, so he lays out a clear choice for Judah through the contrasting reigns of Jotham and Ahaz.[1]

Jotham means *The Lord Is Perfect*, and the short chapter 27 has much to say about how the new king of Judah lived up to his name.[2] He was the son of a Jewish woman and the grandson of a man named Zadok, whose name means *Righteous*. Under their influence, he imitated his father Uzziah's godly years throughout his entire reign. Although he failed to remove the "high places" from his kingdom, he restored the Temple and the walls of Jerusalem after their destruction at the hands of King Jehoash of Israel.[3] He rebuilt the fallen fortresses of Judah and forced the Ammonites to pay him a hefty yearly tribute of 3.4 tons of silver, 1.6 tons of wheat and 1.35 tons of barley. The

---

[1] Jotham reigned from 750 to 732 BC and Ahaz reigned from 735 to 715 BC, including a joint reign of three years. The northern kingdom was destroyed in 722 BC, so God used these two reigns to lay a better choice before Judah.

[2] Don't be confused that 2 Kings 15:30–33 agrees that Jotham ruled for sixteen years but then talks about his *"twentieth year"*. Jotham ruled jointly with Ahaz, so his reign can be dated in different ways.

[3] 2 Kings 15:35 explains what 2 Chronicles 27:2 means by saying they *"continued their corrupt practices"*.

Chronicler leaves us in no doubt as to why the reign of Jotham was so successful. It was *"because he walked steadfastly before the Lord his God."*[4] The Lord made his reign a glorious example of the first possible future that the southern kingdom of Judah could choose.

Ahaz means *He Has Snatched*, and chapter 28 records that he was also a king of Judah who lived up to his name. From the start, he snatched hold of the throne as his own, not as something which had been entrusted to him by the Lord. Although he ruled as joint king with his father for the first three years of his reign, Isaiah 7 makes it clear that he had no intention of sharing power with anyone.[5] Not only did he reinstate Baal-worship throughout his kingdom, but he also worshipped the Ammonite idol Molek, who demanded people prove their devotion to him by sacrificing their babies in the fire. Ahaz murdered at least two of his sons in this way.[6] This was a new low, even for the kings of Judah.[7] Instead of starting well but falling short, Ahaz exceeded his predecessors' sins from the very outset of his reign. When the Chronicler says that *"he followed the ways of the kings of Israel"*, he is using the reign of Ahaz to show us the other possible future that the southern kingdom of Judah could choose.[8]

---

[4] *"All his wars"* in 27:7 refers to his battles with Israel and Aram, which are recorded in 2 Kings 15:32–38. The writer of Kings does not mention Jotham's victory over the Ammonites, but the Chronicler does so in order to make his reign a clear example of the glorious future which Judah might have chosen.

[5] Isaiah 7 recounts the Aramean–Israelite invasion from 735 to 732 BC. The Chronicler pointedly insists that Ahaz only ruled for sixteen complete years. His first three years were merely years of tutelage under his father.

[6] What Ahaz does in 28:3 is condemned by the Lord in Leviticus 20:1–5 and Deuteronomy 12:31. Before we rush to judge, however, bear in mind that our generation aborts over 50 million babies each year globally.

[7] The Chronicler is a very generous judge of the kings of Judah. Joash murders Zechariah yet *"did what was right"* (24:2). Amaziah worships idols yet *"did what was right"* (25:2). Uzziah profaned the Temple yet *"did what was right"* (26:4). Ahaz alone receives nothing but condemnation (28:1).

[8] The Greek name for the *Valley of Ben Hinnom* is *Gehenna*. Jesus uses this ten times in Matthew and Mark as a name for *hell*, because the Lord lays this same choice before people today.

King Ahaz doesn't prosper like his father Jotham. Again, the Chronicler leaves us in no doubt as to why: *"The Lord his God delivered him into the hands of the king of Aram."*[9] The gold and silver which King Asa foolishly plundered from the Temple to buy help from the king of Aram had helped that northern nation to become a superpower. Together, King Rezin of Aram and King Pekah of Israel are able to inflict more casualties on Judah in a single day of fighting than died on the first day of The Somme. They plunder Judah of its treasures and they carry off over 200,000 of its women and children into slavery. Ahaz has sinned by sacrificing his sons in the fire to Molek, so now he loses his precious eldest son on the battlefield. Again, the Chronicler leaves us in no doubt as to why. It was *"because Judah had forsaken the Lord"*.

The Aramean and Israelite invasion of Judah took place from 734 to 732 BC – that is, during the three years when Ahaz was still ruling as joint king with his father. Given the non-stop military successes of Jotham's reign, we might have expected Ahaz to repent of his sins and to beg for wisdom from his father. There is no indication that he did so. In fact, his sinful actions manage to make even the northern kingdom look comparatively godly.[10] When the prophet Oded charges the leaders of Israel with sin for enslaving their fellow Israelites, they repent in an instant. They clothe their naked captives and send them straight back home to Judah, without demanding a penny of ransom money. As they do so, they provide us with a picture of the Gospel. If Ahaz repents of his sin, even at this late stage, he will surely be forgiven. The grace of God truly is that amazing.

Sadly, the Chronicler informs us that Ahaz refused to turn to the Lord for help. He turned instead to King Tiglath-Pileser III of Assyria. When he sees that Edomite raiders are crossing

---

[9] Note that the Lord remained Ahaz's God, even when Ahaz rejected him. Aram was modern-day Syria.

[10] Oded means *Restorer*. In Judah, bringing such discipline from the Lord might result in prison (16:7–10) or in death (24:20–22), but in Israel it results in repentance.

his southern border and that the Philistines are capturing cities on his western border, Ahaz panics.[11] He goes to the Temple, not to pray, but to plunder. He repeats Asa's folly by using gold and silver from the Temple to buy help from another foreign power. Don't miss the way in which the Chronicler refers to the southern kingdom as "Israel" when he explains that *"The Lord had humbled Judah because of Ahaz king of Israel, for he had promoted wickedness in Judah"*. The Lord was presenting a choice to the southern kingdom through the reigns of Jotham and Ahaz – either to go the way of David and be blessed, or to go the way of the northern tribes that rejected David and be destroyed. Tragically, Ahaz embodied the wrong choice for Judah.

The southern kingdom of Judah had some bad kings but Ahaz is at the bottom of the pile. The Chronicler tells us that the Assyrians *"gave him trouble instead of help"*.[12] Buoyed by his gold and silver, they would launch a far more serious invasion of Judah in 701 BC. But let's not get ahead of the story. For now, King Ahaz believes himself to be wise for worshipping the idols of the Arameans who defeated him.[13] Before he dies, he shuts the doors of the Lord's Temple and builds altars to false gods on every street corner, looking for a saviour anywhere but in the God of Israel.

In 722 BC, the northern kingdom of Israel was destroyed by the Assyrians. The Chronicler jumps over this, keeping our attention focused on the choice which lies before Judah. Ahaz isn't buried in the royal tombs of the kings of Judah, as an

---

[11] 2 Kings 16:6 tells us that, shortly after the Arameans captured the Red Sea port city of Elath from Judah, the Edomites retook it from them. The power of Aram was about to be shattered, but not to the benefit of Judah.

[12] 28:20. The Assyrians destroyed the kingdom of Aram in 732 BC and the kingdom of Israel in 722 BC. However, the Chronicler is less interested in our short-term gains from sin than he is in our long-term destruction by it.

[13] 2 Kings 16 explains that Ahaz was as foolish as Amaziah. While visiting Damascus to thank the king of Assyria for destroying Aram, he made notes on how to worship the idols they had just defeated together. If the gods of Damascus had been unable to save Damascus, they certainly wouldn't save Jerusalem!

indication that he has been a disgrace to the name *messiah*. By contrasting the reigns of Jotham and Ahaz, the Chronicler calls on his readers to make a better choice themselves.

Will we surrender everything to the Lord and be blessed by him, or will we go our own way and reap the terrible consequences of rebellion against the Lord? The choice is ours.

Could It Be?
(2 Chronicles 29:1 – 31:1)

"Hezekiah… did what was right in the eyes of the Lord, just as his father David had done."

(2 Chronicles 29:1–2)

Could it be that Judah will make the right choice where Israel failed? As the dust settles after the fall of the northern kingdom, we have reason to hope that it will. Hezekiah is one of Judah's godliest kings. He is a son of Ahaz, but he rules like a true son of David.

Hezekiah was not the eldest son of Ahaz. God had judged Ahaz for sacrificing his sons in the fire to Molek by causing his crown prince Maaseiah to die on the battlefield in 28:7. Hezekiah was therefore an unexpected monarch, who had been left to be discipled by his godly Jewish mother and his godly grandfather.[1] The Chronicler rejoices that Hezekiah didn't merely do *"what was right in the eyes of the Lord"*. He ruled *"just as his father David had done."* In other words, he looked like a real *messiah*.

In chapter 29, Hezekiah begins his reign by restoring the Temple of the Lord after its desecration and dereliction by his father. He reopens its doors and recommissions the Levites to cleanse its courtyards of any trace of the idolatry of the previous regime. He makes it very clear as he commissions them why his father's reign was unsuccessful. Ahaz made the wrong choice and he incurred the wrath of the God who had just destroyed

---

[1] His mother's name Abijah means *The Lord Is My Father*. His grandfather Zechariah's name means *The Lord Remembers*. He may well have been the same Zechariah who mentored Uzziah in 26:5.

the northern kingdom.[2] This stirs our hope that Hezekiah will make a better choice than his father, as he sets his heart to renew Judah's covenant with the Lord.

The writer of 1 and 2 Kings devotes three chapters to the reign of Hezekiah, focusing mainly on the Assyrian invasion of Judah in 701 BC. The Chronicler devotes four chapters to his reign, three of which focus on the revival which preceded the invasion. This different focus is deliberate, since the Chronicler wants to highlight to his readers the importance of the Temple in God's purposes for his people.[3] In 29:6, Hezekiah describes the Temple as the Lord's *mishkan* – that is, his *Tabernacle* or his *Dwelling-Place*, with a history stretching back to the days of Moses. In 29:11, he recommissions the priests *"to stand before him and serve him, to minister before him and to burn incense."*[4] Instead of being disappointed that the Lord has not yet restored a king from David's dynasty to the throne of Judah, the Jews after the exile ought to be thrilled that he has restored their fallen Temple – something the best kings of Judah prized more highly than they did their throne.[5]

The Levites spend sixteen days reconsecrating the Temple and its courtyard, burning anything idolatrous in the Kidron Valley, which lies between the Temple that Solomon built for the Lord on Mount Moriah and the temples that he built for pagan idols on the Mount of Olives. It is the same valley where Asa burned his grandmother's Asherah pole in 15:16, and this act of consecration marks out Hezekiah as a true son of David.

---

[2] The events of chapter 29 take place in 715 BC, so the *"captivity"* described in 29:9 must be the one recorded at the hands of the Arameans and Israelites in 734–732 BC (28:5 and 8).

[3] The list in 29:12–14 includes all three clans of Levites (Kohath, Merari and Gershon) and all three families of worship leaders (Asaph, Heman and Jeduthun). It is clearly directed at his Jewish readers after the exile.

[4] Under the New Covenant, every Christian has become a priest of God (1 Peter 2:4–5). This is therefore our job description. We are to *fellowship* with God, *work* with God, *worship* God and *pray* to God.

[5] Because the Chronicler wants to present the priests and Levites as the true custodians of Jewish history, he chooses not to note that the high priest Uriah helped King Ahaz to desecrate the Temple (2 Kings 16).

After sixteen days of reconsecrating the Temple, Hezekiah restores its blood-sacrifices and heartfelt worship. The Chronicler emphasises that, as the priests slaughter their sacrifices, the Levites lead the people in worship *"in the way prescribed by David and Gad the king's seer and Nathan the prophet; this was commanded by the Lord"*. In case we miss this as a restoration of all that was good in the Tabernacles of Moses and David, he adds that *"Hezekiah and his officials ordered the Levites to praise the Lord with the words of David and of Asaph the seer."*[6] This marks such a complete turnaround from the sinful regime of Ahaz that we find ourselves wondering: Could this be the *Messiah* we are waiting for?

In chapter 30, Hezekiah goes a step further by celebrating the Passover.[7] As one of the first acts of his reign he sends out invitations to the Festival, not just throughout Judah, but to the Israelite survivors in the former territory of the northern kingdom. He invites all twelve tribes of Israel to reunite as one nation around the blood of the Passover Lamb, recognising the Lord as *"the God of Israel"*.[8] Sadly, most of the Israelite survivors laugh at the royal messengers and refuse to come.[9] Only a few of them are willing to travel south to repent of their sins and find salvation in the Lord. Those who do so experience such God-given unity with the people of Judah that they decide to observe the Festival of Unleavened Bread for fourteen days, instead of the usual seven. When the Chronicler says that *"since the days of Solomon son of David king of Israel there had been*

[6] Hezekiah kneels down in worship, like Jehoshaphat in 20:18, hailing the Lord as the true King of Judah.

[7] Because he became king only a few days before the Passover, Hezekiah celebrates it a month later than usual. This had precedent in Numbers 9:10–11.

[8] Hezekiah's letter to the northern tribes offers us a masterclass in evangelism. We will win more people to Christ by extolling God's goodness towards them than by berating them for their sinfulness towards God.

[9] These verses prefigure the parables which Jesus told about God inviting sinful people to his banquet in Matthew 22:1–14 and Luke 14:15–24. *"Foreigners"* are included in the Passover instead of Israelites in 30:25.

nothing like this in Jerusalem", we begin to wonder again: could this be the long-awaited *Messiah*?

Here we see two of the Chronicler's greatest themes at play: the twelve tribes of Israel are reunified under God through the blood-sacrifices that they offer together at the Temple.[10] In 30:27, he emphasises that the Lord's true *dwelling-place* is heaven, not the Temple in Jerusalem, yet what happens in these chapters nevertheless feels like a foretaste of heaven.[11] In 31:1, the people return home to spread revival throughout Israel and Judah. We have seen nothing like this since the days of David and Solomon.

Could it be that Hezekiah will make the right choice where his father failed? Could it be that he is the *Messiah* that we are waiting for? As the dust settles on the destruction of the northern kingdom, the Chronicler gives us fresh reasons to believe.

---

[10] The Chronicler describes forgiveness *"for all Israel"* in 29:24. Painful though it was, the destruction of the northern kingdom paved the way for a reunification of the twelve tribes of Israel under the true *Messiah*.

[11] The Hebrew word for *dwelling-place* in 30:27 is not the same word used in 29:6. It is *mā'ôn*, which normally describes the *lair* of a lion (also in 36:15). The Presence of God is to be feared as well as prized (Hosea 11:10).

Signs of Revival
(2 Chronicles 31:1–21)

"They were faithful in consecrating themselves."

(2 Chronicles 31:18)

The nineteenth-century evangelist Charles Finney began his famous *Lectures On Revival* by describing several signs that are present in any spiritual revival. After defining it as: *"the renewal of the first love of Christians, resulting in the awakening and conversion of sinners to God"*, he asserts boldly: *"You see why you have not a revival. It is only because you do not want one. Because you are not praying for it; nor anxious for it, nor putting forth efforts for it."*[1]

We may or may not agree with Charles Finney's methodology, but we cannot deny that spiritual revivals happen. Hezekiah means *The Lord Is My Strength*, and he lives up to his name by transforming the spiritual temperature of his nation. One moment the Temple doors are shut and the people of Judah are worshipping the idol Baal. The next moment King Hezekiah is leading his new subjects in a renewal of their covenant with the Lord. The Chronicler seems almost as surprised at the speed of this as we are. He says in 29:36 that *"Hezekiah and all the people rejoiced at what God had brought about for his people, because it was done so quickly."* Let's therefore examine some of the signs of this sudden revival.

Hezekiah's revival is *both top-down and bottom-up*. On the one hand, we can trace its origins back to the king. Having watched his father sacrifice his brothers in the fire to a foreign

---

[1] The quotes in this chapter come from Charles Finney's first and second *Lectures on Revival* (1835).

idol and compromise the independence of his kingdom to the king of Assyria, Hezekiah has resolved in his heart that he will follow the Lord.[2] At the same time, we can also trace the success of the revival back to his subjects. In 29:34, the priests are amazed that the Levites are even more zealous for God than they are. In 30:15, the priests and Levites are amazed that the ordinary worshippers at the Temple are even more zealous still. It is the common people who seek to purify the city of Jerusalem during the Festival (30:14) and who return home to demolish the "high places" across Judah and the former territory of Israel (31:1). This teaches us that lasting spiritual revival is seldom purely a top-down or a bottom-up affair. Revival only takes root when both leaders and followers receive a fresh desire to follow the Lord.

Hezekiah's revival is *a work of grace from start to finish*. God doesn't revive the land of Judah in spite of the sins of Ahaz. He revives the land of Judah through the sins of Ahaz! The greatest mystery of Hezekiah's reign is how such a godly king could arise from such a wicked father. The answer is quite simple. Ahaz had expected his eldest son Maaseiah to reign after him, so he saw no danger in Hezekiah being mentored in the ways of the Lord.[3] It was too late for him to reverse this when his eldest son was killed in battle, at the very moment that his failures were making many of his subjects hungry for revival.[4]

Charles Finney argues that *"Frequently the most outrageous wickedness of the ungodly is followed by a revival."* That is certainly the case here, throughout chapters 29–31. God permits his people to celebrate the Passover on the wrong

---

[2] Isaiah and Micah prophesied during the reigns of Jotham and Ahaz, and it appears from Jeremiah 26:16–19 that the young Hezekiah was deeply convicted by what they said.

[3] Hezekiah was crowned king in 715 BC, but 2 Kings 18:1 says that he began to reign in 729 BC. This indicates that his father reluctantly recognised him as the new crown prince after the death of his brother.

[4] Hezekiah says in 29:8 that all could see that Ahaz's sins made Judah *"an object of dread and horror and scorn"*.

day (30:2–3) and without some of its lawful stipulations (30:17–20) because he delights to see their wholehearted revulsion against sin.[5] When Hezekiah urges the northerners not to fear to join them because *"the Lord your God is gracious and compassionate"* (30:9), he is assuring them that his revival isn't really his at all. It was *"what God had brought about for his people"* (29:36).

Hezekiah's revival is marked by *deep unity* among God's people (30:12), by *joyful worship* (30:21–26 and 31:2) and by *heartfelt prayer* which reaches up to heaven (30:27). Charles Finney treats these things as causes of revival, but it seems fairer to conclude from these three chapters that they are actually the first signs that revival has begun. The Chronicler insists that these things were proof that *"the hand of God was on the people"* (30:12).[6]

Hezekiah's revival is marked by *deep repentance over sin*. The blood of the Passover Lamb symbolised forgiveness through the death of the *Messiah*. The Festival of Unleavened Bread which followed it symbolised that, in order to receive it, we must be willing to die to ourselves.[7] It is remarkable, therefore, that the worshippers at the Temple insist on celebrating the Festival for fourteen days, instead of the usual seven. It shows that they are equally determined to demolish the idols in their hearts as they are to demolish the idols on the street corners and at the "high places" in 30:14 and 31:1.

Hezekiah's revival is marked by *lavish generosity* towards the Lord. Jesus teaches us that money is the greatest idol that vies with God for our affection, so in one sense this is simply the outworking of their deep repentance and recommitment to

---

[5] They justified their actions through a generous interpretation of Numbers 9:10–11. The Chronicler's statement in 30:4 that this *"seemed right both to the king and to the whole assembly"* prefigures Acts 15:28.

[6] In other words, the hymns of Charles Wesley did not bring about revival; revival brought about the hymns of Charles Wesley! The same is true of the other great worship songs which have accompanied revival.

[7] 1 Corinthians 5:7–8; 2 Corinthians 5:14–15, and Galatians 2:20; 5:24 and 6:14.

the Lord.[8] For many decades, the people of Judah and Israel have withheld their tithes and offerings from the Temple, but in chapter 31 they follow the king's repentant lead by bringing so many gifts to God that it takes the priests and Levites four whole months to process and pass on their offerings.[9]

Hezekiah's revival is marked by *bitter spiritual warfare*. It is easy for us to focus on the fact that it resulted in prosperity for Judah (31:21).[10] It is easy for us to focus on the fact that it led to many Gentiles coming to faith in the God of Israel (30:25). But let's not miss the fact that it also led to mockery and rejection (30:10), to lots of hard work (31:21) and to a military invasion by the Assyrians (32:1).[11] The Devil never takes revival lying down. If you want revival, then you'd better be prepared to fight for it.

Which brings us back to where we began, with Charles Finney's famous statement about revival:

> *It is the renewal of the first love of Christians, resulting in the awakening and conversion of sinners to God... You see why you have not a revival. It is only because you do not want one. Because you are not praying for it; nor anxious for it, nor putting forth efforts for it.*

If you want to see fresh spiritual revival in your own day, then bring these signs to the Lord in prayer. The God who revived ancient Judah still longs to revive us today.

---

[8] Matthew 6:24 and Luke 16:13. The word *"they"* in 31:4 probably indicates that these generous gifts enabled the priests and Levites to work full time in the Temple, but it could also mean that such lavish gifts enabled the givers to devote themselves more deeply to the Lord. Jesus teaches us in Matthew 6:21 and Luke 12:34 that our hearts become devoted to wherever we give our treasures, and not just the other way around.

[9] It is characteristic of the Chronicler to highlight repentance which results in renewed honour for the Temple. He records their offerings in great detail for the sake of his Jewish readers after the exile.

[10] 2 Kings 18:8 says that God enabled Hezekiah to recapture the cities that his father lost to the Philistines.

[11] We saw earlier that revival provokes a spiritual backlash. See 19:4 – 20:1; Exodus 17:5–16 and 1 Samuel 7:1–7.

Surprise, Surprise!
(2 Chronicles 32:1–33)

"After all that Hezekiah had so faithfully done, Sennacherib king of Assyria came and invaded Judah."

(2 Chronicles 32:1)

For the Chronicler, life is very simple. If we set our hearts to follow the Lord, then we will prosper. If we turn away from the Lord, then we will suffer.[1] So it comes as a surprise to us when he suddenly informs us that *"After all that Hezekiah had so faithfully done, Sennacherib king of Assyria came and invaded Judah."* What on earth went wrong?

First, it appears that the revival which began in 715 BC was waning by 701 BC. We can tell from Isaiah 30:22 and 31:7 that *"idols overlaid with silver"* and *"images covered with gold"* had reappeared across the land of Judah. Revival not only needs to be sought from God; it also needs to be maintained through prayer to God. After allowing the Assyrians to destroy the northern kingdom of Israel in 722 BC, the Lord lets them add the southern kingdom of Judah to their shopping list in 701 BC to rekindle the flame of revival.

Second, it appears that Hezekiah's heart was also drifting from its earlier devotion to the Lord. The Chronicler explains that God used a visit from some Babylonian envoys *"to test him and to know everything that was in his heart."* We know from the fact that 2 Kings 20 and Isaiah 39 name the leader of the Babylonian envoys as Marduk-Baladan, who was deposed as

---

[1] 11:4; 12:2, 12; 14:7; 15:15; 17:3–5; 19:2; 21:10–15; 22:4–7; 24:18–24; 25:20; 26:5; 27:6; 28:3–6, 19 and 31:20–21.

king of Babylon in 702 BC, that the events of 32:24–31 took place before Sennacherib besieged Jerusalem in 701 BC.[2] The Lord saw that the best way to root out the pride that was revealed in Hezekiah's heart was to permit this Assyrian invasion.[3]

When the Babylonian envoys arrive in Jerusalem, it is like the arrival of the Queen of Sheba at the court of Solomon. They have heard that the Lord has miraculously healed Hezekiah of a fatal illness, so this is his opportunity to take them to the Temple and to encourage them to worship the God of Israel with him.[4] Instead, he takes them to the Temple storerooms and boasts to them about his wealth and power. The Chronicler leaves much of this detail to 2 Kings and Isaiah, noting simply in verse 25 that *"Hezekiah's heart was proud"*. When Isaiah warned him that the Babylonians would return to plunder the treasures he had shown them, instead of repenting, he shrugged his shoulders: *"Will there not be peace and security in my lifetime?"* The Assyrian invasion was God's way of answering emphatically: *No*.

Third, it appears that the Chronicler wants to correct a view that living under God's blessing will always guarantee easy living. The truth is, those who set their hearts to serve the Lord will often feel his hand of discipline upon them, as he responds to their heart's desire to become more like him. In John 15:2, Jesus explains that God *"cuts off every branch in me that bears no fruit, while every branch that does bear fruit he prunes so that it will be even more fruitful."* Those who love the Lord still feel his knife, but in different ways. In that sense, the Assyrian invasion is not God's response to Hezekiah's

---

[2] Marduk-Baladan twice tried to liberate Babylon from Assyrian rule, in 721–710 and 703–702 BC. After failing for a second time, he disappears from history.

[3] The Chronicler is exceedingly generous towards Hezekiah. He does not mention that he foolishly sought to make Egypt his saviour (Isaiah 30:1–5 and 31:1–3) or that he plundered a ton of gold and 10 tons of silver from the Temple in a failed attempt to buy off the Assyrian army (2 Kings 18:13–16).

[4] The Chronicler only devotes a single verse to this amazing miracle (32:24). He expects us to have read the full account of it in 2 Kings 20 and Isaiah 38–39.

sin but to his thirst for ever greater holiness. It results in a strengthening of his faith in the Lord.

When Hezekiah hears that his border fortresses have fallen to the Assyrian army, he does all that his own hands can do.[5] He prepares Jerusalem for a long siege by blocking up the Gihon Spring, outside the city walls, and diverting its water to the Pool of Siloam, inside the city walls.[6] He reinforces the walls of Jerusalem and builds additional walls and towers. He stockpiles weapons for his soldiers. He does all that his own hands can do, but he knows deep down that his hands are no match for the hands of the Assyrians.

If Hezekiah's zeal was flagging before the Assyrian invasion, then it definitely isn't now. He encourages the people of Jerusalem to place their faith, not in what his own hands have done for them, but in the hand of the Lord. *"Do not be afraid or discouraged because of the king of Assyria and the vast army with him, for there is a greater power with us than with him. With him is only the arm of flesh, but with us is the Lord our God to help us."*[7]

What follows is a classic example of spiritual warfare. The Devil tries to use deception to scupper the revival that is taking place in Judah. Sennacherib responds to Hezekiah's rallying cry by sending messengers to preach his own rival sermon to the people of Jerusalem. It is full of lies. If the hand of the Lord did not succeed in rescuing the northern kingdom from the hand of Sennacherib, then what reason does Judah have to believe that it will rescue the southern kingdom from him? Besides, hasn't Hezekiah offended the Lord by demolishing his "high places" and forcing everyone to worship at the Lord's

---

[5] The royal annals of Sennacherib boast that he captured forty-six fortified cities and carried off over 200,000 captives from Judah, reducing Hezekiah to *"a prisoner in Jerusalem his royal residence, like a bird in a cage."*

[6] To understand 32:2–4 and 30, take a look at 2 Kings 20:20. Hezekiah's Tunnel is an amazing piece of ancient engineering. Tourists in Jerusalem still queue up to wade through his 520-metre-long tunnel today.

[7] 32:7–8. The Chronicler says literally in verse 8 that *"the people were upheld by the words of Hezekiah"*. That's what leaders are called do for God's people. Hezekiah's words are similar to those of 2 Kings 6:15–17 and 1 John 4:4.

Temple instead?[8] If the gods of Assyria have strengthened Sennacherib's hand to conquer every other nation in the region, then won't those gods surely strengthen his hand to conquer Judah just as easily?

Hezekiah stands firm in his faith. He remembers that the gods of those conquered nations are mere idols, *"the work of human hands"* (verse 19). He enlists the help of Isaiah, and the two of them cry out to God in prayer. They plead with him to hear this blasphemy against his name and to prove the power of his hand by crushing the Assyrian invasion.[9] What follows is one of the most stunning reversals in the whole of military history. An angel of the Lord comes down from heaven and, in a single night, puts to death the entire Assyrian army. Sennacherib wakes up to find with horror that he is surrounded by 185,000 corpses. He panics and flees home to Nineveh, where the Lord grants him twenty years to repent. When he refuses to do so, he is assassinated by his own sons.[10]

After the siege of Jerusalem is lifted, no one is left complaining that the Lord permitted the Assyrian invasion. Surprising though it was, it has brought about an even greater blessing for Judah. There are no longer any foreign idols left in the land. Its spiritual revival has been granted fresh forward momentum. We are told in verse 23 that many foreign rulers came to Jerusalem with gifts for Hezekiah. *"From then on he was highly regarded by all the nations."* He was able to testify to each of his foreign visitors about the Lord, just as King Solomon had been able to testify to the Queen of Sheba.

---

[8] The Devil's lies are effective because they are often partly true. Hezekiah *had* removed the "high places" where the Lord was worshipped in ways contrary to his Law (Leviticus 17:1–9). The Lord was delighted by this obedience, but there was enough truth in Sennacherib's accusation to make people wonder.

[9] For a lot more on how Hezekiah prayed a prayer of repentance at the Temple, as envisaged by Solomon in his prayer of dedication, see 2 Kings 18–19 and Isaiah 36–37. A staggering 185,000 Assyrian soldiers died!

[10] Note God's grace here. Sennacherib fled home in 701 BC and was not murdered by his sons until 681 BC. Only then was he murdered while worshipping in the temple of the Assyrian fertility-god Nisrok.

"Manasseh led Judah and the people of Jerusalem astray, so that they did more evil than the nations the Lord had destroyed before the Israelites."

(2 Chronicles 33:9)

We have seen that the Chronicler presents his history of the kings of Judah as a story of "six plus one". Three times over, he gives us six *messiahs* followed by a seventh false *messiah*. You may remember that the first cycle went like this:

Rehoboam (930–913 BC) – "bad"
Abijah (913–910 BC) – "bad"
Asa (910–869 BC) – "good"
Jehoshaphat (872–848 BC) – "good"
Jehoram (853–841 BC) – "bad"
Ahaziah (841 BC) – "bad"
[Athaliah (841–835 BC) – "antichrist"]

The antichrist at the end of the first cycle is a usurper to the throne. Queen Athaliah does not come from the dynasty of David but from the evil house of Ahab. The second cycle is different, since it is the only cycle where the antichrist comes from David's own dynasty.

Joash (835–796 BC) – "good" then "bad"
Amaziah (796–767 BC) – "good" then "bad"
Uzziah (792–740 BC) – "good" then "bad"
Jotham (750–732 BC) – "good"

Ahaz (735–715 BC) – "bad"
Hezekiah (715–686 BC) – "good"
Manasseh (697–642 BC) – "antichrist"

Hezekiah has been humbled through the Assyrian invasion of
Judah. Having shrugged his shoulders in 2 Kings 20:19, asking
"Will there not be peace and security in my lifetime?", he now
repents of his self-centredness and begins to plan for the next
generation. He installs his twelve-year-old son Manasseh to
start ruling with him as joint king.[1]

Sadly, it is too little too late. Manasseh means *Forgetfulness*,
and he lives up to his name. He remembers nothing of what his
father teaches him about stewarding the throne of David for the
true King of Judah. He rebuilds the "high places". He constructs
shrines for Baal and Asherah.[2] He sacrifices his children in the
fire to cut a deal with the demon-god Molek.[3] He forges further
pacts with demons by consulting witches and occultists.[4]

Terrible though Manasseh's idolatry is, the Chronicler is
even more horrified by the way that it defiles the Temple of the
Lord. He is appalled that Manasseh dares to erect pagan altars
in the Temple courtyards – in the very place the Lord promised
to make the earthly footstool to his heavenly throne.[5] Having
forgotten what his father taught him, Manasseh soon forgets the
Law of Moses too. He leads the people of Judah so far astray

---

[1] Several of the kings of Judah did this as a way of training up their sons. We know that
Manasseh's reign ended in 642 BC, so the first nine years of his fifty-five-year-rule must
have overlapped with the final years of his father. Manasseh was the longest reigning king
of Judah, as well as being its most sinful king.

[2] *"The image"* which is mentioned in 33:7 was an ornate Asherah pole (2 Kings 21:7).

[3] As mentioned earlier, the Greek name for the *Valley of Ben Hinnom* is *Gehenna*. Jesus
uses this ten times in Matthew and Mark's gospels as his name for *hell* because the fire in
the valley spoke of the demons which were at work behind it.

[4] The *host of heaven* in 33:3–5 means more than simply sacrificing to the sun, moon
and stars. It is the same Hebrew phrase that is used in 18:18 to describe the demons
which inhabit the heavenly realms. This embracing of sorcery marks a new low for Judah.
Manasseh has become the prince regent of Satan.

[5] Before we rush to judge Manasseh, let's reflect on what false teaching and practices we
may have brought into the Church ourselves. See 1 Corinthians 10:6.

from the instructions that the Lord gave Moses at Mount Sinai that they become even more depraved than the Canaanites who inhabited the land before them. Manasseh resurrects *"the detestable practices of the nations the Lord had driven out before the Israelites"*, and he entices his subjects to do the same.[6] When the Chronicler laments that *"Manasseh led Judah and the people of Jerusalem astray, so that they did more evil than the nations the Lord had destroyed before the Israelites"*, he is telling us that Manasseh was the worst king that ever came from David's dynasty. He wasn't just a failed *messiah*. He was an *anti-messiah*.

Manasseh is hurtling towards the same destruction as Queen Athaliah, when suddenly the Chronicler surprises us. Since Manasseh had refused to listen to his prophets, the Lord brings about a fresh invasion of Judah by the Assyrian army.[7] When Manasseh is taken off to Babylon as a common prisoner of war, he finally remembers what his father taught him.[8] He repents of his sin and is released from prison.[9] He returns home, removes the idols from the Temple courtyards and reconsecrates the Temple to the Lord. Although he is by far the worst king of Judah, Manasseh proves that God will forgive anyone who puts their hope in a better *Messiah*.[10] He escapes the fate of Queen Athaliah.

---

[6] The Hebrew verb *tāʾah* in 33:9 normally describes a man *seducing* a married woman. Godly Hezekiah and sinful Manasseh both demonstrate just how much influence leaders have over their people. When Manasseh sacrifices his own children (33:6) the people of Judah quickly do the same (Jeremiah 7:30–32 and 19:1–6).

[7] Manasseh did not just refuse to listen. He became known as "the Nero of Judah" because he murdered God's prophets – probably including Isaiah. See 2 Kings 21:16; 23:26–27 and 24:3–4, and Jeremiah 15:4.

[8] Don't be confused by the reference to Babylon as an Assyrian city. Marduk-Baladan's rebellion had failed.

[9] King Ashurbanipal of Assyria invaded Judah in about 650 BC. Some of the reliefs on his palace walls depict him leading away prisoners of war with a hook through their nose or lips to make them as docile as a bull with a ring in its nose. See also 2 Kings 19:28.

[10] Despite the sins of Manasseh's reign, the Lord remains *"his God"* (33:12) and *"the God of Israel"* (33:16).

Sadly, in 33:21–25, the Chronicler laments that Manasseh's repentance comes too late to influence his son. Amon's name means *Master Builder*, but his reign is exceedingly destructive. He reverses any traces of his father's belated repentance, pursuing all of the same sins that dominated the bulk of his father's reign. The best thing that we can say about his reign is that it only lasted two years, before he was assassinated by his courtiers.[11] Amon begins a third and final cycle of "six plus one", which looks like this:

> **Amon (642–640 BC) – "bad"**
> **Josiah (640–609 BC) – "good"**
> **Jehoahaz (609 BC) – "bad"**
> **Jehoiakim (609–598 BC) – "bad"**
> **Jehoiachin (598–597 BC) – "bad"**
> **Zedekiah (597–586 BC) – "bad"**
> **[Nebuchadnezzar – "antichrist"]**

We are now entering the final furlong of the history of Judah. After two cycles of "six plus one", we are still waiting for a true *Messiah* to come forth from David's dynasty.

---

[11] The Chronicler tells us that four kings of Judah were not buried in the royal tombs of David's dynasty because they were such bad *messiahs*: Jehoram (21:20), Joash (24:25), Uzziah (26:23) and Ahaz (28:27). We are also told in 2 Kings 21:18 and 26 that Manasseh and Amon were buried in the royal garden rather than in the royal tombs, because they were terrible *messiahs* too.

Fresh Start
(2 Chronicles 34:1–33)

"The king stood by his pillar and renewed the covenant in the presence of the Lord – to follow the Lord and keep his commands."

(2 Chronicles 34:31)

Whether it is baking or playing computer games or making things out of LEGO®, we all know that there are times when it's best to give up on a bad job and to start all over again. When Josiah came to the throne of Judah, it had been so ravaged by his grandfather Manasseh and his father Amon that even an eight-year-old could see that little could be salvaged from their rule. Josiah knew that he needed to make a fresh start for Judah.

In 34:1–7, the reign of Josiah offers a fresh start for *David's dynasty*. The assassination of Amon proves to be a severe mercy from the Lord, because it means the eight-year-old Josiah has no time to learn any of his father's evil ways. Josiah means *Given A Foundation By The Lord* and, sure enough, the priests and prophets lay a much better foundation for him as to how to steward his throne for the real King of Judah.[1] In 632 BC, aged only sixteen, Josiah begins to express his personal faith in the Lord. In 628 BC, he proves that faith by beginning to cleanse his territory of his father's idols.[2] The Chronicler presents this as a

---

[1] The prophet Zephaniah was a member of the royal family of Judah (Zephaniah 1:1), so it appears that the young Josiah was deeply influenced by his call to choose between God's judgment and God's salvation.

[2] This was enormously courageous of Josiah, since his father had been assassinated by his subjects. People who are willing to sacrifice their own children are not likely to let a twenty-year-old king stand in their way.

fresh start for the royal family of Judah by telling us twice that Josiah sought to walk in the ways of *"the God of his father David"*.

Josiah longs for the reunification of the twelve tribes of Israel, but not through the false unity of his fathers. After destroying the "high places" in his own kingdom, he travels north to do the same in what used to be the northern kingdom too. As he does so, he calls any survivors from the ten northern tribes to repent of their sins and to return to the God of Israel. Under Josiah, all twelve tribes can enjoy a fresh start with the Lord.[3]

In 34:8–13, the reign of Josiah offers a fresh start for *the Temple*. After demolishing the pagan shrines, the king sets his heart in 622 BC towards purifying the Temple from its desecration by the last two kings of Judah.[4] He asks the high priest Hilkiah to set the priests and Levites to work to repair it, funded by generous donations from the people.[5]

In 34:14–21, the reign of Josiah offers a fresh start for *God's Word* at the heart of Judah. We can tell how much its people neglected the Scriptures during the reigns of Manasseh and Amon from the way that Hilkiah seems surprised to find a copy in the Temple, and from the way that the royal secretary Shaphan looks at it blankly and, almost as an afterthought, tells Josiah that *"Hilkiah the priest has given me a book"*.[6] It feels a lot less like a person finding their missing set of car keys than

---

[3] 2 Kings 23:4–20 gives more detail about this. Josiah demolishes the shrine of Molek in the Valley of Ben Hinnom so that nobody can sacrifice their children there. He stops male prostitutes from selling their bodies in the Temple courtyards. He then goes north to Bethel to fulfil the prophecy spoken against Jeroboam in 1 Kings 13:1–2 that a king named Josiah would burn the bones of his false priests on their own pagan altars.

[4] The Hebrew text of 34:11 does not just say that those kings allowed the Temple to fall into ruin. It says that they actively *"destroyed"* it.

[5] The Chronicler encourages us in 34:9 that many survivors from the northern kingdom responded to Josiah's missionary tour by bringing their donations to the Temple too.

[6] Hilkiah means *My Portion Is The Lord*. He has not been a good high priest up until this moment, showing little initiative to repair the Temple and allowing the desecration of its courtyards (Zephaniah 3:4). But now he steps up and becomes the person who brings the Scriptures back to centre stage in the life of Judah.

a person being reminded that they even own a car![7] The king, however, recognises the book instantly. When Shaphan reads it out loud to him, he rips his royal robes in repentance.[8] He urges Shaphan and Hilkiah to seek out a prophet of the Lord urgently, since he has concluded that *"Great is the Lord's anger that is poured out on us because those who have gone before us have not kept the word of the Lord; they have not acted in accordance with all that is written in this book."*

In 34:22–28, we catch our first clue that this fresh start isn't going to be enough to save the kingdom of Judah from destruction. The prophet Huldah is the wife of a man named Shallum, which means *Payback*. He is the "keeper of the wardrobe", which probably means that he was a Levite tasked with looking after the priests' sacred robes.[9] She sends word back to Josiah that the Lord has seen his repentant heart and forgiven his sins. The destruction of the southern kingdom has been postponed but it has not been cancelled altogether.[10] We are now in a third cycle of "six plus one" without finding any true *Messiah* in David's dynasty. It has become abundantly clear that the twelve tribes of Israel can only be reunified by passing through the "death and resurrection" of exile.[11]

In 34:29–33, Josiah is determined that his reign may yet bring about a fresh start for *the people of God*. He refuses to

---

[7] *"The Book of the Law"* was technically just the first five books of our Bibles, but in common usage it included the Psalms, the Prophets and the other books of the Old Testament (John 10:34 and 1 Corinthians 14:21).

[8] This is a great illustration of Romans 3:19–20. Without God's Word, we convince ourselves that we are doing fine (2 Corinthians 10:12), but with it we discover our need of Jesus Christ (Galatians 3:24). Tragically, Josiah's son Jehoiakim would burn the Word of God, instead of repenting before it, in Jeremiah 36:20–32.

[9] Huldah is the only female prophet named in 1 and 2 Chronicles. Her name means *Weasel*, which is unflattering, yet despite the fact that Jeremiah and Zephaniah are in Jerusalem, the high priest goes to her.

[10] The Lord effectively tells Josiah: *Because you listened to my Word, I will also listen to your words.* Isaiah 66:2 agrees that how we respond to God's Word to us hugely affects the depth of our relationship with him.

[11] It is 622 BC, exactly 100 years since the exile of the northern kingdom, so don't miss the references to *"Israel and Judah"*, to *"the God of Israel"* and to *"all the territory belonging to the Israelites"* in 34:21, 23, 26 and 33.

treat Huldah's prophecy as an excuse for fatalism, but rather as a springboard for further faith. He gathers the people together in the Temple courtyard, as in the days of Solomon and Jehoshaphat, to read out the Book of the Law to them.[12] He then leads them in a renewal of the covenant that God made with the twelve tribes of Israel, as they stand together in the Presence of the Lord.[13]

The chapter ends on such a high that it is hard to believe that there are only two chapters left in the Chronicler's scroll. But Huldah isn't wrong. It will take a lot more than this type of fresh start to cleanse the southern kingdom from its persistent sins. Jeremiah 3:10–11 delivers the Lord's verdict on this crucial moment in the Temple courtyard: *"Judah did not return to me with all her heart, but only in pretence."* Although Josiah's motives were sincere, many of his subjects didn't really mean what they said. They renewed their covenant with God because everybody else was doing it and because it seemed like a good way of currying favour with their ruler. As a result, Jeremiah continues: *"Faithless Israel is more righteous than unfaithful Judah."*[14]

This shocking verdict prepares us for the final cycle of "six plus one" kings of Judah. Even the greatest king of Judah after David was unable to revive the southern kingdom from the outside in. Only a far better *Messiah*, who knew how to transform sinful people from the inside out, could ever enable Judah to follow God in truth, not merely in pretence.[15] Huldah is right that the twelve tribes of Israel will only truly be reunited as God's people and truly reconsecrated to him through the "death and resurrection" of the exile.

---

[12] This is what happens when we study the Word of God. We get so excited by it that we refuse to take no for an answer. We feel we have to pass it on to other people too.

[13] The two tall bronze pillars of the Temple porchway represented the joining of heaven and earth through the Temple. We can infer from 23:13 and 34:31 that it became a tradition for the king to stand next to one of the pillars and for the high priest to stand next to the other.

[14] Zephaniah issued this same warning in the reign of Josiah. Like a used-car salesman's smile, the tears at the Temple were superficial and would not be enough to prevent the destruction of Judah (Zephaniah 1:4–6).

[15] Jesus says he has come to do this in John 4:23–24.

Innocent Blood
(2 Chronicles 35:1–27)

"Josiah celebrated the Passover to the Lord in Jerusalem, and the Passover lamb was slaughtered on the fourteenth day of the first month."

(2 Chronicles 35:1)

The penultimate chapter of 2 Chronicles feels like a Quentin Tarantino movie. It is wall-to-wall bloodshed from beginning to end. Having warned us that the twelve tribes of Israel will only be reunited through the "death and resurrection" of the exile, Chronicles begins to show us what will happen to them through the blood of the *Messiah*.

King Josiah invites the twelve tribes of Israel to celebrate the Passover Festival with him at the Temple.[1] Unlike Hezekiah, who celebrated the Passover on the wrong day and without its proper regulations, Josiah is meticulous about observing every detail. Celebrate it on the fourteenth day of the first month? *Check*. Honour the Presence of God above the Ark of the Covenant in the Most Holy Place of the Temple? *Check*.[2] Make sure that the priests and Levites are in their proper places to slaughter the Passover lambs, according to the rules laid down for them by David and Solomon? *Check*. Chronicles speaks a lot about the innocent blood of these Passover lambs, because they are being presented as a prophetic picture of what God will

---

[1] The Chronicler emphasises that this Passover was for *"all Israel"* in 35:3, 4, 13 and 17–18.

[2] The Ark had evidently been removed from the Temple to hide it from Manasseh and Amon. Since this is the last mention of the Ark in the Old Testament, it was probably lost while hiding it from the Babylonians.

accomplish for the twelve tribes of Israel through the death of his *Messiah*.[3]

Like King David at the end of 1 Chronicles, King Josiah leads the way in generosity. The power of an ancient ruler was measured by the size of his flocks and herds, so Josiah gladly sacrifices his royal status by providing 30,000 sheep and goats, and 3,000 bulls, as innocent blood-sacrifices for the twelve tribes of Israel. The priests and Levites follow his lead by providing further animals for the people. The Chronicler assures us that, when the priests shed the innocent blood of these Passover lambs, they do everything *"as it is written in the Book of Moses."* The Levite worship leaders also lead the people in grateful songs of praise as *"prescribed by David, Asaph, Heman and Jeduthun"*. Everything here points to the utter perfection of the true Passover Lamb who is to come.[4]

Once this innocent blood has been shed for the people of Israel, they observe the Festival of Unleavened Bread for seven days, as stipulated by the Law of Moses. We have already noted, during the reign of Hezekiah, that those seven days were meant to serve as a reminder that forgiveness *for* sin should always lead to freedom *from* sin. The blood of the Passover Lamb is able to save God's people to the uttermost. It enables them to step out from under the guilt of sin and it empowers them to shake off the yoke of slavery to sin.[5] Our sanctification is as much a gift of God's grace as is our justification.

In 35:19, the Chronicler emphasises that it is 622 BC, exactly a hundred years after the destruction and exile of the northern kingdom of Israel. That's quite a centenary, but there is nothing here to suggest that Judah will go the same way any time soon.

---

[3] The Chronicler devotes nineteen verses to this Passover, even though he is running out of scroll. By way of contrast, the writer of 1 and 2 Kings only devotes three verses to it, in 2 Kings 23:21–23.

[4] Josiah's Passover is a lot more regimented than Hezekiah's Passover. Is it significant that there is no mention of *rejoicing* in this chapter? His intensity didn't produce sincerity.

[5] The Apostle Paul explains the meaning of Exodus 12:1–28 to us in 1 Corinthians 5:6–8. Men like Daniel and his friends probably caught their passion for God's holiness during this revival under Josiah.

King Josiah is aged only twenty-six and he rules the southern kingdom in a godlier fashion than any of his predecessors. He only seems to be getting started in his righteous reign.

It is therefore quite shocking, in 35:20–27, when we discover that the innocent blood that is to be shed at the end of the chapter is the blood of King Josiah. The Assyrian Empire is coming to an end. It is about to be supplanted by the Babylonian Empire. Their final showdown will not take place until the Battle of Carchemish in 605 BC, but plenty of skirmishes are taking place in the run-up to that decisive battle. Pharaoh Necho rides out from Egypt with his army in 609 BC in order to support the beleaguered Assyrians. When Josiah refuses to allow him to pass through the land of Judah, he tries to reason with him. He claims that he is being obedient to a vision in which the God of Israel commanded him to lend his weight to the fight against the Babylonians. If Josiah refuses to let Necho pass through the land of Judah, he may find himself resisting the Lord.

Suddenly, Josiah begins to act like King Ahab at the Battle of Ramoth Gilead. He refuses to believe Necho's testimony about the Lord. He rushes headlong onto the battlefield, disguising himself so that the famous Egyptian archers cannot make him a special target for their arrows. Like King Ahab, however, he is shot at random, escaping in a chariot to die of his wounds after the battle.[6] His death in 609 BC marks the beginning of the end for Judah. Over the next twenty-one years, it will experience three waves of exile to Babylon, the city which Josiah so foolishly tried to defend. In that sense, we might even say that the reunification of the twelve tribes of Israel through the "death and resurrection" of the exile begins with the innocent bloodshed of this godly *messiah*.[7]

---

[6] 2 Kings 23:29 says Josiah died at Megiddo, whereas the Chronicler says he was brought home in a chariot to die in Jerusalem. Evidently, he was alive at the start of his journey but declared dead on arrival.

[7] The Greek transliteration of the Hebrew for *Hill of Megiddo* in 35:22 is *Armageddon*, so Revelation 16:16 treats this event as a prophetic picture of the forces of evil being defeated through the death of the *Messiah*.

Many readers speculate about what sin Josiah must have committed for his reign to end so abruptly. Aged only thirty-nine, he still had everything to live for. The prophet Isaiah responds that Josiah did nothing wrong at all. We have misunderstood the Chronicler if we think he is telling us that nothing good will ever happen to the wicked and that nothing bad will ever happen to the godly. Isaiah 57:1–2 unpacks what the Chronicler tries to teach us in 34:26–28. The Lord did not require the life of King Josiah on the battlefield because he was sinful, but because he was good. He wanted to spare him from witnessing what was about to happen to the southern kingdom of Judah.[8]

> *The righteous perish, and no one takes it to heart. The devout are taken away, and no one understands that the righteous are taken away to be spared from evil. Those who walk uprightly enter into peace; they find rest as they lie in death.*[9]

There is a general truth we can learn from these verses. Premature death is not the worst thing that can happen to those to whom the Lord has granted life beyond the grave. But the Chronicler also has a more specific lesson for us here. As the greatest *messiah* of the southern kingdom of Judah spills his innocent blood on the battlefield, he becomes a prophetic picture of the true *Messiah* who is coming to be a better Passover Lamb than the thousands of animals that were slaughtered at the Temple in the days of Josiah.

---

[8] 2 Kings 23:26–27 says that the fate of Judah had already been sealed by Manasseh's sins. Josiah's personal repentance could save him, but not his stubborn nation too. They would need to be disciplined through exile.

[9] Isaiah 57:1–2. Zechariah 12:11 indicates that the grief was so great over Josiah's death that it became proverbial for any lavish mourning. Jeremiah probably sang something similar to Isaiah 57:1–2 in his lament for him (35:25). He learned from this to write the Old Testament book of Lamentations about the fall of Jerusalem in 586 BC.

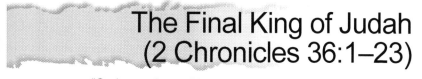

The Final King of Judah
(2 Chronicles 36:1–23)

"God gave them all into the hands of Nebuchadnezzar."
(2 Chronicles 36:17)

Josiah is the final king of Judah who sets his heart on seeking the Lord.[1] After him come four other kings who set their hearts on other things. The final kings of Judah are:

> **Jehoahaz (609 BC) – "bad"**
> **Jehoiakim (609–598 BC) – "bad"**
> **Jehoiachin (598–597 BC) – "bad"**
> **Zedekiah (597–586 BC) – "bad"**

In 36:1–4, we are told about Jehoahaz. He is the fourth son of Josiah and his throne name expresses his surprise that the people have made him king instead of his older brothers.[2] Jehoahaz means *The Lord Has Taken Hold Of Me*, but he refuses to take hold of the Lord and, as a result, reigns for only three short months as king. It is likely that the people chose him because of his fiery anti-Egyptian rhetoric, so Pharaoh Necho quickly replaces him with an older brother who is more willing

---

[1] Four more kings rule after him, but Josiah is the last to be buried in the royal tombs of David's dynasty.

[2] Jehoahaz was originally named *Shallum* (Jeremiah 22:10–12). His older brothers are listed in 1 Chronicles 3:15. Johanan may have died young, since he is the only one of the four brothers not to rule as king of Judah.

to serve as his puppet ruler. Jehoahaz dies a prisoner in Egypt, as a prophetic warning of what will happen due to Judah's sin.[3]

In 36:5–8, we are told about Jehoiakim. Pharaoh Necho emphasises that he is Egypt's puppet ruler by changing his name from Eliakim, which means *God Raises Up*, to one which means *The Lord Raises Up*, as a commemoration of Necho's vision of the Lord in 35:21. Jehoiakim rules for eleven years, during which time he bankrolls the Egyptian campaign against the Babylonian Empire. Sadly, he is less willing to submit the throne of Judah to the Lord.[4] The rest of the Old Testament tells us that he burnt Jeremiah's prophecies, murdered the prophet Uriah and set up pagan idols in the courtyards of the Temple. When King Nebuchadnezzar of Babylon defeats Pharaoh Necho at the Battle of Carchemish in 605 BC, Jehoiakim thinks nothing of breaking the oath he made in the name of the Lord in order to switch sides. His treachery fails. He is killed and his corpse is left to rot outside the walls of Jerusalem. Several of his predecessors had been judged by not being buried in the royal tombs, but Jehoiakim isn't buried at all.[5]

In 36:9–10, we are told about Jehoiachin. He reigned for three months – about as long as it took the Babylonian army to reach Jerusalem and demand the tribute his father had stopped paying. Nebuchadnezzar had already taken a first group of Jews into exile after the Battle of Carchemish in 605 BC. Now he takes a second group into exile in 597 BC. Jehoiachin is among them, thrown on the scrapheap of history at the age of eighteen.[6]

---

[3] Jehoahaz was taken captive at Riblah, on the River Orontes, the very place where the princes and priests of Judah would be slaughtered by the Babylonians in 586 BC (2 Kings 23:31–35; 25:5–7, 18–21).

[4] Jehoiakim might deny it, but the Chronicler insists in 36:5 that the Lord remained his God.

[5] This extra detail about the reign of Jehoiakim can be found in 2 Kings 23:36 – 24:7; Jeremiah 22:18–19; 26:20–23 and 36:1–32, and Ezekiel 8:5–18. Josephus also confirms it in his *Antiquities of the Jews* (10.6.3).

[6] Some Hebrew manuscripts say that he was aged eight, but 2 Kings 24:8 indicates that this is a copying error. The Babylonian royal annals say that Jerusalem fell a second time to Nebuchadnezzar on 16 March 597 BC.

In 36:11–16, we are told about Zedekiah, another son of Josiah and the final king of Judah from David's dynasty. His name means *The Lord Is Righteous*, which serves as a warning to the southern kingdom, but he is every bit as forgetful as Manasseh.[7] He fills the Temple courtyard with idols. He forges an alliance with Egypt, reneging on the oath he swore in the name of the Lord to serve Nebuchadnezzar. He is so ungodly that he imprisons Jeremiah and fails to notice when the Presence of God leaves the Temple on 17 September 592 BC.[8] Even when the Babylonians besiege Jerusalem for thirty months, from 15 January 588 BC to 18 July 586 BC, Zedekiah refuses to surrender to the Lord.[9]

When Zedekiah abandons Jerusalem in order to save his own skin, he is captured along with the remaining members of David's dynasty. They are put to death before his eyes, then his eyes are gouged out so that the end of David's dynasty becomes the final sight emblazoned on his brain. Blind and childless, he is taken as a prisoner to Babylon, never to be heard of again. David's dynasty appears to die out with this final king of Judah.

King Nebuchadnezzar of Babylon is the *anti-messiah* who comes at the end of this third cycle of the history of the Jewish kings. Foreign kings have already plundered the Temple six times, but Nebuchadnezzar plunders it three more times. The last time, he burns down the Temple and brings the southern kingdom of Judah to an abrupt end.[10] Having carried off two

SMALL THINGS ABOUT JUDAH

---

[7] His original name was Mattaniah, which means *Gift Of The Lord*. The kings of Babylon changed the names of those they conquered as a means of asserting their supremacy over them (Daniel 1:7).

[8] You can read about these wider events of Zedekiah's reign in 2 Kings 24:17 – 25:7; Jeremiah 32:1–5; 34:1–22 and 37:1–21, and Ezekiel 8:1; 9:3; 10:4–5, 18–19; 11:22–23 and 17:15–19.

[9] It is a terrible thing to be told in 36:16 that now *"there was no remedy"* for the southern kingdom, but we are issued a similar warning ourselves in Hebrews 12:16–17. We must surrender to the Lord while we still can.

[10] The Temple was previously plundered in 1 Kings 14:25–28 and 15:18, and 2 Kings 12:18; 14:14; 16:7–8 and 18:15–16. Nebuchadnezzar plunders and destroys it in 2 Chronicles 36:7, 10 and 18–19.

groups of Jewish prisoners into exile in Babylon in 605 BC and 597 BC, he now carries off a third group of exiles in 586 BC. In that sense, Nebuchadnezzar can claim to be the final king of Judah.

But the Chronicler tells a very different story. He is light on the detail of the destruction of Jerusalem, so that he can focus our eyes on the way that Nebuchadnezzar resembles Queen Athaliah.[11] He too is a destroyer of David's dynasty, and he too fails to kill its final heir. The writer of 2 Kings ends his story by reminding us that Jehoiachin is still on the scrapheap in Babylon. The Lord brings him back to the royal palace, as he did Joash, and ensures that Jehoiachin's grandson Zerubbabel is chosen to lead the Jewish survivors back home from their exile to the Promised Land. David's dynasty is not extinguished. There is a final King of Judah yet to come.

Rather than focusing on Jehoiachin, the Chronicler ends his account, by focusing on King Cyrus of Persia, who overthrew the Babylonian Empire in 539 BC. He insists that the Lord's Temple remains the focal point of history, despite its destruction (36:15–16). He insists that whatever the Lord speaks with his mouth through his Law and Prophets, his hand will certainly fulfil (36:21).[12] The final two verses of 2 Chronicles are almost identical to the first two-and-a-half verses of Ezra, since they probably share the same author, who invites us to read the second instalment of his story.[13] The Chronicler ends the first instalment with a cry of triumph. King Nebuchadnezzar of Babylon has not proven to be the final king of Judah. His throne has fallen to King Cyrus

---

[11] He is also like the *anti-messiah* Manasseh, since the Lord brings him to repentance in Daniel 1–4.

[12] 2 Chronicles 6:15. Seventy years' worth of sabbath days was what the Lord warned would happen in Leviticus 26:34–45. It takes Jewish history back to about 1050 BC, the year when Saul became the first king of Israel.

[13] We saw in the introduction to this commentary that 1 and 2 Chronicles, Ezra and Nehemiah were originally two books, not four. The Jewish tradition seems valid that both were written by Ezra the scribe.

of Persia, who now paves the way for a new cycle of Jewish history to begin.[14]

The fall of David's dynasty was tragic, but the Lord used it to set up a new era in the history of his people. He used it to clear the stage for his true *Messiah* to arise from David's fallen dynasty – who alone would be the final, everlasting King of Judah.

---

[14] The Chronicler makes the words of Cyrus sound devout and he notes that they fulfil God's promise in Jeremiah 25:12–14 and 29:10. Isaiah 44:28 – 45:1 also predicted he would do this a century before he was born.

Conclusion: The God of Small Things

"The Lord, the God of their ancestors… had pity on his people and on his dwelling-place."

(2 Chronicles 36:15)

The Guardian newspaper has made some serious errors of judgment over the years. During the American Civil War, it sided with the South and declared that the election of Abraham Lincoln was *"an evil day both for America and the world"*. During the Indian Mutiny against British rule in 1857, it defended the status quo due to *"unfaltering confidence in our right to rule over the native population by virtue of inherent superiority"*. It opposed the suffragettes. It promoted the virtues of asbestos. It fretted that the National Health Service might swell the ranks of the *"less gifted"*. It even reassured its readers in June 1914 that, *"It is not to be supposed that the death of the Archduke Francis Ferdinand will have any immediate or salient effect on the politics of Europe."*[1]

However foolish these errors of judgment may be, they pale into insignificance compared to the folly of thinking that God has given up on his promises to his people. The Jews were tempted to believe that he had done so after the exile, since their homeland remained a subjugated province of the Persian Empire, without any new king from David's dynasty on its throne. It was difficult for the original readers of 1 and 2 Chronicles to fathom what God was doing amidst their confusion but, for us

---

[1] To its credit, *The Guardian* confessed these errors in an article entitled "What We Got Wrong" (7 May 2021). Material copyright Guardian News & Media Ltd, 2022.

reading many centuries later, the Chronicler's message rings out loud and clear.

In **1 Chronicles 1–9** we saw that the Chronicler turns the spotlight onto several **small things about Israel** which should reassure his readers that God's promises towards their nation have not failed. The exile of the twelve tribes of Israel to Assyria and Babylon has become a "death and resurrection" for their nation. God has brought them back home from the exile, united as one nation, to usher in a brilliant new era of Jewish history.

In **1 Chronicles 10–29**, we saw that the Chronicler turns the spotlight onto several **small things about David** which bring further reassurance to the Jews about God's promises. He introduces the theme of God's *Messiah*, using David as a prophetic picture of the greater King of Israel who is to come. He also talks a lot about David's Tabernacle, which quickly turns into a new theme of *the Lord's Temple*. For the Jews who first read the Chronicler's new history of Israel, this was of paramount importance. Even if God hadn't yet restored his *Messiah* to the throne, he had magnificently restored his *Temple*.

In **2 Chronicles 1–9**, we saw that the Chronicler turns the spotlight onto several **small things about Solomon** which should reassure his readers even further. He describes the building of the Temple in lavish detail to remind his readers that its restoration under Zerubbabel was as big a miracle as would be the restoration of David's dynasty. After presenting Solomon as a prophetic picture of the *Messiah* who is to come, he lets Solomon's prayer reassure his readers, in 6:15, that God never forgets his promises: *"With your mouth you have promised and with your hand you have fulfilled it – as it is today."*

In **2 Chronicles 10–36**, we saw that the Chronicler turns the spotlight onto **small things about Judah** which should also reassure his readers. He expresses the history of the southern kingdom as a story of three times over "six plus one". Six flawed *messiahs*, then the *anti-messiah* Athaliah. Six flawed *messiahs*, then the *anti-messiah* Manasseh. Six flawed *messiahs*, then the *anti-messiah* Nebuchadnezzar. Finally, he turns the spotlight onto King Cyrus of Persia to reassure his readers that another, better *Messiah* is now on his way.

The Chronicler's retelling of Jewish history forms the final two books of many Hebrew Old Testaments. In manuscripts where it doesn't, it is only because Ezra and Nehemiah supplant them, since most readers recognise those books to be the second instalment of the same story. Either way, the Hebrew Old Testament ends with the Chronicler's reassurance that God's promises towards his people can never fail. Jewish history did not end with the fall of the southern kingdom. It is only just getting started.

It is therefore significant that the first book of the New Testament presents itself as the follow-up to the Chronicler's great story. We noted in the introduction to this commentary that the Greek name for 1 and 2 Chronicles is *Paraleipomenon*, which means *Things Omitted Earlier*. It is self-consciously a closing summary of the Old Testament, which looks forward to a new stage of Jewish history which will be orchestrated by the true *Messiah*. That's why Matthew begins his gospel with a cry of triumph: *"This is the genealogy of Jesus the Messiah the son of David".* It is why he then launches into seventeen verses of genealogy which deliberately echo the long lists of names in 1 and 2 Chronicles. It is why he presents that genealogy as a story of three times over "six plus one" times two. Matthew declares that Jesus is the fulfilment of 1 and 2 Chronicles. He is the final King of Judah.[2] *"There were fourteen generations in all from Abraham to David, fourteen from David to the exile to Babylon, and fourteen from the exile to the Messiah."*[3]

Niccolò Machiavelli famously argued that *"Whoever wishes to foresee the future must consult the past; for human events ever*

---

[2] For example, Matthew 12:6, 23, 28 and 42 ask us: *"Could this be the Son of David?"*... *"Something greater than the temple"*... *"The Kingdom of God has come"*... *"Something greater than Solomon".*

[3] Matthew 1:17. In order to make it a perfect three time "six plus one" times two, Matthew leaves out several people from this family tree, just as the Chronicler often does. For example, Ahaziah, Joash, Amaziah and Jehoiakim are all missing.

resemble those of preceding times."[4] In other words, this retelling of Jewish history forms a mirror in which we can see our own concerns and disappointments with Church history. We too might be tempted into thinking that the Lord's promises have failed towards us. The Church looks weak and compromised in many ways. The Gospel doesn't seem to be triumphing in every nation. Very often, it doesn't even seem to triumph with our closest friends. There are plenty of reasons for Christians today to become as disappointed and disillusioned with the promises of God about his *Messiah* as it was for the original readers of 1 and 2 Chronicles.

The original Hebrew name for these two books is *Dibrēy Hayyāmīm*, which means literally *The Things of The Days*. Perhaps that's because it's easier for us to spot the faithfulness of God through the grand sweep of history than it is to spot it on any single day of our lives. But the God that we discover in the small details of 1 and 2 Chronicles is just as faithful in the small details of our own lives today.

So, as we end our study of these two books of the Bible, the Chronicler turns to us and encourages us to have faith in the *Messiah* in our own generation too. No matter how dark events may appear to you, and no matter how much you are tempted to doubt God's promises towards his Church in your own day, the Chronicler urges you to make the words of Solomon your own prayer of faith to the God of small things:

"With your mouth you have promised and with your hand you have fulfilled it – as it is today."[5]

---

[4] Niccolò Machiavelli wrote this in 1517 in his *Discourses* (3.43.1).

[5] 2 Chronicles 6:15.

Other titles in the
Straight to
the Heart
Series

Printed in the United States
by Baker & Taylor Publisher Services